HARPER TORCHBOOKS / The Cloister Library

(*Continued on next page*)

† *Included in The Library of Religion and Culture, edited by Benjamin Nelson.*

HARPER TORCHBOOKS / The Academy Library

HARPER TORCHBOOKS / The Science Library

Spiritual Problems
in
Contemporary Literature

EDITED BY

Stanley Romaine Hopper

HARPER TORCHBOOKS / The Cloister Library

HARPER & BROTHERS, NEW YORK

This volume is based on lectures given at
The Institute for Social and Religious Studies
of The Jewish Theological Seminary of America
during the winters of 1948–1949 and 1949–1950.

First HARPER TORCHBOOK edition published 1957

Library of Congress catalog card number: 57–10118

PREFACE TO THE TORCHBOOK EDITION

One of the most heartening appraisals of this book when first published (1952) was that of Theodore M. Greene, who said of it in *The New York Times Book Review* (February 15, 1953): "Most published symposia are disappointing; this collection of eighteen essays is a notable exception. I wish it could be read, and reread, by thoughtful men and women in every walk of life. It is a most illuminating commentary on modern literature in our contemporary society—on the predicament, and the failures and achievements of the writer, but also on our cultural situation, our spiritual hazards and opportunities. It is in the best sense a civilized and civilizing volume." This captures very well what the symposium aims at; it is only important to add that the essays have lost nothing of their relevance since 1953—indeed, their pertinence is sharpened by the interval and by the increasing demand for competent studies which explore and unfold the relation of literature to the deeper understanding of our inmost concerns.

For this reason it has seemed to me undesirable to tamper with the text in any basic way. The *Foreword* indicates the origin of the essays and the circumstances under which they were first presented. Unfortunately the manuscripts of Mr. Philip Rahv and Professor Meyer Schapiro, both of whom spoke in the original lecture series, were unavailable for inclusion in the published symposium. On the other hand, I was fortunately a delegate to the International Conference on Christianity and Art, at the Ecumenical Institute, Chateau de Bossey, Celigny, Switzerland, in May, 1950, where M. Denis de Rougemont presented his superb paper on "The Mission of Art as a Creative Expression of the Human Spirit"—a paper which coin-

vii

cided so evidently with the interests of these studies that I procured his permission to translate it and include it with the others. Because of its high importance, and because of the number of times it has been cited by other authors, I have often wished that the translation might have been more felicitous at certain points. Since, however, there is an edge of intractability about words whereby one set of terms is never permitted to stand absolutely for another set of terms (let alone the terms of one language for those of another), I have left this essay also unmodified as to translation.

According to de Rougemont, "Art is an exercise of the whole being of man, not to compete with God, but to coincide better with the order of Creation, to love it better, and to re-establish ourselves in it." This statement provides a useful baseline from which the scrutiny of the essays as a whole may be undertaken. Nevertheless the reader will soon discover that the opinions expressed represent solely the views of each individual contributor and that no attempt has been made, either editorially or otherwise, to coerce any artificial synthesis of interpretations or unity of design beyond that afforded by the best readable arrangement of the essays as presented. The contributors were chosen because of the special contribution each could make to the general knowledge and understanding of the subject. It is hoped that this new edition, through making this material more generally accessible, will continue to serve as a useful resource to that rapidly increasing number of scholars and students and general readers who are finding its topics among the most insistent and clarifying of our age.

STANLEY ROMAINE HOPPER

Drew University
April, 1957

FOREWORD

The following studies were presented originally in the form of lectures in two series on "Contemporary Spiritual Problems as Reflected in Contemporary Literature," at The Institute for Religious and Social Studies of The Jewish Theological Seminary of America in New York City. The Institute is a graduate school conducted with the cooperation of Catholic, Jewish, and Protestant scholars. It is one of the few places where this sort of concurrent study of contemporary problems can be made, openly and without prejudice, with a view to intelligent appraisal and mutual enlightenment.

Especially is this important to the present studies. For the field of letters and the arts is also, and by its very nature, necessarily open and without prejudice; and it is desirable, in times of stress such as we experience today, that appropriate forums for the free expression of the men of religion and the men of letters be fostered and maintained as a safeguard for those very freedoms and values which have been so greatly cherished by the creative spirits of all ages.

But from still a further point of view this meeting—of religion and letters—is desirable: for the problems of the literary artist today bring him more and more firmly upon the crucial centers of all human reflection. These are the "limit-situations" with which so many of our formal thinkers are today preoccupied; they are the centers of perplexity and pain experienced in every time of crisis or radical change: they are the focal points of mystery and decision which it is the office of religion itself to clarify. In short, contemporary letters and contemporary religion are occupying, and to a far greater extent than is commonly recognized either by artist or religionist, a common ground.

This is not to suggest that their *functions* are the same. They are not, and it is not the purpose of these studies to confuse the realm of esthetics with the realm of religion. On the contrary, it is the interest of these studies to clarify if possible, the curious hiatus that has arisen between the men of letters and the men of faith which has made for a deplorable lack of understanding and communication between these groups. Many theologians and clergymen feel today that they have no clarity regarding the spiritual insights to be found in our best literature; indeed, they are frequently confused and bewildered by it, oftentimes writing it off as a prime example of the confusion and bewilderment discernible everywhere in the realm of the spirit today. And similarly there are many otherwise creditable (and even distinguished) literary people whose knowledge of what is taking place in theology today is almost sublimely unenlightened. Their creative works are therefore legitimate but uninformed fumbling after solutions to problems of the spirit, works which could have been more efficiently ordered and more accurately construed had the author or the artist been working within the framework of a well articulated world-view. Where esthetic skill and theological awareness meet (as in poets such as T. S. Eliot and W. H. Auden) a poetry of unusual penetration and genius results. And where the theologian possesses also some understanding of the interpretive significance of the arts (as in the work of Paul J. Tillich, or Gabriel Marcel) a superior penetration into the religious mysteries appears.

With a view to bridging, at least to some extent, this gulf between the artist and the student of religion, a number of poets and critics, prominent in the world of letters, were invited to participate, and to address themselves to the general subject of contemporary spiritual problems as reflected in contemporary literature. Also a few men, representative in their fields, were selected to review the relation of the literary artist to the adjacent fields of interpretive study—sociology, philosophy, religion, and the other arts. Finally, and to bring the foregoing studies to a focus at the level of the contemporary interaction between the literary artist and specific patterns of belief, a few outstanding interpreters of religious ideas and beliefs were selected—scholars whose works have already shown a lively and competent interest in contemporary letters, as well as in theology.

The studies were designed to bring into sharper focus the religious significance of the deeper themes of current literary works, with their intense expression of modern man's search for a soul, for comradeship, for inner peace, for a "place in the cosmos," for hope, for creative satisfactions. It is an odd paradox that just as religious dogmas were being relaxed through the liberalizing movements of the nineteenth and early decades of the twentieth centuries, the literary world should have been renewing these and making them a point of appeal. Thus not only has man's knowledge of himself been multiplied, and the inner motivations of his soul laid bare, but the return existentially upon the ultimate dilemmas of life and destiny is everywhere made plain in contemporary art and letters.

This significant fact has not been understood sufficiently, either by the creative artist or by the religious interpreter. The creative artist experiences, explores, and expounds through his medium these essentially religious themes, but without the benefit of theological support. His work, therefore, is frequently a *negative* disclosure of the nature of human need, bearing witness to the *absence* rather than the presence of God. The theologian or the religious interpreter, meanwhile, proceeds on his dialectic way, unaware of (or not comprehending) the richest mine of confessional experience and spiritual exploration as exemplified in literature, available since the Renaissance.

This book aims, therefore, to bring together both literary and theological opinion upon these themes, with a view to throwing some interpretive light upon the problems shared by artist and religious interpreter alike.

It was almost inevitable that the studies, so prepared, should fall into three parts. Part I includes those studies which explore the place of the poet, dramatist, and novelist in the modern world, the question as to his vocation and creative task, the relation in which this stands to the other arts, and the manner in which this task is illuminated *vis à vis* the tasks of the sociologist, the philosopher, and the religionist. Quite clearly, the focus of attention here is upon "Religion and the Artist's Situation."

Part II moves at an entirely different level: for here the problem of vocation explored in Part I accepts responsibility for itself, and, no longer moving at the level of general interest, turns in upon the artist's problem in such a way as to explore the real nature and implications of the esthetic options that are open to him in a world whose traditions and conventions no longer sustain him—no longer offer him, that is, frameworks and systems of order and unity which the majority of his readers accept and understand. The absence of such basic conventions in a culture thrusts the artist back upon origins, and upon himself, and in the way in which all other sensitive souls are thrust back upon origins and upon themselves in a time of cultural crisis. The artist becomes Tiutchev's orphaned man, "unravelled, alien"—or, as another translation has it

> without home,
> orphaned, alone, impotent. . . .

This is the inner side of the literary artist's problem. The other side—the outer side—has to do with his recognition of the lack of agreements, conventions, and general understandings in a time of general uncertainty, such as ours. "The issue is between the unified and the dismembered universes," as Archibald MacLeish once described it. "It is merely the fundamental problem of the location of man in the universe." Such a problem is certain to be felt by the artist and by the religionist, for their tasks are both interpretive and constructive. MacLeish himself recognized that the problem, primarily, "is not a poetic problem": but in a day when the religious primacies are called in question he was sanguine enough to add—"though it will probably be solved by a poet." [1] This discounts the theological vitality of our time. Moreover it is not likely that it will be solved by a poet, for poetry has always been the handmaiden of religion, and, by definition, a problem of faith and order will not be solved at the esthetic level. Nevertheless the poet must use such means as are at his disposal. Part II is an attempt to study these means.

At the esthetic level this represents a search for what Eliot termed the "objective correlative"—the artist's formula for bringing together and unifying the otherwise disjunct materials and facets of

---

[1] Archibald MacLeish, *A Time to Speak,* Houghton Mifflin Company, Boston, 1941, p. 154.

experience which comprise the raw material of his specific project. The literary artist's use of mysticism, of myth, of metaphor, are here explored; and the oblique disclosures of religious implication as found in literary existentialism, the artist's experience of moral isolation, and the entire problem of religious theodicy which his own task imposes on him at the point of creative interpretation, are here explored as they relate to the literary artist's creative ordeal. Part II is thus, in some respects, the *Purgatorio* portion of these studies— at once the most difficult in analysis and the most necessary to the artist—as it addresses itself to "Religion and the Artist's Means."

Part III moves more openly at the level of religious emergence, where specific religious orientations are accepted and more or less visibly employed. The traditional frameworks—Judaism, Catholicism, Protestantism—are here specified and their patterns noted as they are being used in contemporary letters. Here again it must be remembered that the aim of the studies is not, at this point, to insinuate any partisan or parochial strictures upon the artist, but to note rather the way in which the artist resolves the common problem by way of an adoption of religious truths as structural media intrinsic to his vocational tasks and aims. The studies conclude with "Religion and the Artist's Beliefs," a return upon the question of vocation, or mission, from the religious standpoint, and with a résumé of the responsibilities now held in common by religious and literary interpreters alike. The two—the men of letters and the men of faith—ought not, and in fact do not, work in isolation from each other. They must, not merely for their own mutual interest, but for the benefit of all

> Learn from each other where their love will
> lead them.

I should like to express my personal thanks to the contributors; to the Reverend Earl A. Holmer, who was most helpful in discussions leading to the original lecture series; and to Miss Jessica Feingold, whose aid throughout both the organization of the lecture series and the preparation of the book was invaluable.

STANLEY ROMAINE HOPPER

CONTENTS

xv

III

RELIGION AND THE ARTIST'S
BELIEFS

SPIRITUAL PROBLEMS
IN
CONTEMPORARY LITERATURE

RELIGION AND THE ARTIST'S SITUATION

Oh save me in this day,
  when Now
Is a towering pillar
  of dust which sucks
The ruin of a world
  into its column.

Stephen Spender, in "Time in Our Time"

I

THE LITERARY ARTIST AND THE OTHER ARTS

BY

JAMES JOHNSON SWEENEY

"The artist," as Wyndham Lewis once wrote, "goes back to the fish. The few centuries that separate him from the savage are a mere flea bite to the distance his memory must stretch if it is to strike the fundamental slime of creation. And it is this condition, the very first gusto of creation in the scale of life in which we are set, that he must reach, before he in his turn can create." [1]

In approaching contemporary art in no matter what field, there are two points which must be kept in mind: first, that no matter how unfamiliar the surface aspects of a contemporary work of art may appear, underneath a fundamental characteristic relates it to all the art of past times; second, that if a contemporary work is truly art, it must offer a surface aspect essentially different from all the art which has preceded it. This is true of every veritable work of art, in no matter what field—writing, painting, sculpture, music, architecture, or the dance. And through this duality of reference what art has provided for every period is a model, in T. S. Eliot's words, for "controlling, ordering and giving shape and significance to the immense panorama of futility and anarchy which is contemporary history."

I

I believe it was Bernard Shaw who said that fine art is the only teacher except torture. But, pointed as the epigram is, it does not do

[1] Wyndham Lewis, "The Caliph's Dream," *The Artist from "Blast" to Burlington House,* Laidlaw & Laidlaw, Ltd., London, 1939.

full justice to the level on which art speaks to us. Shaw's countryman, the late W. B. Yeats, expressed it more perfectly in his poem "Byzantium":

> A starlit or a moonlit dome disdains
> All that man is,
> All mere complexities,
> The fury and the mire of human veins.[2]

In fact, that poem and his earlier "Sailing to Byzantium" are two of the most suggestive statements of the spiritual value of art in twentieth century writing.

> That is no country for old men. The young
> In one another's arms, birds in the trees,
> —Those dying generations—at their song,
> The salmon-falls, the mackerel-crowded seas,
> Fish, flesh or fowl, commend all summer long
> Whatever is begotten, born and dies.
> Caught in that sensual music all neglect
> Monuments of unaging intellect.
>
> O sages standing in God's holy fire
> As in the gold mosaic of a wall,
> Come from the holy fire, perne in a gyre,
> And be the singing masters of my soul.
> Consume my heart away; sick with desire
> And fastened to a dying animal
> It knows not what it is; and gather me
> Into the artifice of eternity.
>
> Once out of nature I shall never take
> My bodily form from any natural thing,
> But such a form as Grecian goldsmiths make
> Of hammered gold and gold enamelling
> To keep a drowsy emperor awake;[3]

[2] W. B. Yeats, "Byzantium," *Winding Stair,* copyright 1933 by The Macmillan Company, New York, and used with their permission.

[3] "Sailing to Byzantium," *The Tower,* copyright 1928 by The Macmillan Company, New York, and used with their permission.

In those lines, and in the closing stanza of "Byzantium," Yeats stated the poet's ideal of that final quality which true art held for him:

> . . . . . The smithies break the flood,
> The golden smithies of the Emperor!
> Marbles of the dancing floor
> Break bitter furies of complexity,
> Those images that yet
> Fresh images beget,
> That dolphin-torn, that gong-tormented sea.[4]

For us, in the present period, Yeats's concept of the spiritual value of a work of art has a peculiar relevance. For today, if ever, we need help toward breaking the "bitter furies of complexity." In an age of decaying faith we are sorely in need of that reassurance that "monuments of unaging intellect" can give, and of the stabilizing influence of a gathering "into the artifice of eternity." We see all around us chaos and lack of standards for judging quality. Our civilization, so-called, is a mob civilization. For "the tendency of unlimited industrialism," as the poet T. S. Eliot has written, is "to create masses of men and women—detached from tradition, alienated from religion and susceptible to suggestions: in other words, a mob." And "a mob," he adds, "will be no less a mob if it is well fed, well housed and well disciplined."

Yeats in these two poems envisages the human soul in its relation to works of art. He finds that the architect and goldsmith have set up miracles of workmanship to stand in mockery of "all that man is" —models of order, an order that does not exist where "that sensual music" of the world makes its insistent demands. They give us examples of order amid "the perplexities, the fury, and mire of human veins."

This is one of the basic values of a work of art, whether of literature, painting, sculpture, music, or architecture. This is what a work of art, a true work of art, holds for us: this pattern of organization and har-

[4] *Winding Stair, op. cit.*

mony amid seeming chaos; this means to a conception of macrocosmic unity through an assimilable microcosm.

II

Every true work of art, like Yeats's cathedral dome, mosaic pavement, and golden bird, has a potential power of purgation for natural beings; for a true work of art always combines a unity of general form with a variety in its elements. The satisfaction that this combination gives is essentially a blending together of our responses into a unified whole, providing us a model for the organization of our emotional life and the problems of daily existence. This is what we loosely term "beauty" in a work of art.

This is the value that the individual, authentic art expression has for the observer. But this is only half the story. This would hold true of an authentic work of art of any period, not necessarily a "modern" expression. But an authentic contemporary work of art has an added and more poignant significance for us. For this additional significance we have to go beyond the individual work of art to its relationship with what has preceded it. We are given the lead in the phrase, "detached from tradition," quoted above in T. S. Eliot's description of the spiritual effects that unlimited industrialism has had on our civilization. For today we have equally as much need of the assurance provided by a sense of tradition in human expression, as we have for those models of organization for our emotional lives which brilliant individual examples will provide.

"No poet, no artist of any art," T. S. Eliot wrote in *Tradition and the Individual Talent,* "has his complete meaning alone. His significance, his appreciation is the appreciation of his relation to the dead poets and artists. You cannot value him alone; you must set him, for contrast and comparison, among the dead. I mean this," he says, "as a principle of aesthetic, not merely historical, criticism."

In other words, art as a spiritually unifying experience is not complete in its isolated expressions. The poet, Eliot continues—and it holds for the painter, sculptor, and musician as well—"can neither take the past as a lump, an indiscriminate bolus, nor can he form himself . . . upon one preferred period. . . . The poet must be very conscious of the main current, which does not at all flow invariably through the most distinguished reputations. He must be quite aware of the obvious fact that art never improves, but that the material of art is never quite the same. He must be aware that the mind . . . of his own country—a mind which he learns in time to be much more important than his own private mind—is a mind which changes, and that this change is a development which abandons nothing *en route,* which does not superannuate either Shakespeare, or Homer, or the rock drawings of the Magdalenian draughtsmen."

Tradition, therefore, is no mere antiquarian prejudice, the implication in a work of art of some pleasing archeological reconstruction. It does not consist merely in

following the ways of the immediate generation before us in a blind or timid adherence to its successes. . . . Tradition is a matter of much wider significance. . . . It involves, in the first place, the historical sense, . . . and the historical sense involves a perception, not only of the pastness of the past, but of its presence; the historical sense compels a man to write not merely with his own generation in his bones, but with a feeling that the whole of the literature of Europe from Homer and within it the whole of the literature of his own country has a simultaneous existence and composes a simultaneous order. This historical sense, which is a sense of the timeless as well as of the temporal and of the timeless and of the temporal together, is what makes a writer (or an artist in any field) traditional.[5]

Consequently, "tradition" may fairly be said to consist, not in preserving a form or set of forms, but in keeping alive an interest in the solution of contemporary problems in contemporary terms or materials. As the sculptor Jacques Lipchitz has expressed it, from a slightly different point of view, "As a workman I feel I must always keep before me that ideal of a great river which is always changing and can never be arrested. And it is the individual creative freedom which alone feeds it."

[5] T. S. Eliot, "The Sacred Wood," *Tradition and the Individual Talent,* Methuen & Company, Ltd., London, 6th edition, 1948.

III

What is timeless in art, therefore, is the spirit which brings the artist consciously or unconsciously "back to the fish," as Wyndham Lewis expressed it. The rest, the surface aspects of his art, are never timeless and never should be expected to appear so. They should be rooted in and reflect the time in which the work of art is produced: the artist's aims, his environment—spiritual as well as physical, the social setting. As a consequence, from period to period, from day to day, all art that is not plagiarism must be different in surface aspect from all art that preceded it. And to keep familiar with its living changes we must keep in touch with them. If we do not, we will always be surprised at what has taken place in our absence. If we are long enough out of touch with them, the effort required to renew an easy intercourse with them will be almost as great as the first effort we had to expend to put ourselves in stride with the constantly changing idiom of the living present, instead of the static idioms of the dead past.

In connection with this factor, tradition, let us take a special case among the arts—painting and sculpture. Actually, much of the modern layman's trouble in approaching contemporary painting and sculpture is due to his misunderstanding of tradition. He forgets the ages of art that lie behind modern expression and attempts to base his taste on one preferred period—the Renaissance. He takes Renaissance art and its derivations to represent all art. Actually the Renaissance is only a tiny corner of art history. There are the Egyptian, the Minoan, the Sumerian, centuries of Greek art before the naturalistic idiom developed. There is the art of the early dynasties in China, the art of Europe in the Middle Ages, dozens of centuries of art in a dozen quarters of the world. And all are part of the true tradition of art, all on an equally high level—on a level as high as our own art of the past six hundred years, if not higher—and all as far from the naturalistic, single perspective representation of the Renaissance and post-Renaissance as what seems strangest in modern art today to the Philistine. Yet the Philistine persists in judging contemporary art solely by the standards of this relatively limited and specialized period in the history of world art. He forgets that a similar approach to that which he condemns has given us practically all the great art of the world, whereas the naturalistic imitation of nature based on an artificial perspective on tradition has produced only a tiny fraction of the total in the past few hundred years. The Philistine talks of tradition and anti-traditional expressions, yet it is the truly modern artist who is the real traditionalist and who aspires to be so.

To appreciate the importance of keeping in stride with the growth of expression for the full appreciation of contemporary art, it is interesting to compare what has happened in painting and sculpture. Many of the critical analyses in T. S. Eliot's lecture, *From Poe to Valéry*,[6] illuminate by analogy much also that has come to pass during that same period in literature's sister arts.

"All poetry," Eliot declared, "may be said to start from the emotions experienced by human beings in their relations to themselves, to each other, to divine beings and to the world about them. It is therefore concerned also with thought and action which emotion brings about, and out of which emotion arises." The same holds for painting and sculpture. "But," Eliot continues, "at however primitive a stage of expression and appreciation, the function of poetry can never be simply to arouse these *same emotions* [my italics] in the audience of the poet. . . . In the earliest poetry, or in the most rudimentary enjoyment of poetry, the attention of the listener is directed upon the subject matter; the effect of the poetic art is felt without the listener being wholly conscious of this art." We see here the persevering analogy with painting—the popular art of the late Middle Ages and early Renaissance and much subsequent narrative and history painting even down to the present.

With the development of the consciousness of language (Eliot continues) there is another stage at which the auditor, who may by that time have become the reader, is aware of a double interest in a story for its own sake, and in the way in which it is told; that is to say, he becomes aware of

[6] T. S. Eliot, *From Poe to Valéry*, Harcourt, Brace & Company, New York, 1948; delivered at the Library of Congress, Washington, D.C., in 1948.

style. Then we may take a delight in discrimination between the ways in which different poets [or painters] will handle the same subject—an appreciation not merely of better or worse, but of differences between styles which are equally admired. At a third stage of development, the subject may recede to the background; instead of being the purpose of the poem [or the painting] it becomes simply a necessary means for the realization of the poem [or the picture]. At this stage the reader, or listener [or observer], may become as nearly indifferent to the subject matter as the primitive listener was to the style. A complete unconsciousness or indifference to the style at the beginning, or to subject matter at the end would, however, take us outside of poetry altogether (just as it would take us outside of painting as an art)—for . . . a complete unconsciousness of anything but style would mean that poetry had vanished.

What has happened in the case of Valéry is a change of attitude toward the subject matter. We must be careful to avoid saying that the subject matter becomes "less important." It has a different kind of importance: it is important as *means:* the *end* is the poem. The subject exists for the poem, not the poem for the subject. A poem may employ several subjects, combining them in a particular way; and it may be meaningless to ask "What is the subject of the poem?" From the union of several subjects there appears, not another subject, but the poem.

One could scarcely find a better description of what has happened to painting during the past few centuries, and with increased speed during the past seventy years. Perhaps subject matter in the plastic arts has always been more of a means to an end than it was in early poetry. At any rate, Cennino Cennini, in the Renaissance, already saw it in that light. In his book, *The Book of the Art of Cennino Cennini,* he wrote: "It is an art we signify when we use the verb 'to paint.' It requires imagination and manual cleverness; it seeks to find new things hidden within known natural forms and seeks to express them through the hand in such a way as to make one believe that something, which does not exist, exists." [7] Even in his time we see that Cennino Cennini did not predicate the imitation of any aspect of nature. He did not recommend, for example, that the artist should make an identical copy of a tree, a false tree, as it were. He recommended that

[7] Christiana J. Herringham, *The Book of the Art of Cennino Cennini,* George Allen & Unwin Ltd., London, 1922.

the artist find new things hidden under the commonplace appearance of nature, and he proposes in his book the means by which the artist may do this. The artist is, Cennino writes, by his knowledge alone, that is to say, through the fullness of his artist's nature, at complete liberty to bind things together, to find correspondences, to compose, to transmute, to unify in such a fashion as to make the observer believe in Cennino's phrase that "what does not exist, exists." In other words, the painter should be free, according to this Renaissance artist, to create *out of* nature new objects—new picture objects as we might express it in current-day jargon—and to employ nature, that is, subject matter, in Eliot's usage, as a means. And the end, to paraphrase Eliot, is the painting.

IV

Again, if we apply Eliot's analysis of the evolution of modern poetry to the evolution of modern painting, we recognize at once a common trend—the steady growth of interest in style and emphasis on it, accompanied by the retirement of subject matter interest to a subordinate position. It becomes easy to see why the broad, unfamiliar public, lacking interest to make sufficient effort to familiarize itself with the new idiom, will find as little gratification in most contemporary painting and sculpture as it will in most valid contemporary poetry or contemporary music on the same exploratory level.

But are the artists justified in adopting such an intellectually or esthetically exclusive attitude? The answer is that, the facts faced, they have no choice, no alternative. The evolution of the arts cannot be reversed. To insist today on the all importance of subject matter, as Eliot says, "to insist that the poet should be spontaneous and irreflective, that he should depend upon inspiration and neglect technique, would be a lapse from what is in any case a highly civilized attitude to a barbarous one."

For an artist wilfully to disregard the maturity of viewpoint his predecessors have won for him, would be to deny his heritage and to impoverish himself spiritually. An engineer or physicist who would disregard what his predecessors had found out in their practice, would not be taken seriously. The engineer or physicist must know as much as possible of what people knew in the past, then go in some direction a step further than they had gone. That step is his originality. The untutored artist has no more value in our modern world than the untrained engineer or uneducated physicist.

To take another paragraph from Wyndham Lewis's critical writings of thirty some years ago:

The Child and the Naif are two of the principal mainstays of dilettante criticism. And this "phenomenon" with all the sentimentality of which its exploitation clearly is susceptible, is one of the trump cards in the amateur's game and a fruitful source of confusion. It is one of the most obvious avenues, flooded with an effusive critical craft, by which the thoroughly undeserving can slip through into a position of artificial respect.[8]

"There are two types of Naif," he continues, "the Child-Naif and the Primitive-Naif. It is difficult to say which is the more boring of the two." And this structure of Lewis's holds as well for the American scene Naifs of the Grant Wood era in our middle nineteen-thirties as it does for the Grandma Moses of today.

"Every artist," the sculptor Jacques Lipchitz has said, "should be allowed and encouraged to make use of his vision of nature as he sees fit. But when I say 'freedom *vis-à-vis* nature' I do not mean the freedom we find in the paintings of children, the mentally unbalanced, or the so-called modern primitives. These are not free; they are cut off from some of the richest assets of the heritage of art."

The artist, every true artist, is then in the proper sense of the word a traditionalist, for a real tradition is not a relic of the past; it is a living force which animates and informs the present. And this is the base of the second important spiritual contribution that a true work of art provides.

Thus we see that the individual work of art, taken in its discrete unity, affords a model of organization amid the confusion of the visible and apprehensible world. In its traditional character a work of art offers us another key to the understanding of the universe. It

[8] Lewis, *op. cit.*

stands not merely as a discrete unit, but also as an essential element of a totality. Through it, in its character of link in a long and continuing tradition, we are given a sense of that larger unity of which it is impossible to discern the discrete borders, but in which the work of art has an organic position in its framework of tradition.

This from a spiritual viewpoint, is the major contribution of the creative literary artist and the other arts. And this also is the reason why the observer, auditor, or reader, as well as the artist, must not limit himself to one or two private admirations, nor to one preferred period, but must force himself to see art at once both intensely and large, if he hopes to derive from it its full spiritual contribution. To see it this way full recognition must be given to the living contemporary artist in his eternal role of explorer. For the past relives in the artist and we can learn to read its fundamental message only through the hornbook he fashions for us.

II

SOCIOLOGY AND THE LITERARY ARTIST

BY

ALBERT SALOMON

In this particular moment of history, we are dominated by two conceptions of man which have reached an almost critical stage of competition. While they extend and are the extensions of myriad branches of man's creative activities, they are the foremost symbolizations of the conflict which lies at the very heart of modernity. It is the conflict which rages between sociology and the literary arts which is ultimately the heart of the matter.

The simplest formulation of the incompatibility might be stated in the following way: Literary arts conceive of truth in terms of the whole through the use of symbols and images. Further, it is the truth about the whole seen as the dynamic unity of the interacting relationships between God, world, and man. Throughout the history of literature, the great literary patterns, the epic, the drama, the idyll, and pastoral poetry, testify to this thesis.

Sociologies, on the other hand, conceive of truth in terms of societal relationships and the social process at large. They deal with man as a member of society, and start from the hypothesis that the social process is the very universe of man. It is this hypothesis which appears in contrast to the totality of works of philosophizing and imagination prior to the appearance of sociology, works which demonstrated a philosophical and poetic conception of man which neither restricts man to or by the social process. The poet and the philosopher saw man in the totality of the universe, as a part of it.

As a result, the great literary forms are lasting and continuous forms of human expression. The great works of poetry are intelligible, and can be understood beyond and despite the moment of their historical origins. We are still able to understand, despite the sociologists and historical relativists, Homer, Dante, Aeschylus, Sophocles, and Shakespeare. Further, the nature of the poet is a perennial one; there is the consistency of intent to interpret man's complex character, his relation to his fellow man, his living in the world, and his belonging to the universe of a divine and absolute meaning.

The patterns of sociology, however, are diametrically opposed to the patterns of poetry. Sociology is a historical discipline which came into existence at the end of the French Revolution, and at the unification point of the Industrial and Social Revolutions. It is a modern invention which is distinguished from social philosophy in so far as its primary intention is the application of the totality of scientific methods toward the transformation of the social world into a most perfect and human enterprise. It is essentially the synthetic philosophy of scientific methods and the eschatology of the "scientific method." It is, further, the theory that the last and perfect state of the world and the salvation of the world can be achieved through the utilization of all the scientific methods, the benefit and improvement of the whole of mankind being its telos. For this reason, the sociologist, in contrast to the poet, is primarily the messianic bohemian, the philosopher who no longer exists within the context of the eternal positing of truth preservation. He is the new type of philosopher, concerned with the summarization and synthesis of all previous scientific methods (specifically, the "scientific method" of the natural sciences), directed at the transformation and total change of the world of man into the control of nature and society, more pointedly the complete secular salvation of man. The sociologist, therefore, stands in total contradistinction as social engineer to the poet who is concerned with the maintenance, preservation, and continuation of the truth about the whole, the truth of the unity of God, world, and man.

I

However, we have so far been concerned primarily with the logical articulation of the thesis which needs careful analysis in terms of the related historical phenomena. To make our thesis more comprehensible, we must consider another problem, namely, that of sociology as an attitude prior to sociology as science and philosophy. Sociology as an attitude is a prescientific awareness of the fact that the individual life is determined by the dynamic process of groups, by the pressure of collective institutions, and by the stereotypes and uniformities prescribed by societal control. Such an attitude arises with modern society.

What is of crucial importance is the fact that modern society does not find its inception in terms of the industrial bourgeoisie, but in terms of the society of the court of the absolute state, which is the first competitive society. The society of the court includes the urban educated and patrician wealth. Its literary accomplishment, in the final analysis the accomplishment of sociological awareness, is the modern novel. The novel emerges as a new literary form, not because bourgeois, patrician, and people as such are different from the knights of chivalrous romance, but because sociological awareness, the totally new factor, becomes the focusing element of plot. In the simplest possible terms, society is now the destiny of the individual; the horizon under which the individual lives is determined by the pressure, power, and control of society. The novel, from *Don Quixote* on, is the manifestation of this new outlook.

This idea has two different aspects in the development of the novel: the constructive and the destructive. It is constructive in so far as society is conceived of as the educator, the guide, the leader which affords the individual the possibility of realizing his own potentialities. This is the avenue which leads from *Don Quixote* to Goethe's *Wilhelm Meister* and Galsworthy's *Forsyte Saga*. The other trend in the development of the novel, the destructive aspect, in terms of the concept of society as the destiny of man, finds the individual suffocated by the social stereotypes and the obligations imposed by society upon the individual soul. This is the trend that leads through Gustave Flaubert, Jacob Wasserman, and Henry James.

There is one case in both literary history and the history of sociology where there is a unification of the novel and sociological analysis—Montesquieu's *Lettres Persanes*. The *Lettres Persanes* is satire, novel, and, at the same time, the first sociological treatise, a treatise which deals with the analysis of the variety and the various departmental strata of social conduct, extending from the external behavior to the motives of conduct of the human being. It establishes the thesis that the best sociologist is a stranger, the man from another country who comes to see another civilization in all its varieties and in all its various departmental strata. We have here the fullest expression, and the culmination, of what has been termed the sociological attitude.

But we are also concerned with sociology as a philosophy of history and as universal method in the period of collective social organizations. The St.-Simonians and the Marxists have both dealt with the problem of literature quite extensively, but always in an unsatisfactory manner with respect to the interests of the man of letters, especially the man who knows something about poetry and tragedy in general. Both the St.-Simonians and the Marxists have promulgated the general thesis that the literary arts are functional expressions and are specifically expressive of the division and distribution of power. The function of the poet is the appraisal of the established situation of power and the eulogization of the ruling society in terms of its assumed wisdom, intelligence, and right to social eminence.

However, this is only the very superficial sociological problem and is not at all satisfactory. It refers only to the fringes of poetry. Such sociological analyses explain completely only the literary works and authors who write with the intent of satisfying the desires of certain groups or majorities. They are concerned with the eternal literary businessman who writes for the perennial magazines of entertainment in terms of the prescriptions of the publishers and the assumed demand of the public: fifteen per cent crime, fifteen per cent adventure, forty-five per cent sex, and twenty-five per cent bourgeois respectability. This phenomenon existed at all times, from medieval to modern. It is a general sociological type.

However, as a kind of sociological imputation, this is not valid for the great poet, even when forced to write for popular magazines, such as the case of Balzac or that of Dostoievski. However, the Marxist writers have undergone a process of refinement and have converted their social approach into a constructive method. Lukacs, the man who later on became a Bolshevist author, in particular has done a very remarkable piece of work on the sociology of the drama and the metaphysics of the novel. A summary of his main position reveals the following: esthetic value is not subject to sociological imputations. However, the sociologist is capable of determining the conditions which make possible the realization of esthetic values and promote or prevent the development of certain literary forms. As an example, he asks, in the sociology of the drama, how it is possible, and how, as sociologists, can we understand that the Greek tragedy is a unique phenomenon which does not recur in the Western world, and why do we have the continuous change between the patterns of the tragedy as they arise in the Renaissance, in the work of Shakespeare, in the work of the French classicists, and in the nineteenth century works of Ibsen and his followers?

Lukacs decides that the decisive problem for the sociologist is the understanding of what the determining elements are which condition the poetical imagination, the imagination of the poet. How far is the poet influenced by the intellectual and philosophical horizon, by the society in which he lives? It is this idea, which was the guiding star of his inquiry into the sociology of the drama, which resulted in the discovery that the drama, specifically in terms of great tragedy, was vanishing more and more from the scene in the modern world, because, with the growth and increasing power of scientific and technological thinking, the idea which is indispensable for the tragic poet, the idea of destiny, the destiny with which the human being is in conflict, was disappearing more and more from the scene. The reason for its disappearance was the fact that everything could be manipulated by the sociological and sociopsychological techniques of the modern world. Lukacs similarly indicated in his book, *The Metaphysics of the Novel,* that the great forms of the epic are disappearing from the modern world. They vanish necessarily because the sociological conditions and the intellectual attitudes which made possible the patterns of the epic from Homer to Ariosto and Milton are gone. These conditions were focused around the homogeneity between man and society, the individual and his world. The world of the epic was a process of life in which human beings left home, and migrated through the world in order to come home again. It was, in the last analysis, a closed and eternal universe in which men trusted and were in harmony with the gods and the powers of nature.

II

In terms of the sociology of language, it is sociologically of the greatest relevance to find out how far the general language of a society lends itself to the poetical, to the needs of the poet and his imagination; it is further important to determine how far the problem which we are currently facing, and have been for fifty or sixty years, the necessity of the poet to construct his own language, is indicative of a certain situation of the poet in modern society. If the situations of poets such as Pope and Goethe are considered with regard to the language of their society, it is still possible to demonstrate that these poets are still involved with and concerned with the language of their society proper; they are still able to use the emotional language of their nations, in order to concretize the factors of poetic imagination.

But something happens around the end of the nineteenth century. The poet then feels that the language which is used by his society does not lend itself any longer to his specific needs and requirements. He is forced to create a language of his own. The problem of the alienation of man and the alienation of the poet as the most complete human being is apparent in this kind of phenomenon (as discerned by Hegel and Marx). The sociologist, as antagonist, is, nevertheless, fully capable of recognizing this phenomenon.

Therefore, there seems to be adequate reason to believe that sociology can make a contribution, though modest and humble, to the problem of the literary arts. The sociologist is able to explain and understand why literary forms are in continuous change, why the intellectual and moral horizon of the artist's society has a tremendous impact on imagination, with reference to the building up of plots and creating the possibility of the organization and contribution of one or another literary form, whether the epic, the tragedy, the drama, or the comedy. For this reason, the theoretical incompatibility between sociology and literary art remains a purely logical phenomenon. On the plane of history and in the development of the social process, the literary arts are subject, as are all historical and social phenomena, to social changes, to the transformation of society, to change in the ruling classes, to the general transformation of the intellectual and moral horizon, to the transformation of the emotional and attitudinal relationships of human beings, their specific society, and situation. There is an instrumental value which can be accorded the sociological method, in terms of its ability to explain the changes in literary forms, the rise of new and the decay of old ones.

What appears to be a rejection of the primary thesis is, rather, a compromise. Specifically, it goes without saying that poetry transcends the horizon of society, as does philosophy. Sociology, which today appears only to be a very humble discipline, appeared as the philosophy of total progress, and science and philosophy of society claimed to establish the social process, the historical development, as an ultimate horizon of human beings. The great poet, not the literary businessman, and the great philosopher have always known that society and the social process, that history and historicism, are not the ultimate universe of human beings. Human beings live in a universe which is larger than the social process, larger than history proper, the universe in which God, the universe, and man are united in a continuous interaction with each other. The great poet understands human life as a symbol of something more than life, the universe of God, world, and man.

The great poet has, therefore, a position superior to that of the sociologist, the sociologist of the primordial and early stages of sociology, as well as that of the contemporary sociologist who is of the opinion that sociology is a science which makes it possible to manipulate the completeness of human beings, without taking into account the area of spiritual personality, of dignity, which is not manipulatable. The poet understands that humans transcend the social process in the few moments in which they establish homogeneity and integration between social stratification and individual characters. The poet is able to grasp this specific universality and totality of human beings, because, by his very nature, he is imagining and visualizing the totality of life beyond the sphere of everyday routine relationships. He knows that all human beings, all members of society, despite the routine of their lives, despite the necessity of the mechanisms of the social process, long to transcend this kind of routine; they long for homogeneity and integration of a type in which all human beings are united beyond their individual characters and beyond all the elements of social stratification.

III

There are four different attitudes in which human beings are united in this way beyond the sphere of social process; these attitudes are the specific material problems for the poet. First, they are united in the lust for having fun; second, men are united in the lust for making fun; third, men are united in fear of the gods; and fourth, men are united in the communion of suffering. These are the elements which make possible the work of the great poet beyond the pale of social institutions, and which should be commented on. With reference to the first, the longing for having fun finds its eternal form in the literary field from the naturalistic comedy of Aristophanes, to the Western show business. The cliché which is important to the sociologist is the categorization of fun in terms of wine, woman, and song.

With reference to the unification in the lust for making fun, the second eternal type of literary presentation comes into existence, namely, the literary comedy, as over against the naturalistic comedy. Here is the expression of the wish to transcend the routine of everyday life in the having of fun *of* the fellow man, fun *of* everything. There is the third desire of human beings involved in the unification into a homogeneous group in and through fear of the gods. Here we find the relationship to Greek tragedy, which is not primarily an esthetic phenomenon, but a religious phenomenon. It is a phenomenon in which the Athenian citizenry received the symbols of their religious worship, and it is the struggle with the gods and the struggle of the gods with heroes which is the subject matter of this form. All tragedy referred to the divine power, to the power of destiny, at least at the fringe of their plots. Only in the modern tragedy, in the tragedy of the scientific technological bourgeois society, in the work of Ibsen and his followers, do we find that tragic plots are constructed along psychological lines, but not along the lines of vision and destiny, of the struggle of a human being with destiny.

There is, further, the Christian drama, which is of extreme importance in the Middle Ages. It is not a tragedy, because in the Christian world, tragedy is not possible because of the immanence of salvation. But the Christian drama and tragedy are both vanishing. It is in this context that the grim fact of secular society is apparent. Secular society involves the elimination of destiny and the categories of religiosity from the crucial relation to everyday existence.

The fourth homogeneity of human beings has been called the communion of suffering, nowhere more visible than in the great epic. *The Odyssey* and *The Iliad* are concerned with the suffering of human beings imposed upon them by the stupidities, meanness, wickedness, and ridiculous human behavior of the gods; their own passions, their own lack of reason, and their own lack of moderation are responsible. There is a most beautiful witness for the renaissance of the understanding of the Homeric epic as the literary form of suffering in the writings of a young lady who died of starvation, Simone Weil. "The Iliad: or The Poem of Force" is one of the most beautiful interpretations of the relevance of Homer for ourselves, for our own life, of how perfectly alive Homer is in a situation in which we have passed through the hells of human possibilities, the perfectly clear elaboration of the fact that humans are capable of the most wicked and most sublime acts at the same time.

The idea of the epic as the literary form in which the communion of suffering is established, has a specifically modern application, too. From a sociological point of view, and in applying the sociological method, we can see that the modern novel, as described above, is in a state of transformation. This transformation begins during the middle of the nineteenth century. The work of Balzac is not any longer the middle class novel, no longer the novel which focuses around the idea that society is the ultimate destination of human beings. Balzac organizes the *Comédie Humaine* as a new work in which all the novels are united and transformed into a new homogeneity. What is indicated is that Balzac knows that human beings do not live in society alone, but in the universe of theosophic insight, the struggle of the vital and spiritual forces in humans.

What happened in the uprooted and unleashed forces of modern society in a state of revolution is only the general struggle which is going on between the spiritual and vital forces in the universe. What happened in the work of Balzac is the transformation, for the first time, of the novel into a new pattern, a new type of epic which is continued by Dostoievski and Proust. This is a new pattern of epic, a work in which the literary form arises from the idea that there is a new homogeneity of human beings, a new homogeneity of suffering, a new poetry of evil, as Balzac says, in which human beings are suffering through the powers of the vital energies, being aware that there is a spiritual reality to which they should ascend and which they cannot reach.

The work of Dostoievski and Proust transcends the novel as a specific literary form of the eighteenth and nineteenth century. They indicate a progression toward a new vision, a new insight, a new manifestation of the insight of literary forms, a new epic, whatever might be a specific integrating and unifying element. Whereas we are able to comprehend fully the changes in literary form and to see how the poets mirror the gap between the forces of the universe, the powers of vitality and those of the spirit, this is the totality of sociological insight. Not the sociologist, but the poet is able to describe the labyrinth of the world and the paradise of the heart. Poetry transcends the horizon of society, only when integrating the hell and paradise of human life into the symbols of the whole, a task which the sociologist is incapable of realizing.

III

PHILOSOPHY AND THE LITERARY ARTIST

by

IRWIN EDMAN

There is an ancient warfare, or apparent warfare, between philosophy (or the philosopher) and the creative literary artist, and it is perfectly easy and clear to see why. Philosophy in the past century has become extremely academic in both a good and bad sense—it has become a technical, esoteric jargon interested more and more in scrupulous and responsible analysis of terms and the dialectical connection between ideals. In the interests of such responsibility and precision and scrupulousness, philosophical language has become a special professional jargon which is almost impossible for many laymen to read, and which is almost impossible for many educated readers and those with literary interests to read with endurance. The pages of the philosophical journals are, in this country—not so much in England—marked by an almost deplorable absence of lucidity and directness.

On the other hand, there has been an increasing rebellion in the literary tradition against a kind of semi-philosophical generalization as in, say, Emerson or Thoreau, the general intellectual content and temper of nineteenth century essayists, such as Leigh Hunt and William Hazlitt. Poets have especially wanted to emphasize the vital particular, the concrete living detail, rather than the generalities and abstractions of analysis. Thus there has been a mutual suspicion between the camps of poets and men of letters, on the one hand, and the philosophers, on the other.

At the same time there has been a parallel and opposite phenomenon. It has been perfectly clear from the dawn of modern literature, and indeed earlier than that, but it has been especially clear since the beginning of the nineteenth century, or the late eighteenth, that, to take just two examples, poets such as Wordsworth and Coleridge, were immensely stimulated and immensely controlled by quite specifically identifiable philosophical ideas. Coleridge was, as it were, the poetic ambassador of the transcendental notions of late eighteenth century German philosophy. Wordsworth translated, or better transmuted, in the poetic and meditative imagery of his poem "The Prelude," the chief sediment, or spiritual deposit, of the German romantic tradition, in philosophy and of Platonism in the Western world; and Shelley combined the poet's sensibility to Platonism with a revelationary interest in such analytically political ideas as those of Godwin's *Political Justice*.

Coming nearer to our own time, it is perfectly clear that such diverse men of letters as T. S. Eliot, Thomas Mann, and Marcel Proust, have expressed in the forms of poetry and the novel, themes that obviously are animated by such diverse philosophies as those of Jacques Maritain, of Bergson, of Nietzsche, of Schopenhauer, and Kierkegaard. There is in the air (if one examines, for instance, a poem such as W. H. Auden's "The Age of Anxiety") or in the intellectual climate, precisely those leading themes which animate and absorb and academically preoccupy professional philosophers.

I

What then may we say is the proper, and what may we also say is the promise, or indicated relation, of philosophy to creative literature, or of the philosopher to the creative literary artist? It is a well known and curious fact, historically, that the divorce between philosophy and literature is a relatively recent one. This does not mean that there has not been technical discussion before the nineteenth and the twentieth century. All one has to do is to examine medieval ecclesiasticism, to see how very technical philosophical analysis could become. But in the great classic tradition of philosophy until very recently, in the modern world, the distinction between philosophy and literature was almost impossible to draw.

George Santayana once remarked that in the seventeenth and the eighteenth century philosophers wrote like gentlemen, not like professors. In England, for example, in David Hume and Berkeley, in Hobbes and in a great deal of John Locke, the man of letters and the man of thought were identical or were fused. There was a very good social reason for this; it was not an accident of temperament. The social reason was that philosophers were addressing themselves not to a special subject of professional analysis or to a special group of professional readers. They were addressing themselves to what Samuel Johnson called the "common reader." They were addressing themselves to the general educated public, and to the widest problems of human life.

In the early nineteenth century in this country, the great appeal of such philosophical writers as Theodore Parker, of Emerson, and Thoreau, was that ideas, presented in imaginative form and presented in the appropriate garment of effective English prose, appealed to the same public that was at the same time reading the novels of George Eliot and of Dickens and of Thackeray. Eliot is a peculiarly good illustration of the connection between fiction and philosophy, for here was a writer who, writing novels that are just beginning to be recognized as good stories, was also one of the leading moral teachers of the general public in England in the nineteenth century.

Again in France, the line between philosophy and literature is to this day almost impossible to draw, and in the great classic writers of French philosophy, Descartes, Pascal, Voltaire, Maritain, or the contemporary or recent philosophical writers in France, Bergson, for example, the line between philosophy and literature is never sharply drawn. The technical esoteric tradition of philosophical writing originated, along with other barbarities, in Germany. Someone once said that German philosophy could not have been invented without the German language. That is not accurate, for philosophical German is not the German language. It is a special jargon which happens to use words in certain coincidences resembling ordinary German words, but actually often the invention of the philosopher himself. The whole scheme of elaborately oversystematized verbal structure is almost a German invention, and it must be remembered that, historically,

American academic philosophy, like so many other branches of the academic tradition in America in the latter half of the nineteenth century, was peculiarly under German influence.

I say this to explain why it is in the past fifty years, and especially in this country, that while a general interest in ultimate questions has grown, philosophers have become a group talking to themselves in almost a private code language which is as far as possible from the normal cadences and overtones of literary discourse, and certainly as far as possible from literary expression as one can conceive.

If one goes back in the history of thought in France or England, or in the ancient world to Plato himself, the divorce between philosophy and literature was unknown; though it was Plato who remarked that there is an ancient enmity between poetry and philosophy; but it is Plato, himself, who is also a poet and a man of letters. (In the nineteenth century in Germany there are two remarkable exceptions to the prevailing private esoterica that constitute so much of German philosophy. Those two brilliant variants are Schopenhauer and Nietzsche, who happen to be great poets and stylists as well as impressive thinkers.)

II

So much for a brief glance at the history of our theme. To come more directly to the theme itself: it is apparent that to the more reflective writers of our generation the prevailing winds of doctrine have swept over their imagination. Their works became expressive of the current intellectual climate, as well as expressive of their private temperaments and their personal issues and problems. Writers in our age may select from the dominant winds of doctrine, so to speak, certain winds by which they will elect to be stirred, and driven, but there is hardly a contemporary poet or a contemporary novelist who is not sometimes plagued by, sometimes inspired by, precisely the kind of moral and ultimately logical or epistemological and metaphysical issues which preoccupy theologians and philosophers.

If contemporary men of letters are affected subconsciously, often quite explicitly, by current movements in those general ideas we call philosophy, in what sense do they express philosophical ideas? How adequate is literature, generally speaking, as a vehicle of philosophical instruction and edification, or of philosophical analysis? In what sense can we derive from an examination of contemporary writing of the more reflective kind, but nonetheless literature—in what sense can we from such reflective literature derive a reliable index to what is going on in the intellectual imagination of the present time? That is a peculiarly important question, because as a critic put it a generation ago, during the so-called flaming youth of the twenties, young men are taught the doctrine of ethics out of Aristotle by an elderly professor, but they get their ethical ideas out of novels by F. Scott Fitzgerald and Ernest Hemingway. They get their ideas through the imaginations of men of letters, and not through the analysis of philosophers.

In what way does the general reader learn philosophical ideas from writers? To give utterance to a private hobby and observation of my own about the relation of men of letters to philosophy, and at the risk of making a blunt and pretentious generalization, I will say that generally speaking there is a time lag between men of letters of any generation and philosophical ideas; so that, though it is not always recognized, the ideas that get current in literature are generally a thinned out version of ideas that the philosophers have ceased to deal with a generation earlier, or have ceased to deal with in the same way.

To give the first of the illustrations, there is the now rampant mode of literary philosophy called Existentialism. Someone remarked recently that one had to be in a soundproof room not to hear the word, "Existentialism." I remember being asked by an eminent lady, full of good works and a sincere but fluttery interest in ideas, "Now, tell me about Existentialism," which during the course of her good works she had got around to. I replied, "Just wait a year to ask that question, and you will not even be interested to ask it, and you will not even be interested in the answer." There are modes in ideas, and existentialist novels, existentialist plays, have been a vogue.

But if one examines the philosophical ideas in Existentialism, he finds that their sources are in a certain romantic tradition of subjective psychology, of an untenable half lyrical celebration of personal questioning, spiritual anguish, derived from a Danish philosopher named Kierkegaard and with additional roots in Schopenhauer and in Nietzsche. That kind of romantic self-pity and self-examination, self-anguish, acute introspection, is very old in philosophy; it is the latest thing, or recently was the latest thing, in literature.

Take another example. About 1920, there began to appear a series of novels by a brilliant young Oxonian satirist, a witty skeptic and cynic, named Aldous Huxley. His satire was based on his despair with a world in which he saw no meaning, in a world that implied the brute march of unconscious power, the movement of matter on its meaningless and relentless way. Huxley was writing in terms of an alien world, founded on the notion of the billiard ball physics of the nineteenth century. He was fond of speaking of the disillusion and desperation which came from the recognition of the Darwinian basis of human psychology. He wrote a poem of twelve lines which has the character of a romantic love lyric of the nineteenth century, but which ends with these two psychologically shocking lines, or lines that thirty years ago seemed shocking:

> And so we sat in blissful calm,
> Quietly sweating palm to palm.

That kind of desperate realization of the physical and biological basis of life and love was made on the basis of a simplified and also simpleminded materialism that had long passed away from philosophy. There was already appearing on the philosophical horizon the Bergsonian critique of pure intellectualism; in science, the simple literalness of Darwinian biology was no longer accepted, even by biologists; but the men of letters were continuing to write on ideas that were already not in the forefront of ideas in philosophical analysis.

Let me cite still another and famous illustration. Thomas Mann is celebrated at the present time as the most philosophical and intellectual of contemporary novelists. The most celebrated of his works in this respect is *The Magic Mountain,* which is marked, among other things, by sometimes interminable conversations between the hero, Hans Castorp, and the nineteenth century liberal, Settembrini. This international cosmopolitan, nineteenth century liberal's ideas are a kind of belated, retrospected encyclopedia of philosophical ideas that were fashionable in the late nineteenth century, particularly in Central Europe.

I call attention to this time lag in literature, or the time lag between the creation and origination of philosophical ideas and a literary expression of them, because literature reaches more people than technical philosophical analysis does, and it is often a surprise to professional philosophers, when they happen to circulate in the general human society, to find hailed as greatly novel and great revolutionary themes, ideas that in the profession of philosophers are old long before they enter contemporary poems and novels. I do not mean for a moment that poets and novelists should not use and exploit ideas. Nor do I mean for a moment that it is a business of poets and novelists to keep *à la page* and use only the latest words or ideas. That is not at all what I mean. The reason I call attention to this time lag is to correct the impression that contemporary literature, even among some very eminent practitioners, is really distinguished as freshness, as originality of thought, or as even a competent analytical presentation of philosophical ideas.

III

There is another important factor. Men of letters tend frequently to live beyond their intellectual income, and they deal with ideas which they cannot competently master or express. There is a striking recent instance in a very gifted man of letters, Arthur Koestler. Koestler published *Insight and Outlook,* which was a most singularly dogmatic collection of odds and ends of psychology and philosophy, uncritically used, enunciating what was supposed to be a new way of looking at experience. Without going into details, from the point of view of anyone versed in contemporary philosophical and psychological analysis, the book was the work of a hopeless amateur. *Insight and Outlook* did not happen to be offered as a work of art, but as a work of philosophy; but in works that are offered as works of art, the first thing we should note is that ideas are likely to be a generation old; secondly, that they are likely to be somewhat superficially, somewhat rhetorically, presented, or if they are presented with careful intellectual responsibility, it is the artistic quality of the work that suffers.

A poet who tries to write a textbook of ideas, is likely to end up by writing a textbook, rather than a poem. A novelist who insists that his novel should be a forum of ideas, is likely to have produced debaters with names attached to them, rather than living characters. The ways in which philosophy influences literature are or should be subtler than a set of explicit ideas which are deliberately incorporated into a work of art.

There is one famous contemporary instance of the finer, more delicate relation of philosophy to literature, and that is the work of Marcel Proust. Some who have read that extraordinary narrative, *Remembrance of Things Past,* will recall that the last volume, *Time Regained,* is a subtly nuanced meditation on the way in which art recaptures the vanished moments of memory, and in which the past becomes immortalized and eternally alive in the frozen recapitulations of artistic form. Many years before Proust wrote—many years as a generation goes—Bergson had published a book called *Matter and Memory* and also a book called *Time and Free Will.* There is no question (and there is plenty of evidence) that Proust was enormously influenced in his sense of what human consciousness is by the writings of Bergson, to whom he was, incidentally, distantly related. The effect of philosophy in the long novel of Proust was not the effect of a system of ideas, but the effect of a certain perspective and temper of approach, that gives the effect of a curiously meditative flowing stream of consciousness to the internal soliloquy and illuminated the author's reflections on what are the purpose of art and of literature. Proust is only one instance of the successful fusion of ideas and literary art.

When one reads that difficult, but not essentially obscure work of T. S. Eliot, *Four Quartets,* he is impressed with a poet at his best— an intellectual poet at his best—who is breathing, rather than analyzing certain great traditional themes of Platonic ideas and of the notions of the relation of time to eternity. Eliot, when he is writing as a reflective poet, is ever so much more effective than when in prose he is trying to be, often very badly and ineptly, an amateur philosopher.

With George Santayana, it is very hard to say, in any particular book, whether one is dealing with a poet or philosopher. It is an ironic coincidence that Santayana writes so well that for nearly a generation the philosophers hardly knew he was a philosopher at all. They have learned better now. For a long time they were extremely suspicious of anybody who wrote so beautifully. It happens that philosophers themselves discovered that below the glamor of his style was straight and responsible thinking.

Santayana is an example of a man who is his own philosopher and his own poet at once, who happened, however, to be more successful as an imaginative writer in all his books than in the one novel he wrote. *The Last Puritan* is an example of a philosopher living beyond his technical resources as a writer. Santayana did not happen primarily to be a novelist, but in his philosophical prose he comes as near to combining poetry and responsible analytical thought as anyone in this generation. And long after some of the little technical cults in philosophy have vanished, Santayana's prose and his philosophy will live. He once said that all his philosophy is contained in his sonnets. If he had continued as a poet, if he had written poetry on a large scale, he might well have written the philosophical poem of our generation.

IV

Roughly to summarize the relation of philosophy to creative literary art: philosophers work out new conceptions that become agents of critical reconstruction of our experience. The reason there is a time lag in the imaginative use of ideas by men of letters, is that men of letters, being creatures of imagination, are compelled to wait until ideas have become the general imaginative climate. When ideas are still in the academy, when they are still the subject of purely intellectual discussion, they are not appropriate to literary uses. They are simply abstractions which can only be barely and bleakly used. It is when they become incorporated into more general flavors of, and perspectives of experience, that they become the subject matter of creative literary art.

There is another way in which philosophy animates and sustains creative literature. The classical illustration is the relation of Dante to St. Thomas Aquinas. Dante's *Paradiso* in the *Divine Comedy* is an image, but it is a highly complex and imaginative image, incorporating the basic theme of Scholastic philosophy. In our own day there will doubtless in good time arise some imaginative poet or novelist who will be able to make a sustained image, in which all the spiritual tensions and all the daring intellectual hypotheses of our own day will not be made into a system, but transmuted into an artistic coherence like that of a symphony or a great painting.

About thirty years ago the then English Poet Laureate, Robert Bridges, who had been greatly influenced by Santayana, wrote a poem not very widely known called the "Testament of Beauty." It was an attempt to express Santayana's naturalism in poetic form. It was too deliberate, too academic an attempt. It was a translation, a word by word translation almost, of prose into poetry. But we could imagine there being born, by the good luck of statistical accident, some really great imaginative poet even in our own time, a poet such as Dante, who, having a wide and ranging intellectual vision, should also have the gift of literary art and in one sustained symphonic synthesis, as it were, express rather than state, disclose rather than argue, those relations of appearance to reality, the present to the future, of time to eternity, of the animal basis of human nature to man's spiritual possibilities, of the conflict in our own time between the necessity for security and the human passion for freedom. One could imagine a poet, who, catching these ideas by a kind of osmosis, having the antenna of his imagination—to change the metaphor—stirred or vibrated by these waves of ideas, could produce a work that should be at once an esthetic image, a work of art, and a work of philosophy.

IV

MUTATIONS OF BELIEF IN THE CONTEMPORARY NOVEL

BY

HORACE GREGORY

Whenever we are about to enter a new decade of an extremely self-conscious twentieth century, another critical effort is made to sum up, however faintly they may be discerned, the mutations of belief as they have been expressed in contemporary literature. Our self-consciousness is, I think, inherited from a habit formed during the nineteenth century, a century which in its middle years began to look upon itself in terms of scientific and material progress—I speak of our Western world which in its optimism and material wealth fondly embraced a popular notion of Darwinian evolution—and saw progress as though it were the continuous advancement of enlightened apes and men walking slowly onward and upward along an inclined plane.

In saying this I have probably done great injustice to the truly enlightened intellectuals of the nineteenth century, for not all of them conceived of Darwinism in such naive and popular terms, but here I am concerned with a general concept, however inaccurate it may be, that spread its branches into the popular arts, sciences, and philosophy.

Although Tennyson inverted the image of the inclined plane downward in the least fortunate of his metaphors, the notion of change was no less continuous in his enthusiastic lines:

Not in vain the distance beacons. Forward, forward let us range.
Let the great world spin forever down the ringing grooves of change.

35

So that today the popular notion, which is self-consciously temporal, still persists in a forward motion (as we approach the midcentury mark of 1950).

So much then for the popular notion of continuous change. But I would like to remark that the notion more properly describes changes in fashion than changes in art, and it can be applied with spectacular effect to the evolution of certain strictly mechanical inventions, extending from the first gasoline engine to the latest model of passenger airplane. What I wish to suggest is that the various conditions of imaginative being are not continuous, that man in the growth and decline of his civilizations does not move in a straight line up and down or backward and forward, that the ringing grooves of change, which Tennyson mistakenly conceived as a cultural railroad track, are quite irrelevant to the circular, often spiral movement of human imagination and belief.

I

I, of course, am not the only one who has this conception of change in literature. Paul Valéry, twenty years ago, in one of his books, remarked that literature was always discontinuous, that what he discerned as new movements in literature did not proceed directly from one movement to another. And if I may refer to, let us say, American poetry in the nineteenth century, we have Walt Whitman. Walt Whitman was a very different kind of poet from the poet who came after him, Edwin Arlington Robinson. To my mind that kind of change, that kind of mutation is a change of the greatest significance; and it does not move in a straight line.

It is my belief that what we often describe as changes in belief, as they transform painting, literary expression, and indeed all the various media of imaginative life, are, in reality, a series of intersecting spirals, and that as one intersects the other, we call that transformation "change." With the spirals that seem at times to widen and suddenly contract are impure elements of philosophic and religious belief existing as contradictions in a work of art, because no purely scientific, or rational, or irrational, or even purely esthetic work of art exists. The names given to various schools of art are there for the purpose of intellectual convenience. We merely agree to broad definitions of what is classical and romantic, neo-classical and neo-romantic, realistic and non-objective, spiritual and material, or religious and rational.

I have found in James Joyce's first draft of *The Portrait of an Artist as a Young Man* a very illuminating redefinition of the terms that we think of as either romantic or classical. He also refers to the spiral movement here, by saying that he imagines the domain of an art to be cone shaped. To Stephen, Joyce's hero, the term, "literature," seemed a term of contempt,

and he used it to designate the vast middle region which lies between apex and base, between poetry and the chaos of unremembered writing. Its merit lay in its portrayal of externals: the realm of its princes was the realm of the manners and customs of societies—a spacious realm. But society is itself, he conceived, the complex body in which certain laws are involved and overwrapped and he therefore proclaimed as the realm of the poet the realm of these unalterable laws. Such a theory might easily have led its devisor to the acceptance of spiritual anarchy in literature had he not at the same time insisted on the classical style. A classical style, he said, is the syllogism of art, the only legitimate process from one world to another. Classicism is not the manner of any fixed age or any fixed country: it is a constant state of the artistic mind. It is a temper of security and satisfaction and patience. The romantic temper, so often and so grievously misinterpreted and not more by others than its own, is an insecure, unsatisfied, impatient temper which sees no fit abode here for its ideas and chooses therefore to behold them under insensible figures. As a result of this choice it comes to disregard certain limitations. Its figures are blown to wild adventures, lacking the gravity of solid body, and the mind that has conceived them ends by disowning them. The classical temper on the other hand, ever mindful of limitation, chooses rather to bend upon these present things and so work upon them and fashion them that the quick intelligence may go beyond them to their meaning which is still unuttered.[1]

I happened to regard this as a theological redefinition of *classical* and *romantic*. In studies of the arts these terms are often so hopelessly abused that it is difficult to know what is meant and what one is re-

[1] James Joyce, *Stephen Hero*, New Directions, New York, 1944, p. 78.

quired to believe, and what had begun as a hopeful basis for agreement often ends today in a retreat to philology, or rather, as the French reintroduced it from German studies in literature, a study in semantics, which is not properly a study of literature at all, but a renewed excursion into a scientific and psychological analysis of language.

II

It has been, of course, no secret that we have been living in what has been called so often a scientific age, but until recently it has taken some courage for intellectuals of the Western world—and particularly the intellectuals of England and the United States—to admit that they were also living in a world where religion and ethics were not totally abandoned. This realization was not a sudden change in the deeper responses of belief, but in the mutations of fashionable attitudes. During the past fifty years the experience of two world wars, and from both the emergence of the totalitarian state in Italy, in Germany, in Russia, as well as for brief intervals in smaller nations, has offered terrifying examples of the political machine—and I use the word, "machine," advisedly—with its demands for absolute power. It has caused some intellectuals to become disillusioned, others fearful, and still others frankly ashamed at the physical presence of a destructive non-morality which had existed within the very center of a material and scientific age.

The very sight of a deliberately blacked out Europe, rained upon by bombs and rockets, all scientifically prepared, was not a reassuring spectacle, particularly if one viewed it as among the wonders that science had contrived for the betterment of mankind. A hundred years ago young men and women, faced by the promises that scientific progress had brought before them, grew doubtful of the kind of earthly security offered them by religion—a security, by the way, which, since the Middle Ages and the loss of temporal power by the Church of Rome, was not among the principal credos of the Christian faith. Today a measure of the same doubt enters the thinking of those who believed too blindly in the security attendant upon scientific progress—and this time doubt has begun to undermine even the cheerful tenets of utilitarianism and pragmatism and the benefits achieved through the widespread practice of psychology.

If there is any change in the temper of imaginative writing between the dates of 1900 and 1950, the loss of faith in material and scientific progress has been among the elements of that change, an impure element, crossing and intersecting other elements of belief. And in saying this, I am aware that in using the phrase, "imaginative writing," I shall have to begin to limit my discussion to contemporary fiction, because the poets of the Western world have for the greater part and with remarkable consistency regarded science through the lenses, opera glasses, if you will, of irony and skepticism. Material philosophies among the poets have been rare. Plato, though he disowned the poets, has had more followers among poets than Hobbes or Marx; and today Kierkegaard has greater weight, as well as Whitehead, than either James or Dewey.

But the writers of fiction, those who write short stories and novels, have in this respect been less fortunate than the poets. Their seriousness, their standards of success and of failure, have been, and are even more pointedly today, modified by considerations of commercial value. Because of the very medium the novelist employs, and because it is generally supposed that the public that reads anything at all enjoys reading fiction, the publisher in both England and the United States tends to regard a work of fiction in the same light that he regards any other piece of merchandise. However strongly a novelist may believe what he writes, his survival depends upon his ingenuity to cope with the fashions of his day, to accept the disciplines exerted by public favor, or whatever his publisher thinks the public wants to read. This general rule, to which there are notable exceptions, applies to thousands of volumes published every year.

From this great mass of literature, in which vague tendencies in popular responses may be charted, it is impossible to arrive at any clear definition of changes in belief. On this level sexual content, however disguised, holds the same measure of interest in fiction as it did twenty or thirty or forty or fifty or one hundred years ago. So does the story of crime and of dual personality; and so does the fiction of historical romance, which in one aspect is a view of the past and in another aspect looks to the future in scientific fantasies, utopias, or political warnings, as in *Nineteen Eighty-Four,* or as in *Looking Backward*. The touch of originality that Upton Sinclair has given his series of historical romances is that he has used directly the fiction drawn from current newspapers.

But this continuous stream of fiction floats far above what I regard as the deeper levels of belief and serious concern. On these levels one clear observation can be made: that between 1918 and the present moment the fiction of naturalism has died a natural death. This does not mean that realism has completely disappeared as one of the elements of contemporary fiction, but that the extremes of techniques in realistic fiction no longer follow the rules by which Zola was so long regarded as a master. Even those who admired his example and admitted his influence—the most noteworthy of these being Theodore Dreiser—began to feel that the so-called natural laws of environment and biology could not and do not explain all the springs and motives of human action, will, and desire. It is significant that in his old age Dreiser created a hero whose merits were derived from the Quaker heritage in which the American example is the figure of John Woolman.

III

I would like to add another note to this by quoting from Joseph Conrad. Conrad was regarded at one time as a realistic novelist, but he is a realistic novelist with a great difference from the realism of his fellow writers. He is also a moralist and I think a very significant one. The following quotation from *Lord Jim* will illustrate this, like the quotation from *Stephen Hero,* this has to do with a novelist's attitude toward art and life:

"He lifted up a long forefinger.

" 'There is only one remedy! One thing alone can us from being our-selves cure!' The finger came down on the desk with a smart rap. The case which he had made to look so simple before became if possible still simpler—and altogether hopeless. There was a pause. 'Yes,' said I, 'strictly speaking, the question is not how to get cured, but how to live.'

"He approved with his head, a little sadly as it seemed. 'Ja! Ja! In general, adapting the words of your great poet: That is the question . . .' He went on nodding sympathetically . . . 'How to be! Ach! How to be!'

"He stood up with the tips of his fingers resting on the desk.

" 'We want in so many different ways to be,' he began again. 'This magnificent butterfly finds a little heap of dirt and sits still on it; but man he will never on his heap of mud keep still. He want to be so, and again he want to be so . . .' He moved his hand up, then down. 'He wants to be a saint, and he wants to be a devil—and every time he shuts his eyes he sees himself as a very fine fellow so fine as can never be . . . In a dream . . .'

. . . .

" 'And because you not always can keep your eyes shut there comes the real trouble—the heart-pain—the world-pain. I tell you, my friend, it is not good for you to find you cannot make your dream come true, for the reason that you not strong enough are, or not clever enough. Ja! . . . And all the time you are such a fine fellow, too! . . . How can that be? . . .

. . . .

" 'Yes! Very funny this terrible thing is. A man that is born falls into a dream like a man who falls into the sea. If he tries to climb out into the air as inexperienced people endeavor to do, he drowns—*nicht wahr?* . . . No! I tell you! The way is to the destructive element submit yourself, and with the exertions of your hands and feet in the water make the deep, deep sea keep you up. So if you ask me—how to be?' " [2]

That phrase, "the destructive element," was something that remained in the minds of serious novelists. Henry James thought over the phrase with considerable care, and later on we hear from him an echo of the statement: "In the destructive element immerse. That is the way." And certain novelists hoped as Celine hoped in *Journey to the End of Night,* to go far enough into darkness so as to see the light, which is a concept that a poet such as Edwin Arlington Robinson had. In Europe and after World War I the apotheosis of naturalism, stripped of its optimism, was reached in Celine's *Journey to the End of Night.* It is well to remember that the central figure

[2] Joseph Conrad, *Lord Jim,* J. M. Dent & Sons, Ltd., London, 1935, pp. 155 f.

in that confession of absolute nihilism was a physician, an unsuccessful practitioner of biological science in the slums of Paris, the touch of whose hand upon a patient was the touch of death. Today the book may be regarded, aside from its temporal value, as a pathological document, as one of the many forewarnings of World War II; and in its complete negation of the human spirit, it had sufficient power to create a vacuum which could be filled only by a reassertion of humane intelligence.

By 1935, it became evident that naturalism in fiction had literally travelled to the end of night, and among writers of serious fiction the tenets of Marxian materialism began to reveal themselves as antagonistic to imaginative writing. Critics of fiction then turned to three sources of newly awakened inspiration: the novels of Henry James, of Herman Melville, and of Franz Kafka. Of these it is of some interest to note that James had gone through three separate stages of interpretation: first, as a psychological novelist, then, as a critic of society, and, third, as a moralist, scrupulous in his attention to Christian ethics. This last stage has had its weight upon younger writers of the nineteen hundred and forty's. The latter two writers of fiction were rediscovered as carriers of a biblical and an Hebraic heritage and what was first admired in Kafka as realism—and the same interpretation attended early readings of James Joyce's *Ulysses*—became transformed into a glimmering vision of Kafka's religious purpose, with its relationships between man and man and the inaccessibility of God. It was then rediscovered that Melville's contribution to our literature was transcendental in its import. These rediscoveries began to fill the vacuum that had been created through the general collapse of realism.

IV

So much then for the general historical background of a change in temper which now affects a group of novelists writing in English on both sides of the Atlantic. In Britain, the change in temper has been attended by the neo-Catholic satires of Evelyn Waugh, extended from *Vile Bodies,* which remains the best of many, to *The Loved One.*

It should be observed that the satires, good as they are, still carry their greatest weight in situations not too far distant from the horrors of *Journey to the End of Night.* Spiritual dryness still pervades the scene. And something of the same horror attends the settings of Graham Greene's entertainments and stories of criminal action. It is still too early to say how deeply the fiction of Waugh and Greene is representative of the contemporary scene, but it should be said that the theological novel in English is a rare phenomenon. One thinks of *Pilgrim's Progress,* or in the late nineteenth century the historical romance of Shorthouse's *John Ingelsant,* and in America a few of the shorter tales of Hawthorne. But aside from these, little of excellence in theological fiction provides a precedent for the young writer who attempts to fill the vacuum that realistic fiction has left in its wake.

I may suggest, however, a few examples which the promise of change that seems imminent in contemporary fiction comes to light. One book is J. F. Powers's *Prince of Darkness,* a collection of short stories, which, so it seems to me, brings forward again into the foreground of speculation certain theological propositions. The title story itself is extremely interesting. It is the story of an ambitious priest, one who wants to get on in his vocation, who through sloth and gluttony failed to accomplish what he wishes. A story in which the theological aspect of gluttony and sloth play any part at all is rare these days. Powers has handled the situation with humor and with insight, and probably he has profited by a reading of James Joyce's, *Stephen Hero,* the first draft of *The Portrait of an Artist,* which in a sense is a theological novel—not a finished one or a tremendously good one, but one that had promise of better work to come. And I think that Powers has also read Joyce's *Dubliners.*

Another writer who has our respect and is being read today is William Faulkner. When Faulkner began writing his novels, they were regarded as realistic novels and among them were *Sanctuary* and *As I Lay Dying.* Today, through his book of short stories, *Go Down Moses,* and his *Intruder in the Dust,* he is being regarded, and rightfully I think, as a moralist. The situation in *Intruder in the Dust* is on the surface, nothing more than the conventional lynching story. It is what he does with that lynching story that makes it significant, bringing up moral problems, ethical problems in relationship to the lynching, making the characters in the book realize that an ethic is at work in the situation. I rather think that in the future the later work of William Faulkner will probably be used as an example of what I have been talking about, of a change in contemporary fiction in the United States—for the implications of Faulkner's recent work all bear upon moral and ethical considerations.

I do not know whether Mr. Powers, who is still a very young man, will grow to maturity with the kind of writing for which he is known today. That is all in the future. I do not know whether we will have other novelists such as Mr. Powers: among younger writers we can discern a subcurrent of religious belief, that is very, very strong, yet only a few novelists of our time have had the art to treat the subject of religion seriously.

I would like to conclude with another quotation from Joyce's *Stephen Hero*. He speaks of human imagination and he says:

The imagination has contemplated intently the truth of the being, of the visible world, and the beauties and splendor of truth has been born. The imagination, though it bury itself fathoms deep in formulas and machinery, has need of these realities which alone give and sustain life and it must await from those chosen centers of civilization the force to live, the security for life, which can come to it only from them. Thus the spirit of man makes a continual affirmation.[3]

[3] Joyce, *op. cit.*

V

MAN'S SPIRITUAL SITUATION AS REFLECTED IN MODERN DRAMA [1]

BY

THEODORE SPENCER

As we look at the history of the drama in Western civilization before the twentieth century, the periods when it has been capable of high and serious presentation, of high and serious human concerns, are seen to be very short. If we think of a generation as lasting thirty-five years, they add up to a total of only about five generations: one and a half in Greece, one in England, one in France, and, less certainly, one in Spain and one in Germany. It would seem, as we reflect on this fact, that society cannot long sustain at a high level the most social of the arts, and that once a particular culture has produced its highest dramatic expression, has had its turn at greatness, it does not get another chance. Some societies, like that of Rome, seem never to have had a chance at all.

One cause for this short winded uniqueness may perhaps lie in the conditions which apparently are necessary before great drama can flourish. Leaving aside technical conditions of the stage and the accident of genius (two very large omissions), and using as evidence our knowledge of the five generations which I have mentioned, these conditions may be briefly and tentatively described as follows:

1. A vigorous self-confidence on the part of the body of society that its standards and methods of behavior are valid and important, a self-confidence so strong, as to be largely unconscious.

[1] Professor Spencer died a few days after he presented this manuscript at The Institute for Religious and Social Studies, January 11, 1949. The chapter, therefore, did not have the benefit of the author's corrections.

2. A vigorous confidence, equally strong and equally taken for granted, that individual human passion is valid and important.

3. A sense of the potentialities of evil as most fiercely latent in the extremes of individualism, and manifested through egoism, pride, *hybris*.

4. A consciousness of the inevitability of conflict between this individualistic evil and the real or apparent well-being of society, as expressed in its standards and methods of behavior.

5. A sufficiently mature series of assumptions about man and society, so that in playwright and audience alike there is possible an awareness of illusion in reality and reality in illusion, for either tragic or comic purposes.

I

These conditions, of course, always exist to some extent, and they are neither all inclusive nor necessarily distinguishable from each other. The most one can say of them is that they seem to be among the elements that are usually predominant in the complex set of relationships which has produced important drama in Western civilization in the past. They loom behind or are reflected within the work of the Greek tragedians, Shakespeare, and Racine. It is likely that if we are to have an important drama today, they will be behind and within that drama, too, and that if they are lacking, the drama will not be as important or as serious as we would like it to be, and the heights and depths of man's spiritual situation will remain untouched.

There are two opposite kinds of cultural climate which seem to be unfavorable to good drama; in one a set of values is too thoroughly and universally imposed by education and authority, as in medieval Europe and in the USSR; in the other, all values are seen to be possible, and, therefore, all acts forgivable, because their origins can be anthropologically or psychologically explained. This last situation is the one into which our contemporary intelligentsia is in danger of falling. But drama cannot flourish when values are flaccid. Great drama has to admit the unforgivable; it has, in other words, if it is to express man's spiritual awareness, to recognize the existence of a force which needs no name but which has been called "fate," or "destiny"; in religious terms, "God"; or, metaphysically speaking, "a power under God."

I will return to this important matter in a moment. Before we look at contemporary drama in the light of it, however, it is necessary to make one more preliminary point, namely, that in speaking about man's *spiritual* situation, we are speaking about something different from man's *moral* situation. The two are, of course, closely, inextricably, connected. They are like two circles, so interlocking that the circumference of one passes through the center of the other. But that means that each occupies an area which the other does not cover. The confusion between them has arisen largely because of the contemporary attitude toward sex, and the emphasis given to the effect of his sexual behavior on the relation of an individual to his psychological well-being and his social environment. Contemporary society, especially in America, puts both too much and too little emphasis on sexual behavior; too much, because it is often looked at as the *only* way in which a human being can behave morally for good or ill, and too little, because in a nervous civilization the potential richness of the fullest kind of sexual behavior is often not sufficiently realized. The resulting confusion between spiritual concerns and values and moral concerns and values, may be illustrated in such a play as Eugene O'Neill's *Days Without End*. The play is a crude one, not by any means one of Mr. O'Neill's best, but it is a significant indication of how a spiritual problem can be made overdependent on a moral issue based on sex. John Loving, the hero of the play, is writing an autobiographical novel. He is a split personality played by two actors—one wearing a mask—representing his positive and negative attitudes toward the Catholic religion his uncle, a priest, has brought him up in. He is married, deeply in love with his wife, but has had a momentary affair with another woman. When his wife finds out about this, she is so upset and unforgiving that she walks out in the rain and gets pneumonia. About to die, she decides to forgive after all, and her recovery is promised. The final scene shows the two sides of John Loving before a crucifix. As the positive side, praying that his wife get well, embraces the love of the cross, the negative side crumples and expires, and the play ends with the hero restored, in a mystic vision, to his faith.

Mr. O'Neill here is obviously dealing with a spiritual struggle. But, as elsewhere in his plays, he seems to think of it only in terms of a moral crisis brought on by the pressure of sexual love. The result is that a literate audience is bound to think of both John Loving and his wife as immature and even foolish. The matter is not discussed on an adult level; the effect is more that of nervous strain than emotional strength, largely because, in spite of the fact that traditional religion is, as it were, one of the protagonists, the hero thinks of it only in relation to his own neurotic state; a sexual slip is made the basis for a possible spiritual disaster, and both the faith and the lack of faith of the hero seem unreal.

"Women are not, as they suppose," says the Elder in Bernard Shaw's *Too True to be Good,* "more interesting than the universe. When the universe is crumbling let women be silent; and let men rise to something nobler than kissing them." [2]

Indeed this play of Shaw's represents an opposite way of presenting man's spiritual problems than that of O'Neill in *Days Without End.* Reading it, we are no longer in O'Neill's murky landscape, where the trees are all full of knots and the soil is that of a bog; Shaw's atmosphere is a daylight atmosphere, though the air is as dry as a desert. The dilemmas that O'Neill's characters find themselves in involve them in the flesh and the nerves; Shaw's dilemmas are those of the mind. They involve a higher grade of passion. How different from the somewhat maudlin ending of O'Neill's play is the ending of Shaw's, where the ex-burglar and preacher, whom Shaw calls a rascal and who is partly Shaw himself, cries eloquently in the wilderness of our time:

How are we to bear this dreadful new nakedness: the nakedness of the souls who until now have always disguised themselves from one another in beautiful impossible idealisms to enable them to bear one another's company. The iron lightning of war has burnt great rents in these angelic

[2] George Bernard Shaw, *Too True to be Good,* Dodd, Mead & Company, New York, 1934.

veils. . . . Our souls go in rags now; and the young are spying through
the holes and getting glimpses of the reality that was hidden. And they
are not horrified: they exult in having found us out; they expose their
own souls; and when we their elders desperately try to patch our torn
clothes with scraps of the old material, the young lay violent hands on us
and tear from us even the rags that were left us. But when they have
stripped themselves and us utterly naked, will they be able to bear the
spectacle?

. . . I am by nature and destiny a preacher. I am the new Ecclesiastes.
But I have no Bible, no creed; the war has shot both out of my hands.
The war has been a fiery forcing house in which we have grown with a
rush like flowers in a late spring following a terrible winter. And with
what result? This: that we have outgrown our religion, outgrown our
political system, outgrown our strength of mind and character. The fatal
word NOT has been miraculously inscribed into all our creeds. . . . But
what next? Is NO enough? For a boy, yes; for a man, never. . . . I must
have affirmations to preach. . . . The preacher must preach the way of
life— Oh, if I could only find it! (A white sea fog swirls up from the
beach to his feet, rising and thickening around him.) I am ignorant; I
have lost my nerve and am intimidated; all I know is that I must find the
way of life, for myself and all of us, or we shall surely perish. . . .[3]

As we think of these two plays side by side, one too mired in the
neurotic sexuality of its emotional dark, one too stripped and abstract
in the rarefication of its rational light, they may be considered as two
possible extremes in the dramatic presentation of man's contemporary
spiritual situation. They may serve as points of comparison, as we
briefly survey the enormous area of contemporary drama, and try to
draw a few valid conclusions from what we see.

II

Maxwell Anderson has written that "from the point of view of the
playwright, the essence of a tragedy, or even of a serious play, is the
spiritual awakening, or regeneration, of his hero,"[4] and though the

---

[3] *Ibid.*

[4] Maxwell Anderson, *The Essence of Tragedy, And Other Footnotes and Papers,*
Anderson House, Washington, 1939, p. 10.

statement needs more amplification and qualification than Mr. Anderson himself gives it, no one would deny, I believe, its essential truth. The problem is to define what contemporary society allows us to mean by the hero, and to be sure we know what we are saying when we speak of spiritual awakening, or regeneration.

In describing the periods in Western civilization when great drama has flourished, I left out, you will have noticed, our own most recent past, and the great drama of Ibsen, Chekhov, Strindberg, of which we are the present heirs. The omission was deliberate. For though it is grossly unfair to put those three writers into the same category, and no generalization can cover all the work of any one of them, it is roughly accurate to say that their plays and those of many of their contemporaries differ from the great plays of earlier periods in that society, as a force for good or ill, as something to be rebelled against or to be worked for, plays a larger and more essential role in their works than in the drama, say, of Racine or Shakespeare. This is a natural and even obvious reflection of the trend of modern thinking. Consequently, the typical hero of modern drama is likely to be a different figure from the hero of earlier drama. The hero at all times is best described in terms of the forces which urge him to spiritual redemption; when Goethe made his Faust end his career by draining a swamp for the benefit of generalized mankind, he fathered a type of hero whose spiritual state and spiritual concern are clearly far away from those of Oedipus or Lear. Humanitarian devotion to social welfare as a pledge for salvation, is not the same thing as the kind of realization that makes Oedipus put out his eyes, or melts the heart of Lear with pity and love. Humanitarian devotion is not in itself even necessarily a spiritual act; Ibsen's Dr. Stockman, in *An Enemy of the People,* battling polluted greed for the good of his community, is not a *spiritual* figure, as are Brand and Solness the Master Builder. The discovery Dr. Stockman makes is not of a new dimension inside himself but of an evil in the society outside him, and though he fights that evil heroically, the result is not a tragic catharsis.

The difficulty is that though society may be an agent of what we feel to be destiny, when we identify it with destiny, we feel that destiny has shrunk. To be herself, to be a fitting opponent for the hero, destiny must be larger than a mere aggregate of human beings, or a mere expression of social patterns. We need once more to keep in mind the distinction between moral and spiritual values. It is also important to keep in mind the distinction between a hero and a victim, a distinction which seems obvious at first, but, as we look at much contemporary literature, actually is not. There are a large number of plays with "social significance" that confuse the two; in fact, any playwright who has a deterministic view of human nature is almost bound to make the confusion sooner or later. Marxist drama, for example, is doomed from the start; I mean drama whose scene is laid in an ideal Marxist community—good drama from a Marxist point of view could still be written when the Marxist hero was fighting a bourgeois environment. But the writer in an ideal Marxist state is doomed, in the first place, because Marxist theory would condemn the playwright to consider his characters merely products, victims, of their environment; and, in the second place, because an individual who represented rebellion against this view, and whom we, and the general tradition of European culture, would call a hero, would have to be described by a Marxist as a villain. (The ideal Marxist state can never resist too many splits. Therefore, there will always be conflict, and hence drama of a potential heroism. But no good Marxist should admit this.) It is not even necessary to be a Marxist to fall into the deterministic pit. Plays such as John Howard Lawson's *Processional,* Paul Green's *Johnny Johnson,* Elmer Rice's *The Adding Machine,* deal with victims, not heroes. They may be given extra importance by being dressed up as symbols, but what they symbolize is mere victimization by social forces. For example, Mr. Zero, in *The Adding Machine,* is told by the supernatural agent who moves him about that "The mark of the slave was on you from the start." [5] He is described as "the ready prey of the first jingo or demagogue or political adventurer who takes the trouble to play upon your ignorance and credulity and provincialism." [6] Obviously there is nothing heroic

[5] Elmer L. Rice, *The Adding Machine,* Samuel French, New York and Los Angeles, 1929. Copyright, 1922, 1929, by Elmer L. Rice. All Rights Reserved. Reprinted by permission of the author and Samuel French.

[6] *Ibid.*

about a type such as this. We may pity him, but he is fundamentally an uninteresting bore. Being purely a victim, he is unable to do what a hero must do, if he is to hold our adult attention; he has no responsibility, and, therefore, cannot make decisions. An adult mind, a mind capable of spiritual aspiration, if it is to recognize itself at its best, needs to be convinced, as it watches the behavior of its equals, of the vigor in a given situation of free will. The free will may be defeated by the forces of destiny—forces which in the highest drama are often within the hero as much as his free will is within him—it may be unable to act, it may be sublimated from conflict with destiny into union with destiny, it may even be shown to be an illusion, but it must, on the evidence of all human experience, be an active force, if we are to believe that we are watching and sharing human greatness. It is a commonplace to point out that the tendency of the times makes free will insignificant, as the psychologists, anthropologists, and sociologists show us how our backgrounds have shaped us into what we are; and one can readily understand why playwrights like Mr. Lawson, Mr. Green, and Mr. Rice, anxious to express the times as accurately as possible, have written plays about victims with no will, or illusion of will, of their own. But time takes its revenge on those overanxious to capture it as it flies, and those three plays I have mentioned, and others like them, seem out of date, almost mere period pieces, as one reads them today. We must turn to plays of a different kind, if we are to find a more positive expression of man's true spiritual situation in modern drama. What we want (and how easy it is for an academic figure to make these huge demands, how difficult for the practical playwright to fulfil them!) is the sort of play that will be as specific and concrete as O'Neill and as generalized as Shaw, without either the naïveté of the one or the aridity of the other, plays that have those qualities of the great drama of the past which I outlined at the beginning, and which at the same time are rooted in the life of the present, plays—

But I am reminded by another occasion:

". . . the prince cried out, 'Enough! Thou hast convinced me that no human being can ever be a poet. Proceed with thy narration.'"

III

It can be said that in general the modern plays which have most successfully presented man's spiritual situation have not had contemporary *intellectual* consciousness as their subject matter or their background. Their characters and locale have been removed either by historical time or cultural time. The nervous urban intellectual, the sophisticate, has either had no deep spiritual consciousness to express, or no playwright has thought of an adequate situation in which to express it. Like Alan Squier in Robert Sherwood's *Petrified Forest,* this sophisticate has, in the drama, done little more than repeat the negatives of Shaw's moral preaching. When asked what he has been looking for all his life, Squier can reply only, "Well—that's rather hard to say. I—I suppose I've been looking for something to believe in. I've been hoping to find something that's worth living for —and dying for." [7] Squier does find something to die for, but in doing so he moves out of his previous background. His redemption, significantly enough, involves a repudiation of the sophisticated values which made him representative of his kind. The significance lies in the inevitability of such a renunciation, for a world permeated by disillusionment cannot create a healthy drama. I do not need to point out that there is plenty of disillusionment in contemporary thinking, but it seems to have its main place in the theater as a backdrop for frivolity and even sentiment, as in the works of Noel Coward, rather than as a possible basis for serious expression. It is too negative for serious expression. As I suggested to begin with, a major requirement for the creation of serious drama seems to be "a vigorous self-confidence on the part of the body of society that its standards and methods of behavior are valid and important, a self-confidence so strong as to be largely unconscious." An important part of the serious dramatist's job today is to set his action in an environment where that self-confidence can be found, and project himself, his characters,

[7] Robert E. Sherwood, *The Petrified Forest,* Charles Scribner's Sons, New York, 1936.

and his audience into it. That is why nearly all the best plays of our time have been set in the historical or cultural past.

Shaw's *St. Joan* is an obvious example; the historical dramas of Mr. Anderson, though on a somewhat different level, are others. But the choice of a historical setting (and the assumption of a set of values belonging to that setting) does not by any means guarantee a play's success. A superficial mind will treat everything superficially, and no matter how remote the environment and its values, there obviously must be something in the environment and the values to which a contemporary audience responds. No one can fail to respond, for example, to Joan's splendid speech when she refuses life imprisonment, a speech that is one of Shaw's finest embodiments of belief in the vigor of individual life, the belief which throughout his career has been his great reply to the blight of determination:

> You promised me my life; but you lied.
> You think that life is nothing but not being stone dead. It is not the bread and water I fear: I can live on bread; when have I asked for more? It is no hardship to drink water if the water be clean. Bread has no sorrow for me, and water no affliction. But to shut me from the light of the sky and the sight of the fields and flowers; to chain my feet so that I can never ride again with the soldiers nor climb the hills; to make me breathe foul damp darkness, and keep from me everything that brings me back to the love of God when your wickedness and foolishness tempt me to hate Him: all this is worse than the furnace in the Bible that was heated seven times. I could do without a warhorse; I could drag about in a skirt; I could let the banners and the trumpets and the knights and soldiers pass me and leave me behind as they leave the other women, if only I could still hear the wind in the trees, the larks in the sunshine, the young lambs crying through the healthy frost, and the blessed blessed church bells that send my angel voices floating to me on the wind. But without these things I cannot live; and by your wanting to take them away from me, or from any human creature, I know that your counsel is of the devil, and that mine is of God.[8]

By imaginatively throwing himself into the past in a way that Shakespeare, though Shakespeare wrote mostly about the past, did

---

[8] George Bernard Shaw, *St. Joan,* Brentano's, New York, 1924.

not have to do, Shaw can give emotional vitality to his conflict, the greatest spiritual conflict that drama can handle, the conflict which Sophocles describes in *Antigone* as the conflict between the law of man and the law of God. T. S. Eliot in dramatizing the death of Thomas à Becket in *Murder in the Cathedral,* takes the same theme, though he introduces a schematization which is different from anything in Shaw. Eliot's characters are deliberately divided into a hierarchy of four spiritual levels: the blindly passive and suffering women of Canterbury who form the chorus, a kind of pedal-point in humanity, then the worldly tempters, themselves representing four levels of increasingly potent worldliness, then the priests who are on Becket's side, but for merely human and literal reasons, and finally Becket, himself, achieving a spiritual pinnacle where he can catch a wink of heaven. As in *St. Joan,* the representatives of the law of man win a temporal victory through murder, but spiritual triumph is the victory of the hero.

When I said a moment ago that though Shakespeare also took the past for the subject matter of his greatest plays, he treated it differently from Shaw—or from Eliot—I was suggesting that Shakespeare's age —one with definite confident convictions—could treat the past in terms of its *own* values, whereas a modern writer, in our unconfident age, an age with a much keener historical sense than Shakespeare's, must move more completely into the past for his values. The world of Shakespeare's *Troilus and Cressida* is not morally and spiritually the world of 1200 B.C.; it is the world of 1602 expressed through antique symbols, and Hector can speak of Aristotle with only a superficial violation of chronology. But a modern playwright cannot afford to neglect historical differences, and the more fully he puts himself into the properly chosen past, the more readily he is able to express spiritual values. There are several implications of this; one is that when handled with skill, as by Shaw and Eliot, the presentation of spiritual values in a historic situation is still deeply moving to a large number of people, a fact which may be taken as evidence that there is a large spiritual reservoir in our society (or rather in the individuals who make up our society) which much contemporary thought does not tap, but which is there to *be* tapped by the right person and the right situation and the right time. Another implication is that if we have to borrow values from the past, if we have to go back to the past to find values to express, then our present is a poor thing, two dimensional and spiritually enervated. If we are to use as evidence certain contemporary expressions of man's relation to the universe, this would indeed seem to be true. The final speech of Esdras, at the end of Maxwell Anderson's *Winterset,* might be taken as an example of much of what passes at present for an expression of spiritual insight and aspiration.

On this star, in this hard star-adventure, knowing not what the fires mean to right and left, nor whether a meaning was intended or presumed, man can stand up, and look out blind and say: in all these turning lights I find no clue, only a masterless night, and in my blood no certain answer, yet is my mind my own, yet is my heart a cry toward something dim in distance, which is higher than I am and makes me emperor of the endless dark even in seeking! [9]

This is obviously well intentioned, but if its somewhat smoky mixture of romanticism and neo-stoicism represents the best available thought about man's spiritual condition at the present time, there is little wonder that playwrights take refuge in the more vigorous dogmas of the past. Even if those dogmas represent merely something for their heroes and heroines to fight against, it is at least something with teeth in it.

The second way, as I have suggested, in which spiritual conflict has been successfully presented in the modern theater is by setting the action in the cultural past rather than in the historical past, by writing about the year 1949, for instance, but removing the scene to a community where older values than those available in sophisticated society are still simple and strong. William Vaughan Moody's *The Faith Healer* did this with some success some forty years ago; a more recent example is Paul Green's *The Field God,* to my mind one of the best plays of our time. It is based on a genuine and profound conflict between two values, both of which are worthy. Hardy Gilchrist,

[9] Maxwell Anderson, "Winterset," *Eleven Verse Plays, 1929–1939,* Harcourt, Brace & Company, New York, 1940. Copyright by Maxwell Anderson and used with permission of Anderson House.

is an agnostic farmer whose invalid first wife is a religious fanatic; he is in love with and desires a younger woman who has come to live in the house. He restrains his desires with difficulty but marries the woman after his first wife's death. But everything goes against him because of the hostility of the neighbors and the continuous influence of the first wife's belief in her husband's unfaithfulness. The core of the situation is that the behavior of Gilchrist the agnostic has been without reproach, but that his religiously bigoted neighbors refuse to interpret with Christian charity the high Christian doctrine that lust in the heart is lust in deed, and consider him guilty. There is here a conflict between two forces—one individual, one communal, both apparently good—of the kind which makes strong and adult drama, for we feel that there is more than mere society at work; the inevitability of the conflict, the inextricableness of the hero from his entanglement, create that sense of destiny which we have seen to be necessary for serious drama. As the hero himself says to a confidante:

"Do you know what it is to love somebody better than heaven and earth? . . . That's how I love her and her me, and I love my people, Mag, and they hate me. This religion—it baffles me; there's something there they've got that's too—too strong. It does something to folks. But what would they do without it? They must have something to believe in. . . . But they all think they're doing right, and I know I'm right. Will they cut off our lives so?" [10]

IV

There are a number of modern dramas which might seem to be concerned with man's spiritual problems but which only play with them; works, for example, like those that take their audiences into a world after death, such as *The Adding Machine, Lost Horizons, Liliom, Outward Bound*, etc. These are interesting, but their connection with our subject is of varying closeness. *Lost Horizons* has almost nothing to do with man's spiritual concerns; Sartre's *No Exit* has a good deal. The fact that both involve a life after death is an accident, not part of their essence.

[10] Paul Green, *The Field God*, R. M. McBride & Company, New York, 1927.

There are also a large number of plays that deal with special problems; the Scottsboro case, the Sacco-Vanzetti case, racial problems, etc., all valuable evidence that the contemporary theater is playing an important role as an interpreter, even as a participant, in contemporary life. But such plays—to take an example at random, a play such as *Waiting for Lefty*—are to the kind of play we are looking for what journalism in the non-dramatic field is to literature; absorbing for the moment, but fading in interest as the paper on which it is printed crumbles, a part of history, to use Aristotle's distinction, but not sufficiently universal to be poetry.

For drama, to describe man's spiritual situation adequately, must stick to universal themes and universal conflicts—those that our little 3,000 years of recorded experience can tell us are universal. At the beginning of this paper I tried to describe what some of these universal themes and conflicts are in terms of the conditions under which great drama has flourished in the past. Though there may be enormous difficulties, some of which I have mentioned, in the way of equalling at the present time that past achievement, the situation is not hopeless. The theater is vigorous, and creative minds will think of their own ways of making it as much as possible a medium for spiritual concerns. There is, for example, the way of symbolism, upon which I have not had time to touch. There is the kind of experiment represented by Mr. Eliot's *Family Reunion,* where the hierarchical set of spiritual distinctions he used in *Murder in the Cathedral* is applied to a modern theme with more success than theater-goers in this country have been allowed to appreciate. There is the continuous possibility that new relations may be explored, and new techniques invented for embodying them. The thing to do is to keep our eyes sharpened for the real vision that goes beneath man's relation to his nervous impulses, beneath his generous concern or selfish unconcern with society, and to recognize man's spiritual needs and values when we see them, to distinguish them from more superficial values with which they may be confused.

VI

THE VOCATION OF THE POET IN THE MODERN WORLD

DELMORE SCHWARTZ

I

To have a vocation is to have a calling, to be called. One may be called by the powers of evil as well as the powers of good, but it is clear that one must respond with the whole of one's being. In this sense it is also clear that to have a vocation is very much like being in love. Being in love and being called to write poetry are often linked, and many people feel the need to write poetry when they are in love: and as there are many errors in love, so there are many errors in the writing of poetry. As there is puppy love, so there is adolescent poetry.

As there are errors and as a calling or a vocation is a very important matter and occurs during the formative and decisive years of existence, there is much doubt and hesitation about the fact of having a calling, and a period of trial is prescribed in some vocations, while one of the reasons for going to school, after a certain point, is to determine if one has a true vocation, if one has truly been called; and it is in some kind of school that we prepare ourselves to be adequate to our vocation.

In poetry, it is particularly true that many are called and few are chosen. And to be a poet in the modern world means a certain important renunciation which does not hold of all vocations: it means that there is little hope or none of being able to earn a living directly by the writing of poetry. This has been true in the past, although in

59

other ways, as well as in the modern world, for Dryden speaks of "nothing having the vocation of poverty to scribble." In the modern world, it is hard to think of any poet who has had from the start any real economic support for the writing of poetry. There are prizes, grants, patrons, and poetry is honored by much generosity and much prestige. Unfortunately, these are provided after the poet has established himself, but during the first and perhaps most difficult years of being a poet the best a poet can do is to get some other job to support his effort to be a poet. In recent years, the job of teaching English has provided a good many positions which help the poet during his first years, but it is not entirely clear that this is a good thing. For to have a vocation means that one must respond with the whole of one's being; but teaching should be a vocation, too, and not a job, and when the poet takes teaching as a job, he may injure or weaken himself as a poet, or he may not be adequate to all that the task of teaching requires. All the temptations of the world, the flesh, and the devil, combine to lure the poet to success as a teacher and to the rewards of successful academic ambition. At the same time that the poet resists these temptations, he must resign himself to the likelihood that a genuine poetic reputation can be achieved only among others who are poets —for it is mostly poets who read any poetry, except what is to be found in anthologies—and the kind of fame (that last infirmity of noble mind, as Milton said) which he has every right to want will come to him, if it comes at all, only in middle age.

What I have just said should indicate roughly the difference between being a poet in the modern world from what it may have been in other historical periods. If we turn again to the tried and inherited wisdom to be found in the origins of words, we remember that to be a poet is to be a maker, to be the maker of something new, to make something new by putting things and words together. The distinguishing mark of the poet, that capacity which more than any other skill of the mind makes him a poet, is metaphor, according to Aristotle. Now metaphor is literally a bearing-across, or a bringing together of things by means of words. And composition, which is what the poet accomplishes by all the elements of his poem when they are brought together in a unity structural, formal, intuitive, and musical

—composition means putting things together, bringing them together into a unity which is original, interesting, and fruitful. Thus the poet at any time may be said to be engaged in bringing things together, in making new things, in uniting the old and the new, all by the inexhaustible means which words provide for him. In this way, the poet as creator, and metaphormaker, and presiding genius of unity, is a kind of priest. He unites things, meanings, attitudes, feelings, through the power, prowess, and benediction of words, and in this way he is a priest who performs a ceremony of marriage each time he composes a poem. Unfortunately, not all marriages are happy.

II

In the modern world, the poet who has been truly called cannot respond as did the poets in idyllic and primitive periods, when merely the naming of things, as Adam named the animals, was enough to bring poems into existence. On the contrary, he must resist the innumerable ways in which words are spoiled, misused, commercialized, deformed, mispronounced, and in general degraded. We can see clearly how much this resistance is part of the vocation of the poet, if we consider the recurrent references to language itself in the works of that truly modern poet, T. S. Eliot. These references occur in his poems from the very start, continue in each volume he has published, and culminate in a passage in his most recent book of poems, *Four Quartets:*

> So here I am, in the middle way, having had twenty years—
> Twenty years largely wasted, the years of *l'entre deux guerres*—
> Trying to learn to use words, and every attempt
> Is a wholly new start, and a different kind of failure
> Because one has only learnt to get the better of words
> For the thing one no longer has to say, or the way in which
> One is no longer disposed to say it.[1]

Elsewhere in his work there is a sensitivity to colloquial speech and a kind of horror or anguish about it—which arises from the fact that for a modern poet, as for any poet, words are the keys to what he

[1] T. S. Eliot, *Four Quartets,* Harcourt, Brace & Company, New York, 1943, p. 16.

wants. Eliot's play in verse, "Sweeney Agonistes," is the best example of this aspect of his feeling about language, which is used to express a profound anguish about human beings and human existence. When language is degraded in speech, then the basis in community life for the art of poetry is diseased; and it is appropriate and perhaps inevitable that the modern poet who should have felt this fact with the most acuteness should at the same time be an author who acquired an English accent after arriving at the age of reason. Nevertheless, just as certain kinds of disease make for a greater sympathy to experience or a more precise observation of reality (the blind know more about how things sound and feel than those who have normal vision), so, too, the disease which degrades language in the modern world helps bring about the remarkable and often multilingual sensitivity of the modern poet to the language which is the matrix from which he draws his poems.

Degradation and disease are strong terms of condemnation, and a great claim is also made, when one says that the degradation and disease to which poetry is subjected in the modern world are also among the fruitful and necessary conditions of genuine poetry and a genuine vocation for the art of poetry. For the sake of justifying these claims, let us examine small and convenient examples. The word, "intrigue," is a noun which has four legitimate meanings. It means something which is intricate; it means "a plot or a plotting intended to effect some purpose by secret artifice"; thirdly, it is "the plot of a play or romance"; fourthly, it is "a secret and illicit love affair; an amour; a liaison" (this fourth meaning probably derives from the third). And the synonyms of intrigue are plot, scheme, machination, and conspiracy. Notice that there is no sense in which the word means something overwhelmingly attractive and fascinating, unless one thinks of secret and illicit love affairs as overpowering in their fascination. However (in the year 1950), the use of the word as a noun has fallen into decay. Although there are still references to schemers who engage in conspiracies and intrigues, the noun has become a verb in popular usage: anyone who is said to be *intriguing,* is said to be very attractive, in fact, fascinating like a Hollywood star, or like Mata Hari, the beautiful foreign agent of the First World War. An intrigue was something unpleasant, dishonorable, underhand, and immoral. But to be intriguing is to be wonderfully desirable or interesting, and has no unfavorable or dishonorable association. The sense of the same word has thus been turned upside down; it has changed, in popular usage, from signifying something unscrupulous, to representing, in a vague but unmistakable way, something which is extremely interesting, desirable, or beautiful, and has no immediate connotations of moral disrepute.

What has happened to one word has happened to many words, and can happen to many more. And the causes are not, as is sometimes supposed, limited to a poor teaching of English, or a disregard of the dictionary. In this instance, the shift is probably involved in the radical trial which conventional morality has undergone in the past twenty-five years, and certainly there is also involved the influence of newspapers, the stage, the films, and the *literary* zest with which most people read of the sins of others.

This example does not make clear how a degradation in the meanings of words can be fruitful, as well as foolish. There is a shift of meaning and a new richness of meaning, of course, but some of the exactness has already been lost, and more is going to be lost. Let me point out two more examples in which the complicated and mixed benefits and losses of the change may appear fully. For a number of years I taught English composition to students at a well known university. I taught because I was unable to support myself by writing poetry (and for the most part I like to teach very much). When I began to teach, I was confounded by simple misuses of language of which intrigue is a fairly representative example. One student wrote that "swimming is my chief *abstraction*," and another student said that "a certain part of my native city is *slightly ugly*." A third student, who was attempting to describe the salutary effects of higher education upon all members of the fairer and weaker sex, said that it was good for a girl to go to college because "it makes a girl *broader*." When I corrected the last word, in accordance with my instructions as to the proper usage of English—and with a physical sense of one of the meanings of broader—the student protested that I had a peculiar mind; otherwise I would not object to the way in which she used *broader* instead of broadens.

These errors—errors at least from the point of view of conventional and prescribed usage—made me reflect upon my character as a teacher of composition. The students thought I was pedantic, when they did not think I was idiosyncratic, and one important difficulty was that so many of them made the same errors, that, in a way, they were no longer errors. Moreover, the longer I thought about some of the errors, the more they seemed to be possible enlargements of meaning and association which might be creative. There was a real sense in which swimming, for an urban human being, was an abstraction, as well as a distraction. So, too, to say that something was slightly ugly, was to suggest that a word or words denoting degrees of ugliness from homeliness and plainness to what was utterly ugly, were lacking in English. And, finally, it was true enough that education might make a girl broader as well as broaden a girl's outlook, although I doubt that this would have occurred to me, if it had not been for this fruitful error.

The experience of teaching English literature and English poetry directly, confronts the poet who teaches English with what must be described as the most educated part of the population. Before the poet has taught English, he may well have been under the impression that no one, except for poets, read modern poetry (with a few and misleading exceptions). When he teaches poetry in the classroom, he finds out something which may be a great hope or a great delusion. It may be a delusion now and a hope for the future. At any rate, he does discover that he can persuade any student to understand any kind of poetry—no matter how difficult, they understand it—as long as the students are in the classroom, and they remain interested in it until they depart from school. As so many poets have more and more undertaken the teaching of English and of poetry, it does seem possible that this may be the beginning of a new audience trained in reading and aware of how marvelous and exalted the rewards of poetry can be. But this is a matter which must be realized in the future. In the present, it is true that as soon as the student leaves school, all the seductions of mass culture and middlebrow culture, and, in addition, the whole way of life of our society, combine to make the reading of poetry a dangerous and quickly rejected luxury. The poet who teaches has immediate experiences in the classroom which give him some reason to hope for a real literary and poetic renaissance. As soon as he departs from the pleasant confines of the university, he discovers that it is more and more the case that fewer and fewer people read serious poetry. And the last straw may be the recognition that even poets do not read very much poetry: Edwin Arlington Robinson confessed that during the latter half of his life he read hardly any poems except his own, which he read again and again, and which may explain the paralysis of self-imitation which overcomes many good poets in mid-career. Here then is another trait which distinguishes the vocation of the modern poet from poets of the past: he not only knows how language is inexactly and exactly used, he also knows that for the most part only other poets will read his poems.

III

One reason that language is misused, whether fruitfully or not, is that in modern life experience has become international. In America itself the fact of many peoples and the fact that so large a part of the population has some immigrant background and cherishes the fragments of another language, creates a multilingual situation in which words are misused, and yet the language is also enriched by new words and new meanings. To make fun of errors in the use of language and to make the most comedy possible of foreign accents —or for that matter, an English accent—is a rich and vital tradition of American humor, which is itself a very important part of American life. Moreover, the pilgrimage to Europe has for long been an important episode in the national experience. The American tourist in Europe, Baedeker in hand, has for generations spelled out the names of places, and works of art, and delicious foods. And most crucial of all, the experience of two world wars has made Americans conscious of the extent to which the very quality of their lives depends upon the entire international situation. Whether the danger is from Germany or from Russia, whether a banking scandal occurs in Paris, or Spain becomes Fascist, or a foreign religious institution intervenes in American politics and American morality and American education, no one at this late date can fail to be aware of the extent to which the fate of the individual is inseparable from what is happening in the whole world. The possibility of a war means that a son or a husband may be drafted for military training; and when there is a war in Korea, the stockmarket falls and affects the entire national economy.

These facts are, of course, in one sense platitudes; and yet it may not be clear how they affect the modern poet in his vocation as such. I want to resort to examples again, before trying to define the way in which the international scene and an involvement with it affect the poet as a poet, and have much to do with his calling.

To quote once more from that truly modern poet, T. S. Eliot, here is a passage from one of his best poems, "Gerontion": Christ, the protagonist says, is:

> To be eaten, to be divided, to be drunk
> Among whispers; by Mr. Silvero
> With caressing hands, at Limoges
> Who walked all night in the next room;
> By Hakagawa, bowing among the Titians;
> By Madame de Tornquist, in the dark room
> Shifting the candles; Fraulein von Kulp
> Who turned in the hall, one hand on the door.[2]

Let us think a little merely of the names of the people he remembers, Mr. Silvero, Hakagawa, Madame de Tornquist, Fraulein von Kulp. Is it not clear that the experience which provides the subject matter of the poet or inspires him to write his poem is not only European, but international, for Hakagawa is presumably Japanese; and involves all history, all culture, for the reference here to Titian is matched elsewhere by allusions to ancient Egypt, Buddhist sermons, and the religion of classical Greece? Another aspect of the same involvement and of how it has a direct impact on the language of the poet, is illustrated in "Sweeney Agonistes," where two "Ameri-

[2] T. S. Eliot, *Collected Poems, 1909–1935*, Harcourt, Brace & Company, New York, 1936, p. 43.

can gentlemen here on business" arrive in London and rehearse the clichés of colloquial American speech: London, one of them explains with great politeness to his English friends, is "a slick place, London's a swell place,/ London's a fine place to come on a visit—," and the other adds with equal politeness: "specially when you got a real live Britisher/A guy like Sam to show you around/Sam of course is at *home* in London,/And he's promised to show us around." In the same work, at a moment of great anguish, another character reiterates the poet's extreme sensitivity to and concern for language when he says: "I've gotta use words when I talk to you." [3]

If Eliot, as a transplanted American in Europe, seems to be a special case (a great poet, however, is always a special case, if one chooses to regard him in that light), the example of James Joyce should help to reinforce the somewhat complicated (because ubiquitous) point I am trying to elucidate. Joyce was an impoverished Irishman. As Eliot had to toil for some time in a bank while he tried to write poems, Joyce supported himself during the composition of *Ulysses* by teaching in a Berlitz school in Trieste during the First World War. The publication of *Ulysses*—an event which was described by a French critic as marking Ireland's spectacular reappearance in European literature—was sufficiently a success to make a rich Englishwoman provide Joyce with financial security almost until the end of his life. One must say *almost,* because the German occupation of France cut off Joyce's funds and made him take flight into Switzerland. Two years before, Joyce had completed his last and probably his best work, the stupendous *Finnegans Wake,* a book which would in itself provide sufficient evidence and illustration of the vocation of the modern poet [4] in modern life. All that has been observed in Eliot's work is all the more the case with *Finnegans Wake*

[3] *Ibid.,* pp. 145, 152.

[4] Joyce's two best works, *Ulysses,* and his last book, are not poems in the ordinary sense of the word; and he wrote several volumes of poetry, most of which consists of verses far inferior to anything in his major books. But any view of poetry which excludes *Finnegans Wake* as a poem and Joyce as a poet, merely suggests the likelihood that Joyce transformed and extended the limits of poetry by the writing of his last book. If we freeze our categories and our definitions (and this is especially so in literature), the result is that we disable and blind our minds.

—the attention to colloquial speech, the awareness of the variety of ways in which language can be degraded, and how that degradation can be the base for new originality and exactitude, the sense of being involved and affected by all history. But more than that, the radio and even television play a part in this wonderful book, as indeed they played a part in the writing of it. Joyce had a shortwave radio with which he was able to hear London, Moscow, Dublin—and New York! In reading *Finnegans Wake,* I was perplexed for a time by echoes of American radio comedy and Yiddish humor, until I learned about Joyce's radio and about his daily reading of the Paris edition of the *New York Herald Tribune.* But to repeat, the most important point of all is that *Finnegans Wake* exhibits in the smallest detail and in the entire scope of the work the internationality of the modern poet, his involvement in all history, and his consciousness of the impingement of *any* foreign language, from Hebrew to Esperanto, upon the poet's use of the English language.

IV

It is foolish to speculate about the future of anything as precarious as the vocation of poetry—an eminent critic said some years ago that the technique of verse was a dying one, but Joyce may have persuaded him to change his mind—but to think of the future is as inevitable as it is dubious. Joyce's last book suggests certain tentative formulations about the future of the writing of poetry. He suggests that there can be no turning back, unless civilization itself ceases, as with the end of the Roman Empire. Yet it is also clear that poets cannot go forward in a straight line from the point at which *Finnegans Wake* concluded. What they can do is not in the least clear, apart from the fact that a literal imitation or extension of Joyce would be as mechanical as it is undesirable: too much in the very nature of his work depends upon personal and idiosyncratic traits of the author, his training as a Jesuit, his love of operatic music, infatuation with everything Irish which obsessed him in this, as in his other books. There are other important elements in Joyce's work and in his life, which do lead, I think, to some tentative generalization about the future of poetry and the vocation of the poet. One of them was pointed out to me by Meyer Schapiro (who has influenced me in much of what I have said throughout); the question has been raised as to why Joyce, both in *Ulysses* and in *Finnegans Wake,* identified himself with Jews, with Leopold Bloom, an Irish Jew, and with the character of Shem in his last book (Shem is, among other of his very many kinships, a son of Noah and he is compared with Jesus Christ, to the ironic denigration of both beings). The answer to the question of Joyce's self-identification with Jews, Schapiro said, is that the Jew is at once alienated and indestructible, he is an exile from his own country, exiled from himself, yet he survives the annihilating fury of history. In the unpredictable and fearful future that awaits civilization, the poet must be prepared to be alienated and indestructible. He must dedicate himself to poetry, although no one else seems likely to read what he writes; and he must be indestructible as a poet, until he is destroyed as a human being. In the modern world, poetry is alienated; it will remain indestructible as long as the poet responds to his vocation.

RELIGION AND THE ARTIST'S MEANS

> With the farming of a verse
> Make a vineyard of the curse . . .
>
> W. H. Auden, in "In Memory of W. B. Yeats"

VII

THEODICY, POETRY, AND TRADITION

BY

DAVID DAICHES

Nearly three hundred years ago John Milton, pondering in his age and blindness over the mysteries of human fate and thinking doubtless of the bitter frustrations and disappointments of his own life, put into the mouth of his hero, Samson, an almost desperate questioning of God's ways with man:

> God of our Fathers, what is man!
> That thou towards him with hand so various,
> Or might I say contrarious,
> Temper'st thy providence through his short course,
> Not evenly, as thou rul'st
> The Angelic orders and inferior creatures mute,
> Irrational and brute.
> Nor do I name of men the common rout,
> That wandring loose about
> Grow up and perish, as the summer fly,
> Heads without name no more remember'd,
> But such as thou hast solemnly elected,
> With gifts and graces eminently adorn'd
> To some great work, thy glory,
> And peoples safety, which in part they effect:
> Yet toward these, thus dignifi'd, thou oft,
> Amidst their highth of noon,
> Changest thy countenance and thy hand, with no regard
> Of highest favours past
> From thee on them, or them to thee of service.

The cry is a familiar one in the history of literature. Why do the wicked prosper and the virtuous suffer? It was a very real question

for Milton as he sat in darkness and heard the bells ring out the end
of all his political hopes, the end of his dream of being the poet and
prophet of a new and regenerate England; as he heard the celebrators
of the restoration of Charles II—

> The Sons
> Of Belial, flown with insolence and wine—

roistering in the streets outside. "Why standest Thou afar off, O
Lord? Why hidest Thou thyself in times of trouble? . . . For the
wicked boasteth of his heart's desire, and the covetous vaunteth himself, though he contemn the Lord." So the Hebrew psalmist had long
before asked the same question. It was Job's question, too. "Behold,
I cry out of wrong, but I am not heard: I cry aloud, but there is no
justice." "Wherefore do the wicked live, become old, yea, are mighty
in power?"

I

This old question of theodicy, of the justice of God, or, if we prefer,
of the way the universe is organized so far as it affects man, has long
been a central theme in literature. The answer is generally given in
terms of attitude, rather than of logic. Job's problem disappears in a
note of wonder—wonder at the grandeur and immensity of creation.
The psalmist finds refuge in faith: "Better is a little that the righteous
hath than the abundance of many wicked. . . . For the wicked shall
perish, and the enemies of the Lord shall be as the fat of lambs—they
shall pass away in smoke, they shall pass away." The Prometheus of
Aeschylus, on the other hand, strikes a note of heroic self-confidence,
"behold me, how unjust are my sufferings." These are very different
answers to a single question; but they are all *literary* answers, rather
than philosophical solutions. By this I mean that the answers have
force and meaning in virtue of their poetic expression, of the place they
take in the myth or fable or situation presented, and of the effectiveness with which they project a mood. Job's solution is no answer, if
detached from its eloquent expression and paraphrased as a philosophical position. Such a procedure would make Job sound merely
pusillanimous, just as it would make the psalmist a naive self-deceiver

and Prometheus a futile exhibitionist. In other words, we see in earlier literature a religious (or mythological) tradition and a literary tradition mutually supporting each other, each depending on the other for full richness of expression and significance.

Let me try to explain this point more fully by turning again to Milton. We know that the justification of the ways of God to men, the professed theme of *Paradise Lost,* was for Milton a major preoccupation throughout his life. We see the problem first stated in "Lycidas," a poem ostensibly lamenting a young friend who died before he was able to fulfil his promise as poet and teacher, but actually concerned with the larger problem of the ambitious idealist in an uncertain and arbitrary world. What is the use of dedicating one's self to a future of service to humanity (in Milton's case, through the writing of poetry "doctrinal and exemplary to a nation"), if one might be cut off at any moment, before even one's period of self-preparation was completed?

> Alas! What boots it with uncessant care
> To tend the homely slighted Shepherd's trade,
> And strictly meditate the thankless Muse?
> Were it not better done as others use,
> To sport with Amaryllis in the shade,
> Or with the tangles of Neaera's hair?

The question is turned this way and that throughout the poem, and every kind of traditional answer suggested before the real answer emerges in the mood and tone of the conclusion:

> Thus sang the uncouth Swain to th' Oaks and rills,
> While the still morn went out with Sandals gray.
> He touch'd the tender stops of various Quills,
> With eager thought warbling his Doric lay:
> And now the Sun had stretch'd out all the hills,
> And now was dropt into the Western bay;
> At last he rose, and twich'd his Mantle blue:
> Tomorrow to fresh Woods, and Pastures new.

Like God's answer to Job in the whirlwind, this is not a logical disposal of the problem, but the distillation of a mood in the light of which the poet is able to carry on. The quiet sunrise which proclaims a new day brings a note of humility and acceptance to the poet, who now describes himself as an "uncouth swain"—that is, an unknown or unlearned rustic—and with that comes the determination to do what one can while one can, to enjoy such beauty as life grants and to turn one's hand to what lies to be done, without too much speculation on possible accidents:

> Tomorrow to fresh Woods, and Pastures new

has the sound both of peace and of purpose.

When his blindness came, some fifteen years later, Milton again raised the question of God's justice in so dealing with him:

> When I consider how my light is spent,
>   Ere half my days, in this dark world and wide,
>   And that one Talent which is death to hide,
>   Lodg'd with me useless, though my Soul more bent
> To serve therewith my Maker, and present
>   My true account, lest he returning chide,
>   Doth God exact day-labour, light deny'd,
>   I fondly ask. . . .

But Patience replies, and stills the poet's questioning with a picture of various services rendered by different men actively or passively, God being best served by those "who best bear his mild yoke"; and the poem ebbs quietly away on the concluding line:

> They also serve who only stand and waite.

Has this answer vindicated God's justice? No; but it has projected a mood in the light of which life seems more interesting, more significant, and more tolerable.

In *Paradise Lost* the justification of the ways of God to men is developed on a more deliberate and even grandiose scale. On the surface, Milton, by telling the story of man's fall in Eden, is showing that man fell by a deliberate abuse of his free will, so that he has himself and not God to blame, and also pointing out that God provided a scheme of redemption which would enable those who made the effort to attain to a state far above that from which Adam fell. Thus man deserved what he got by deliberately doing evil, but God in His mercy brought good out of evil by the Christian scheme of redemption. This is the cold, paraphrasable message of *Paradise Lost;* but it is neither the true meaning of the poem nor the real way in which Milton justified the ways of God to men. The real justification of God's dealings with men lies in the implicit contrast between the ideal idleness of the Garden of Eden and the changing and challenging world of moral effort and natural beauty which resulted from the fall. This argument is presented obliquely and continuously through mood and imagery: when the beauty of Eve in her unfallen state is described in terms of classical myths which give an atmosphere of ineffable loveliness to the whole picture, we get a sense of values which can emerge only in the fallen human imagination. The postlapsarian world (to use the theological term) may lack the bliss of Eden, with its perpetual spring and its freedom from the curse of earning one's daily bread by the sweat of one's brow, but the procession of the seasons which was part of the punishment of the fall provides some of Milton's most moving imagery, while symbols of rustic labor with its beauty and dignity contradict or at least modify the explicit statement that work was imposed on man as a curse. Even prelapsarian nature, ideal nature before the fall, can be made desirable in our eyes only in terms drawn from a postlapsarian consciousness, just as good can be made significant only in terms of moral effort against known evil—evil known only in man's fallen state.

The real theme of *Paradise Lost* is man's essential and tragic ambiguity, illustrated in the fact that love is bound up with selfishness (as when Adam follows Eve's example in eating the forbidden apple because he cannot live without her); that good is bound up with evil; that the beauty which adorns the earth as it passes from seedtime to harvest, from the white of winter to the gay colors of spring, is bound up with change, and change, which means growth, also means decay; that the rich pattern of different human civilizations as Milton passes them under review, with all the magic of exotic and musical place names and the excitement of geographical discovery, was made possible by the curse of Babel; that the dignity and beauty of rustic labor, the basis of some of Milton's finest similes, is the other side of the law which decrees starvation and suffering for those who can find no land or no work. In the personal outburst at the beginning of the third book, what the blind Milton most laments are those sights of seasonal change which resulted from the loss of Eden's perpetual spring:

> Thus with the Year
> Seasons return, but not to me returns
> Day, or the sweet approach of Ev'n or Morn,
> Or sight of vernal bloom, or Summers Rose,
> Or flocks, or herds, or human face divine;
> But cloud instead, and ever-during dark
> Surrounds me, from the cheerful ways of men
> Cut off. . . .

They are "the cheerful ways of men" still, in spite of "the sons of Belial flown with insolence and wine." And the curse that "in the sweat of thy face shalt thou eat bread" can make possible the imagery of such lines as these:

> As one who long in populous City pent,
> Where Houses thick and Sewers annoy the Air,
> Forth issuing on a Summers Morn to breathe
> Among the pleasant Villages and Farms
> Adjoynd, from each thing met conceives delight,
> The smell of Grain, or tedded Grass, or Kine,
> Or Dairy, each rural sight, each rural sound. . . .

This is how Milton justifies the ways of God to men—by showing through the emotional pattern of his great poem how everything worthwhile that we can conceive of is made possible by the results of the fall. Again, this is not a logical but a poetic solution to his problem, like the solution of Job and of the psalmist. A religious tradition and a poetic sensibility cooperated to produce an effect which needed both, but which was wholly produced by neither.

In *Samson Agonistes,* Milton handled this problem for the last time. Samson, the hero, was brought pitifully low, apparently deserted by God, and he recovered only to destroy himself with his enemies. Samson's moral recovery is a main theme of the play; but we know from the beginning that there is no going back to the young heroic Samson doing great deeds for his country. He recovers only to die. Is that fair or just on God's part? Is that the only answer to his great cry: "God of our Fathers, what is man!"? No: the real answer is an esthetic one; it lies in the "katharsis" which the tragedy produces. The chorus sums up the significance of the action in the well known conclusion:

> His servants he with new acquist
> Of true experience from this great event
> With peace and consolation hath dismist,
> And calm of mind, all passion spent.

This is Milton's interpretation of the Aristotelian "katharsis," the purgation of the emotions through pity and fear, which is Aristotle's view of the function of tragedy. The calm of mind produced by the tragic "katharsis" is at the same time the mood which accepts God's dealings with men as just. At the end of his life Milton completely and finally reconciled religion and esthetics, the Christian and the humanist, by justifying the ways of God to men in terms of a mood distilled esthetically by tragedy. What Professor Douglas Bush has called "the dilemma of a sacred poet and a Puritan bred in the congenial air of Renaissance classicism," [1] was resolved by applying a classical notion of the function of tragedy to the solution of Job's question.

II

What I am trying to show is that the interplay between religious and esthetic impulses has always been fruitful in literature and that an appreciation of it is independent of the reader's creed or philosophical system. One could demonstrate a similar interplay in Dante and Shakespeare, as well as in the Greek dramatists: had I the space, it would be interesting to attempt to do so. But I must hasten on, to ask the questions that we are most concerned with here. Has the contemporary literary artist anything to learn from this? Has the disinte-

[1] Douglas Bush, *English Literature in the Earlier Seventeenth Century, 1600–1660*, The Clarendon Press, Oxford, 1945, p. 387.

gration of community of belief, which most observers agree to be a characteristic of our present age, altered the situation so radically that the kind of thing done by Aeschylus and Dante and Milton—posing questions suggested by religion and answering them in literary or esthetic terms—becomes impossible? Is there an unbridgeable gap between the history of literature and the contemporary literary artist?

These are not easy questions to answer, and they certainly cannot be adequately answered in one paper. I am all too conscious of the dangers of facile generalization and of the ease with which a showy thesis can be developed by the manipulation of an arbitrary selection of examples. As I try to cast my mind's eye over the vast array of works of literary art from the *Book of Job* to a poem by T. S. Eliot, and think of the numerous changes in taste and attitude, the immense diversity of works and of writers, and the vastly different conscious objectives which different artists have set themselves, I can see how tentative and inadequate any answer to the questions I have raised must be, even if I were much more of a polymath than I can allow myself to claim. But in the realm of critical ideas nothing significant can be achieved without boldness; so, having listed the dangers, let me now proceed to ignore them.

What does the loss of a common background of religious attitudes and symbols mean to literature? The problem has agitated poets for over a century. Nearly a hundred years ago Matthew Arnold, in his poem, "Dover Beach," expressed a view which is central to our present discontents. Looking out over the Straits of Dover on a calm, moonlit night he listened to the splash of the waves on the shore and thought how Sophocles had heard in that sound "the turbid ebb and flow of human misery." He continued:

> The Sea of Faith
> Was once, too, at the full, and round earth's shore
> Lay like the folds of a bright girdle furl'd.
> But now I only hear
> Its melancholy, long, withdrawing roar,
> Retreating, to the breath
> Of the night-wind down the vast edges drear
> And naked shingles of the world.

> Ah, love, let us be true
> To one another! for the world, which seems
> To lie before us like a land of dreams,
> So various, so beautiful, so new,
> Hath really neither joy, nor love, nor light,
> Nor certitude, nor peace, nor help for pain;
> And we are here as on a darkling plain.
> Swept with confused alarms of struggle and flight,
> Where ignorant armies clash by night.

This mood of what Professor Trilling has called "controlled self-pity," this elegiac note which enables the poet to face a world without faith, represents a rather different use of poetic devices than what we find at the conclusion of *Job* or even in Milton. The earlier writers, it is true, projected a mood, which is what Arnold is doing, but it was a mood which enabled man to achieve new equanimity and go about his business untroubled. In *Job,* in the older Greek dramatists, in Dante, in many of Shakespeare's tragedies, and in Milton, a "katharsis" is achieved which frees writer and reader alike from inhibitive brooding. One might even venture a rash generalization and say that these older works freed man for action, while much romantic literature consigns man to perpetual introspection. In fact, this might be, if not an adequate at least a workable, definition of the two terms, "classical" and "romantic." When Milton grows impatient with God and his destiny, he writes a poem which resolves his doubts through projecting a mood of acceptance and preparation for action. Keats, concerned with the same fear that haunted Milton in "Lycidas," afraid, that is, lest he might die

> Before my pen has gleaned my teeming brain

found an answer in pure introspection:

> When I behold upon the night's starred face
> Huge cloudy symbols of a high romance,
> And think that I may never live to trace
> Their shadows with the magic hand of chance;
> And when I feel, fair creature of an hour,
> That I shall never look upon thee more,

> Never have relish in the fairy power
> Of unreflecting love;—then on the shore
> Of the wide world I stand alone, and think
> Till love and fame to nothingness do sink.

How different this is from

> Tomorrow to fresh Woods, and Pastures new

or even

> They also serve who only stand and waite.

Can we go so far as to say that an art with a religious background can achieve "katharsis" more effectively than one without one? The romantic poets, who substituted introspective plangency for religious assurance, often saw the function of art quite differently from the way Dante or Shakespeare saw it. Differences between Dante, the medieval Catholic, and Shakespeare, the tolerant humanist, are numerous and profound enough, but they are both religious, in the sense in which I am using the term, a sense in which Keats and Tennyson and Matthew Arnold are not religious. The ending of *Hamlet* or *Macbeth,* with the reasserting of the norm and the preparation for daily activity is, in the largest symbolic sense, comparable to the ending of Dante's *Inferno,*

> *e quindi uscimmo a riveder le stelle*
> And thence we came forth to see again the stars.

The release from troubled introspection into action is, however, very far from being the objective or the achievement of, say, Tennyson's "Break, break, break," or Arnold's "Dover Beach"—we can all add indefinitely to the list—which cultivate that very state from which the classical "katharsis" (I am using the term now widely and symbolically) seeks to relieve writer and reader. The cultivation of this state is not, it should be added, peculiar to the English romantic poets: there is, in fact, no more perfect example of it than in that remarkable sonnet *"L'infinito"* by the Italian poet, Leopardi, in which a mood of complete surrender to trancelike contemplation is deliberately cultivated:

> *Così tra questa*
> *Immensità s'annega il pensier mio:*
> *E il naufragar m'e dolce in questo mare.*
> Thus amid this vastness my thought is drowned,
> And shipwreck is sweet to me in such a sea.

The mood of "Dover Beach" or "Break, break, break" is not, of course, uniquely romantic: it is not the mood, so much as the use to which it is put in the poem, that differentiates Arnold's description of the waves breaking on the lonely shore from similar descriptions in the classics—from, say, the picture of Achilles in the twenty-third book of *The Iliad,* mourning for his dead comrade Patroclus as he lay

> In an open space where the waves plashed upon the shingle.

That is one of the most evocative—if you like, romantic—lines in Greek literature, but its purpose is not to exploit the temporary mood of plangent meditation, but to prepare the way for the final "katharsis" of Achilles's anger and grief.

Nevertheless, as Matthew Arnold saw as clearly as anybody, a mood of self-pity, however controlled and beautifully expressed, cannot for long remain a literary norm. In England, the mid and late nineteenth century poets played all possible variations on it, and its potentialities were soon exhausted. A classical reaction set in in the second decade of the present century, with T. E. Hulme calling on the poets, in a misquoted line from the seventeenth century dramatist John Webster, to

> End your moan and come away.

Hulme advocated, and prophesied, a period of "dry, hard, classical verse." The cry was taken up by Eliot and others, and a revolution in poetic taste was achieved within a generation. "The poet," wrote Eliot in 1917, "has not a 'personality' to express, but a particular medium, which is only a medium and not a personality, in which impressions and experiences combine in peculiar and unexpected ways." [2] But, in fact, neither Eliot nor any other significant poet of

---

[2] T. S. Eliot, "Tradition and the Individual Talent," *Selected Essays, 1917-1932,* Harcourt, Brace & Company, New York, 1932.

our time was content to make of poetry the mere arranging of impressions and experiences in peculiar and unexpected ways. If the classical poets—again, using the terms widely and symbolically—had created literature by exploiting the impact of personality on a religious tradition, and the romantic poets had exploited personality by itself, what was the modern poet to do, who shared the romantic poets' confusion about religion and at the same time repudiated their exploitation of personality? They could, of course, take Voltaire's position, and say that if God did not exist, it would be necessary to create Him; and some of the arguments brought forward by Eliot in his prose writing almost suggest that at times this is the line that he took. In his later poetry, however, from *Ash Wednesday* on, Eliot has been concerned with the impact of personality on a religious tradition, and in the *Four Quartets* he has been remarkably successful in distilling a mood in the light of which the religious position becomes meaningful, if not logically demonstrable. And that, as we have seen, is the way classical art works.

But Eliot's solution is not wholly satisfactory, and certainly not one that can be successfully employed by others, because, however sincerely his religious emotion is felt (and it is not for the literary critic to presume to judge that), the materials it works on are academic and its documents not central to any religious tradition. (St. John of the Cross, for example, is a more fundamental source of imagery and structure in many of his poems than the Bible or the prayerbook, and there is a curious air of coy connoisseurship about his handling of religious documents.) There is, in fact, however much Eliot may repudiate personality in poetry, a highly idiosyncratic personality at work here, whose solutions of common problems are *not* really helpful to others, for all the influence of his merely technical procedures on younger poets.

The conflict between faith and reason, between religion and experience, is not the modern problem our contemporary writers have to solve. The more vital the religious tradition, the more real and fruitful has that conflict been: it is, as I have tried to show, in *Job*, the Greek dramatists, *Paradise Lost*, as well as in Dante and Shakespeare. The modern problem is to find a valid tradition with reference to which literary artists can pit their personality with poetic profit. There is always a gap between a traditional formulation of values and individual experience, and across that gap sparks the poetic insight. You can sometimes get away with making your own tradition, as in a sense Eliot has (for his Christian tradition is not, I venture to think, identical with any of the main forms of the Christian tradition in Western civilization), but there is something both artificial and dangerous about this: for how can there be tension between your personal experience and the impersonal tradition, when the impersonal tradition is something you have discovered or created for yourself? Yet there are ways out of this dilemma—dangerous ways, and not always imitable ways—but nevertheless ways which have on occasion been successfully taken.

III

Let us glance briefly at two of these—that taken by W. B. Yeats, and that taken by Dylan Thomas.

There is a well known statement of his early position made by Yeats in his autobiographical work, *The Trembling of the Veil:*

> I am very religious, and deprived by Huxley and Tyndall, whom I detested, of the simple-minded religion of my childhood, I had made a new religion, almost an infallible church of poetic tradition, of a fardel of stories, and of personages, and of emotions, inseparable from their first expression, passed on from generation to generation by poets and painters with some help from philosophers and theologians. . . .[3]

If this is all that Yeats had done, he would not have become the great poet we know him to have been. For to repudiate the religious tradition, and to put in its place a tradition derived from the reflection of that repudiated tradition in art and philosophy, is neither logical nor helpful. What is religion, but the primary expression of those basic myths and values which, in turn, are used by artists in the way I have tried to suggest? The genuine agnostic can understand

---

[3] William Butler Yeats, "The Trembling of the Veil," *Autobiography,* copyright, 1916, 1936, The Macmillan Company, New York, and used with their permission.

and appreciate a religious tradition in life and art, and understand how the tensions between that tradition and individual personality have helped to produce great art, but he certainly cannot go to that art and pick out from it a religious tradition unacceptable to him in its explicit form, though Yeats was not alone in thinking that this could be done. What makes Yeats's statement of his problems so interesting is not the solution he suggests, but the awareness of the problem that it shows. He needed a religious tradition to work with, but he could not accept any tradition specifically denominated as religious.

We know, of course, what he eventually did. He built for himself, out of the oddest and most miscellaneous material, a symbolic system with reference to which he could organize his poetic expression. But if it was his own system, created by himself, how could he set himself over against it, to develop those tensions between individual insight and impersonal system, which I have suggested are the most significant way in which a poet can use a tradition? The answer is that the conflict in Yeats's poems is not between himself and the system, but between two aspects of the system, which, being a dialectical one, a balancing of opposites, afforded him all the tensions he could handle. The system itself, with its lunar phases and towers and spinning tops and spiral staircases, was based on the perpetual merging of opposites. As you climb the spiral staircase, you move through all the points on the circumference of a circle, but when you reach the top of the spiral, which is a circle with an infinitely small circumference, you are at all points in the circumference simultaneously. Yeats's poetic imagery from the beginning had been dominated by a conflict of opposites; in his early poetry we find perpetually the human world contrasted with the supernatural world of faery, the familiar and domestic with the wild and strange, the tame with the heroic, the Christian with the pagan. Later on, his images seem to coalesce into a *tertium quid,* so that simple contrasts disappear, and we find symbolic probings into the underlying affinity of apparent opposites. We have this implicitly in the "Byzantium" poems, and quite explicitly in some of the "Crazy Jane" poems:

> A woman can be proud and stiff
> When on love intent;

> But Love has pitched his mansion in
> The place of excrement;
> For nothing can be sole or whole
> That has not been rent.[4]

Or consider:

> Bodily decrepitude is wisdom: young
> We loved each other and were ignorant.[5]

Or this, from "A Woman Young and Old":

> How could passion run so deep
> Had I never thought
> That the crime of being born
> Blackens all our lot?
> But where the crime's committed
> The crime can be forgot.[6]

"Out of our quarrels with others we make rhetoric," Yeats once remarked; "out of our quarrel with ourselves, poetry." Instead of the two poles being personality and tradition, they become opposing aspects of personality. A self-made tradition can be of value to the literary artist only when it contains self-contradictions.

My thesis has been, as will, I hope, be clear by now, that a religious tradition is of value to the literary artist, as providing a challenge to individual experience, out of which art may result. When that tradition disintegrates, the poet can take refuge in elegiac introspection, or he can create or discover a tradition of his own. The former practice may produce much that is valuable, but in the nature of things it cannot be maintained for long, its potentialities being limited and its possibilities soon exhausted; the latter can work only when the created or discovered tradition is complex enough to contain within itself the tensions which the great artist needs: if it does not contain those tensions, then the artist is merely shadow boxing when he employs the

---

[4] William Butler Yeats, "Crazy Jane Talks with the Bishop," *Winding Stair,* copyright, 1933, The Macmillan Company, New York, and used with their permission.

[5] *Ibid.,* "After Long Silence."

[6] *Ibid.,* "A Woman Young and Old."

tradition, for, being the *product* of his own imagination, it cannot at the same time be a *challenge* to his imagination.

Thus Yeats's dialectical symbolic system—if I may use such an ugly term for lack of a better—enabled him to organize the images and ideas in his poetry, so as to achieve profound poetic statement. Instead of his own personality wrestling with the tradition, we find opposing elements of his own personality fighting it out and becoming reconciled within the tradition that he pieced together himself. This does not mean that we must understand—still less that we must agree with —the fantastic system which Yeats elaborated in *A Vision,* before we can understand or appreciate his poems. Of his best poems it can be safely said that his system is a device to help him achieve the rich and significant patterning of image and idea out of which effective poetic expression is distilled. That significant patterning can be recognized, with all its rich overtones of meaning, in such a poem as "Byzantium" without any reference to *A Vision*—indeed, an attempt to interpret the poem too specifically in terms of Yeats's system narrows the meaning unduly and shuts off the reverberating meanings which are what give the poem its greatness. There are some poems by Yeats which do require the application of the system for their appreciation, but these are his less successful ones.

Dylan Thomas has achieved a very different kind of richly echoing poetic statement, but his success, too, is the result of his creation or discovery of a synthetic tradition, in the light of which the proper tensions can be created and resolved. Christianity, Freudian psychology, Welsh folklore, are only some of the elements which he employs together in profound counterpoint to produce some of the most exciting poetry of our time. For a clearer understanding of what modern problem Thomas is solving by this counterpointing of apparently contradictory elements in our culture, let me quote from an author who, in an earlier phase of his career, was painfully aware of the problem, and who has since tried to solve it in a very different way from that chosen by Thomas. Aldous Huxley, in the opening chapter of his novel *Antic Hay* (1923) makes Theodore Gumbril, the disillusioned school master, meditate in the school chapel as follows:

No, but seriously, Gumbril reminded himself, the problem was very troublesome indeed. God as a sense of warmth about the heart, God as exultation, God as tears in the eyes, God as a rush of power or thought —that was all right. But God as truth, God as $2 + 2 = 4$—that wasn't so clearly all right. Was there any chance of their being the same? Were there bridges to join the two worlds? [7]

Gumbril decided that there were not, and therein lay his dilemma. Or again, take the description of the string orchestra in the third chapter of *Point Counter Point* (1928):

Pongileoni's blowing and the scraping of the anonymous fiddlers had shaken the air in the great hall, had set the glass of the windows looking on to it vibrating; and this in turn had shaken the air in Lord Edward's apartment on the further side. The shaking air rattled Lord Edward's *membrana tympani;* the interlocked *malleus, incus,* and stirrup bones were set in motion so as to agitate the membrane of the oval window and raise an infinitesimal storm in the fluid of the labyrinth. The hairy endings of the auditory nerve shuddered like weeds in a rough sea; a vast number of obscure miracles were performed in the brain, and Lord Edward ecstatically whispered "Bach!" [8]

God as a sense of warmth about the heart as opposed to God as $2 + 2 = 4$; music as a series of sound waves impinging on a physiological organism and music as something significant and moving— these are expressed as irreconcilable alternatives. Both explanations seem to be true, yet each seems to deny the other. If the dilemma is posed this way, the only solution would seem to be either complete skepticism or complete irrationality, and neither skepticism nor irrationality can provide a proper environment for great art. What the modern artist needs is some device which would enable him to hold these conflicting attitudes in suspension, as it were, or perhaps it could be better described as a state of tension, or of counterpoint, so that instead of being inhibitive of value they can increase and enrich value.

Huxley's observation about music is neither new nor original.

[7] Aldous Huxley, *Antic Hay,* George H. Doran Company, New York, 1923.

[8] Aldous Huxley, *Point Counter Point,* Doubleday, Doran & Company, Inc., Garden City, 1928.

Shakespeare's Benedick, in *Much Ado About Nothing,* remarks in an ironic moment: "Is it not strange that sheeps' guts should hale souls out of men's bodies?" Unlike Huxley, Shakespeare was not tortured by this perception: he includes it dramatically as one element in the complex and paradoxical nature of things, so that it enriches rather than frustrates his picture of human values in action.

IV

Returning now to Dylan Thomas, we note that his poetic technique enables him to handle in brilliant counterpoint all the different explanations of human situations given by religion, science, and folklore:

> I, in my intricate image, stride on two levels,
> Forged in man's minerals, the brassy orator
> Laying my ghost in metal,
> The scales of this twin world tread on the double,
> My half ghost in armour hold hard in death's corridor,
> To my man-iron sidle.
>
> Beginning with doom in the bulb, the spring unravels
> Bright as her spinning-wheels, the colic season
> Worked on a world of petals;
> She threads off the sap and needles, blood and bubble
> Casts to the pine roots, raising man like a mountain
> Out of the naked entrail.
>
> Beginning with doom in the ghost, and the springing marvels,
> Image of images, my metal phantom
> Forcing forth through the harebell,
> My man of leaves and the bronze root, mortal, unmortal,
> I, in my fusion of rose and male motion,
> Create this twin miracle.[9]

What the modern artist needs is not so much a faith, as a poetic principle to enable him to counterpoint against each other the different aspects of knowledge of which the modern world has made him

[9] Dylan Thomas, "I, In My Intricate Image, Stride On Two Levels," *Selected Writings,* New Directions, Inc., New York, 1946, p. 16.

aware. Consider this fact. We know, or we think we know, so much about psychological conditioning, about the psychosomatic aspects of illness, about the effect of childhood frustrations on adult vices, that we are in danger of being unable to pass any moral judgment on individuals. This man committed rape or murder, but we know that he saw something terrible in the woodshed when he was three, was brought up in a slum, was bullied by a drunken stepfather, had his emotions and instincts warped and frustrated in this way or that, so that we cannot really blame him for what he eventually was driven to do. *Tout comprendre, c'est tout pardonner,* to know all is to forgive all, says the French proverb; but to forgive all is to make it impossible to write the *Divine Comedy* or *Hamlet* or *Paradise Lost.* If we knew all about the inhibitions of King Claudius's childhood, we could not make him the villain in a tragedy. If we knew all Iago's psychological history, we might be tempted to spend all our sympathy on him rather than on Othello. And it did not take even that much psychology to make the Romantics turn Milton's Satan into a hero. If our judgments of men are to be dissolved in psychological understanding, we can no longer pattern a tragedy or create any significant work of art with a human situation as its subject matter. Certainly a behaviorist psychology—and I use this term in its widest sense—leaves little room for an appraisal of personality as such, and without an appraisal of personality as such, why should Hamlet's death be any more significant than that of Polonius?

Yet Hamlet's death, and all that leads up to it, is significant, because it is implicitly set against a tradition of what is valuable in human personality, and out of the implicit conflict with this tradition—which held, among other things, that a good man was doing right to punish an evil one—the tragedy emerges. Cannot we, too, acquire a double vision and set the fact of value in human personality beside the psychological knowledge that would seem to break down the basis of such value, and contemplate the subsequent tensions in art? Cannot the poet, at least, answer Huxley's question, by accepting simultaneously both of his alternatives as each true in its own way, and finding a richness of observation and expression in which the conflict can be resolved? Even in life, cannot we both forgive a man and pass judgment on him? All the more so, surely, should we be able to achieve this twofold attitude in art, which has so many devices for focusing multiple vision.

The problem of the modern literary artist, therefore, is not to find usable myths so much, as to find ways of handling knowledge in a context of value. Knowledge should explain without ever explaining away; proof that Keats's genius flowered early because he had tuberculosis, neither explains away the genius nor makes tuberculosis a desirable disease; a study of the nervous system can tell us all sorts of fascinating things about what makes us tick, but cannot alter the basic fact that we *do* tick and the conviction that, in the last analysis, that fact is mysterious and ineffable; neither physiology nor psychology nor sociology nor economic history, for all the valuable insights they give us into man's behavior, can alter the fundamental mystery of the god in the machine—man being, as Molly Bloom describes a character in Joyce's *Ulysses,* "poached eyes on ghost."

So I dissociate myself from the myth hunters, who see the modern literary artist's basic need as new myths, as well as from those who deplore the lack of a common religious background in our civilization. I think cultural pluralism is a good thing. I think it is both wise and civilized to realize that no single religious creed represents either the final historical truth about what happened or the final theological truth about the nature of man and his relations with ultimate reality, but that any creed may have valuable insights to contribute. Any piece of faith which is destroyed by new knowledge is only destroyed in its formal expression, not in its fundamental reality—or if it is destroyed in its fundamental reality, then it clearly corresponds to no real need or perception, and ought to be abandoned cheerfully. We need neither new knowledge nor new faith, but rather the ability to handle what we have. And that ability, because it involves the counterpointing of apparently contradictory insights, can best be given us by the artist, whose profession it is to distil rich significance out of such counterpointing.

There is then no inseparable gulf between the modern literary artist and his predecessors. If his predecessors enjoyed a more stable background of belief, they still needed to set their individual insights against that background, before they could achieve the highest kind of art. We have more balls to juggle in the air, more conflicting claims to focus into a rich pattern of significance, more items of knowledge to organize into a profound and total vision of man's fate. That what should be regarded as an opportunity is often regarded as an inhibition, is the result of social and other factors too complicated to be discussed here. Part of the trouble with the modern artist is that he has too many tools and a very indistinct notion of what he should do with them, with the result that he spends a great deal of time simply displaying them. If the artist would spend less time alternately bewailing his "alienation" from society and flourishing his unemployed skills, he might realize the exciting opportunity that awaits him. Everybody is too busy explaining everybody else's lack of success. To the chorus of breastbeaters, prophesiers of doom, *laudatores temporis acti,* beraters of popular taste, deplorers of poets' obscurity, interpreters of the modern dilemma, and all the poetasters, criticasters, and undertakers of the Muse who dance upon the grave of literature in the expectation of being hired to conduct the funeral, I can only say, as the Lord said to Job as he sat wailing among the ashes,

> Who is this that darkeneth counsel
> With words without knowledge?
> Gird up now thy loins like a man.

VIII

MYSTICISM AS A SOLUTION TO THE POET'S DILEMMA [1]

BY

KENNETH BURKE AND STANLEY ROMAINE HOPPER

I

Notes and Commentary on a Lecture by Kenneth Burke [2]

by

Stanley Romaine Hopper

I.

It is not easy to grasp Burke's views on mysticism. This is due in part to the reader's own difficulty in setting aside the associations which have grown up in his own mind concerning the nature of "mysticism"—including both the vagueness of the term itself, and the vagueness (or intensity) of the emotional factors which go to make up the reader's unconscious associations, usually religious in nature. Nevertheless, these must be set aside so far as possible if Burke's thesis is to take hold. For he is concerned with the problem of communication, with "rhetoric"; he is concerned with mysticism as a means, not as an end. And in this study, it is with mysticism as an

[1] This chapter represents a joint effort by Mr. Burke and the editor. Mr. Burke spoke in the lecture series which led to this volume, but mislaid his manuscript and could not take the time to reconstruct it. However, he kindly agreed to reconstruction of his material by the editor.

[2] Part I is the editor's reconstruction and exposition of Mr. Burke's material. Part II and Part III were written later by Mr. Burke.

esthetic means whereby the poet may communicate his message to the reader. Two things, then, must be understood at the outset: first, the nature of the modern poet's dilemma; and the esthetic uses of mysticism as a means of overcoming this dilemma.

Undoubtedly the poet's dilemma begins with what T. S. Eliot describes as "the intolerable wrestle with words and meanings." The poet has slowly to learn that

> . . . last year's words belong to last year's language
> And next year's words await another voice.[3]

The poet wrestles always with this semantic angel: and he must suffer the wound of the limitations of himself and his medium, if he is to win the blessings of victory over them. But it is "semantics with a difference" (as Burke says); and the difference is an esthetic one. For the poet's problem is precisely that of "bodying forth" both meanings and significances in the context of esthetic forms.

This problem is not so acute in cultural periods which are unified: in which the conventions of meaning and expression are well articulated and in which a definable world-view is widely accepted. But in a period in which such conventions and agreements can no longer be assumed, or in a period in which no one of these contexts of unity or order may be said to exist in an unequivocal form, the poet's task is a difficult one. His dilemma, in fact, is this: he must create an ordered and (in some sense) unified work of art within a context whose chief characteristics are disorder, lack of order, or partial orders— that is, ambiguities or strife.

To observe that our cultural setting is of this latter kind, is by now a commonplace. We are all aware of the quakes and shocks sustained by the Western consciousness in the first half of the century. The contemporary artist has had to speak either into or out of the vacuums created by the recessions of former patterns of thought and behavior. And this again constitutes his problem: where highly serious he has had to move into the defile of contemporary disillusionment and to encounter there, not strength or faith or hope, but the absence of these:

[3] "Little Gidding," *Four Quartets*, II, Harcourt, Brace & Company, New York, 1943, p. 35.

he has had to engage *at one and the same time* both the social surfaces of pain and the inmost agonies of spirit, and he is obligated by his art to reconcile these at levels of understanding only achieved heretofore by the very greatest tragedians. Lesser talents have wisely accommodated themselves to lesser themes. Many of our ablest creative minds have found the task too great and have been overborne by it. A few, by dint of genius and extraordinary discipline of spirit, have contributed significantly to man's understanding of himself in this period of alienation and gloom.

Of these, Eliot is surely the most instructive from the esthetic point of view. F. O. Matthiessen's analysis of Eliot's approach to the problem illustrates how Eliot's response to this problem has been one of the most significant and influential as an instruction to other artists. Beginning with the surface complexities, and the feeling that "everybody is conscious of every question, and no one knows any answers," Eliot began the search for those equivalences of meaning which lie beneath the surface contrasts. But believing as he did that poetry must express the whole of an experience—both the complexities of its surfaces *and* the underlying structures of meaning and motive—he sought for means whereby some unifying pattern might be found. This pattern was the much discussed "objective correlative"—that basic or internal motif in terms of which a maximum number of details and relevant experiences might be unified.

What is interesting about this, however, is not so much the strategy of the correlative itself as the basic unities to which he actually appealed. The first of these was anthropological, especially in his appeal to ancient myths. To this were added the fresh perspectives on the human spirit provided by modern psychology. Through these an appeal could be made, and at several levels of experience, to those fundamental rhythms of nature which are dramatized in the recurring patterns of the various myths, and to the "common principle underlying all manifestations of life." As a method this provided a means for representing both the essential equivalences of contemporary life and the surface ambivalences; it was a method susceptible either of indefinite expansion or contraction; and it would permit "a continuous parallel between contemporaneity and antiquity" (as he remarked of Joyce's *Ulysses*) which could be manipulated at will by the artist.

Two other back-lying patterns of unity must be added. These are classical metaphysics (as in *Burnt Norton* and the *Four Quartets* generally) and classical theology. This last is predominantly Aquinian refracted through Dante, and gravitates toward mysticism of the variety of St. John of the Cross.

Thus in Eliot's poetry we have proposed four systems of reference and regulation whose purpose it is to afford to the contemporary artist effective ways "of controlling, of ordering, of giving a shape and a significance to the immense panorama of futility and anarchy that is contemporary history" (Eliot). These reference systems are to be regarded from the standpoint of *their esthetic usefulness,* as systems of correlation by means of which the artist can interpret experience such as he finds it in our time. They are employed, that is, as solutions for the poet's dilemma. Burke's study of *Mysticism as a Solution to the Poet's Dilemma* is almost purely of this sort.

2.

At the outset Burke notes what might easily appear as an insurmountable contradiction in terms. Mystical experience was described by William James as being "ineffable" and hence essentially incommunicable. But communication, or expression, is of the very essence of poetry. In attempting to relate the two we appear to be trying to express the ineffable. Little advantage to the poet would seem to be gained from mysticism as a solution to his esthetic dilemma when the problem is put in this way.

Burke, however, takes another view. For the place of mysticism in the work of some of the major poets of recent times—Hopkins, Yeats, Eliot—is an extremely important factor in their respective poetic achievements. The poetic and the mystical are fused, and are evidently one of the most fruitful means for the esthetic realization of those forms of unity and order so desperately sought after by the literary artist today.

Two principles converge here: the *empirical* (from the side of the esthetic) and the *hierarchical* (from the side of the mystical). The hierarchical principle brings something to the poet's empirical creative task which he greatly needs. It is the ancient principle of the "upward and downward way" (Heraclitus), and it provides, in Burke's view, a sort of ideal paradigm for the poet's distribution of his materials.

The Platonic dialogue provides a useful illustration of this. Its dialectical strategy unfolds through successive stages. It begins with sensory images and ascends through imagination and ideas to the highest generalization in the Absolute. The dialogue first sets up several voices, representing different "ideologies," with a view to unmasking these, or to effecting a mutual exposure of imperfect ideas which are seen to be bound to the sensory image in some form. The Platonic Socrates attempts then to rise above these partial views by way of generalizations which transcend the particular biases of the competing voices. Then follows his vision of the pure end or idea resulting from these moves; and, finally, this purely intellectual vision is translated into the Platonic myth or mythic image.

With the introduction of this mythic image, however, an interesting "double-pointedness" arises. The mythic image aims, on the one hand, to lift the poetic awareness one step higher than in the intellectual vision which precedes it; but it effects also, on the other hand, a step down from the purity of abstractions to the impurity of images. Thus the myth, too, is partisan (like the partisanship of the initial competing "voices"): but its partisanship appears at a higher level, a level at which both the rhetorical and the intellectualistic levels of discourse have been transcended. The motivational properties of the mythic representation are thus higher than the sensory images or the competing ideologies from which it takes its rise.

Again the double-pointedness of the mythic image appears in the fact that it may possess both esthetic and religious signification, esthetic in that it contains the resort to sensory images, and religious in that its dramatization appears at the level of ultimate meanings. The poet could take advantage of this in a variety of ways. Hart Crane, for example, in *The Bridge,* substitutes esthetic myths for religious myths and so obtains for his purpose the same "divine" hierarchical advantages. Ideally, the perfect mythic image would be one in which all the objects under consideration were fused, all of them participating in a common spirit and motivation, and one in which all the levels of significance were hierarchically contained in this highest symbolization.

The characteristic expression of this double-pointedness of the mythic image is in terms of the oxymoron—the figure combining contradictory elements in a single expression. It is clear at once how essential this is to the modern literary artist, and how the search for effective images by the contemporary poet consists precisely in this effort to "pack an image or idea with divergent motives" and at the same time to secure effective communication at as many levels of awareness as possible. Images so employed both reveal and conceal. The poetic objects are not just empirical, but are also to a degree enigmatical, and a certain amount of mystery will arise precisely where there is communication between the levels.

3.

Numerous illustrations from literature are provided by Burke in the first two volumes of his projected trilogy.[4] One of the most useful of these is Henry James's preface to *The Spoils of Poynton* in which James's intentional use of the mystical ambiguities in images is made clear. While at dinner one Christmas Eve a quarrel between a mother and son was reported to him. It was a quarrel "over the ownership of the valuable furniture of a fine old house just accruing to the young man by his father's death." This was the "germ" of his plot. Here the ambiguities attach to and arise from the *things* of the household. The household "goods" emerge dialectically and psychologically as the household "gods." Two hierarchies are thus involved, the celestial and the social (the eternal and the temporal). The things are always the focal center of the narrative; but it is the representative value of these things, the passions and forces centered upon them and evoked through them that introduces another hierarchy of meanings.

---

[4] Kenneth Burke, *A Grammar of Motives,* Prentice Hall, Inc., New York, 1945; *A Rhetoric of Motives,* Prentice Hall, Inc., New York, 1950; *Symbolic of Motives* (not published).

Burke appeals significantly to Aquinas's hierarchical principle: the object of faith may be considered in two ways: (1) from the side of the thing believed (here the object of faith is simple); (2) from the side of the believer (here the object of faith is complex). What Burke calls the "range of mountings" appears from the complex side, and represents the variety of means whereby the ascent may be made. Mountain climbing as a "kinesthetic" image is susceptible of double-pointedness; the Alpinist also, as the agent of a symbolic act; again psychoanalysis (as well as popular speech) has supplied the artist with a vast realm of symbols, many of them sexual, which heap hierarchical significances upon the empirical image; ethical mounting appears in the motivation of the *Divine Comedy,* et cetera. A symbol which would gather up all the resources of ambiguity and transcend them through the principle of ascent, would have what William James called "ineffableness."

The poetry of Gerard Manley Hopkins is a second instance of a literary strategy shot through with the mystical and hierarchical double-pointedness. He had "a precocious gift for almost lushly sensuous imagery." His early poems are full of startling images of this kind. But he renounced all this when he affiliated with the Jesuit order. He regarded it as antithetical to his calling, until it was suggested by a superior that he write a poem commemorating the nuns whose lives were lost in the wreck of the *Deutschland.* Here, suddenly, an authentic use for his early talents made possible a recovery of his esthetic interests at a level transcending his previous levels of experience. Both the sensuous imagery and his religion could be included; and what were held heretofore as contradictions become workable ambiguities. The poem opens with a statement of his own moral shipwreck, then moves on to the shipwreck of the nuns. His reference to the shipwreck as a "harvesting for God" would seem to suggest that his own guilt had been a roundabout means for renewal at a higher level. The sinking down is succeeded by a raising up. Exaltation follows.

But Burke goes on to trace, in Hopkins's poetry, an hierarchic identification betwixt God and nature and Hopkins himself, of such a sort as that the natural images will convey the religious exaltation which he experiences mystically: that is, when the mythic image succeeds in containing all the manifold meanings and implications of Hopkins's esthetic celebrations. But when these mythic images fall short of this, then the mystic accidie (the sense of emptiness and drought) "sets in precisely at the moment when the happy combination is somehow broken, and the motives that were thus being transcended are left like ashes after a bright fire." Thence the bitter cries, when, the identification breaking down, the poet is left in himself alone: "I am gall, I am heartburn. . . ."

The *Last Poems* of William Butler Yeats provide a clear example of acceity or drought, as his earlier poems illustrate the use of mysticism and various symbols of the upward and the downward way— the "ladder" of his happy days, the "tower," the "winding stair," etc. How these were tied in with spirit messages, and the Plotinian world-view, and the "phases of the moon" with its intricate psychological system (itself compounded of Nicholas of Cusa's "coincidence of opposites" and Heraclitus's "we live each other's death and die each other's life")—all this is by this time familiar to most students of his poetry. But the reduction of all these esthetic means, in his later years, to the level of offal, is a startling reversal of the mystical thirst for exaltation:

> A mound of refuse or the sweepings of the street,
> Old kettles, old bottles, and a broken can,
> Old iron, old bones, old rags, that raving slut
> Who keeps the till. Now that my ladder's gone,
> I must lie down where all the ladders start,
> In the foul rag-and-bone shop of the heart.[5]

Burke comments, "when several of the peaks in the 'range of mountings' have ceased to figure, . . . the 'mound of refuse' predominates in its starkness."

We are led to note here that the fact of several of the peaks in the range of mountings ceasing to figure is a fact of considerable importance—not, perhaps, from the esthetic standpoint: but from the re-

[5] "The Circus Animals' Desertion," *The Collected Poems of W. B. Yeats,* The Macmillan Company, New York, 1951, p. 336.

ligious point of view this is a datum of considerable moral significance. It suggests that whereas the several mysticisms may offer solutions of structure and strategy to the artist of a purely esthetic kind, their power to sustain the artist in his interpretation of life, experience and reality, is insufficient *if* they are appropriated in a purely esthetic way. This is clearly visible in Yeats, and perhaps not less so—though in more intricate ways—in a poet so devout as Hopkins.

4.

For this reason the use of Eliot as a final example of the uses of mysticism is the happiest choice of all, precisely because the theory of the "objective correlative" supports it, and because Eliot himself has attempted a synthesis of beliefs and artistic expression which takes into account all of the factors involved. Moreover, as Burke very rightly remarks, many of the images used by the poet in his earlier writings are used again in the later poems with fuller connotations and implications—of the sort made possible by the mystical range of mountings. One of the simplest, and at the same time most evident, of these is Eliot's talk of the rose garden. By the time it reappears in the *Quartets* it has acquired maximum implication: (To quote Burke) "Talk of a rose garden can now stand ambiguously for: (1) purely secular delights; (2) vague adumbrations of exalted delights; (3) the final mystic unfolding and enfoldment."

The richness of the symbol would appear, in this instance, to be progressive and cumulative. But a contrast may also be drawn, as between the down-turning mood of the early poems and the transformation and synthesis of the *Quartets*. In the early poems Burke sees this down-turning mood characterized by lamentation, fragility, a certain deliberate crabbedness, as well as by a sort of spectator mood, viewing the city's dramas impersonally and almost statistically, with an ironic kind of aloofness suffusing the whole. In *The Waste Land* these moods approach the mystic's accidie, or drought, already noted in Hopkins and Yeats. The last episode, or "What the Thunder Said," contains a transitional element, anticipating the later manner of the *Quartets*. In this perspective, *Ash Wednesday* "represents the new climb" (compare the "stairs" of "Prufrock" with the stairs of *Ash Wednesday*) : the stairs are still arduous, but, as in Dante, they should become easier the higher one climbs.

The movement of the whole really completes itself in the paradoxes of the *Quartets:*

> When the tongues of flame are in-folded
> Into the crowned knot of fire
> And the fire and the rose are one.[6]

"In sum (Burke concludes), we feel that, to approach the *Quartets* in terms of symbolic action, we should first ask ourselves what primary dialectical resources there are here, for exploitation. For, so far as verbal method is concerned, it is apparently the pyramid of dialectical mountings (the resources of Heraclitus) that this poet relies upon mainly, as the means that can endow the earlier down-turning images with new motives, by placing them in the upward-turning configuration that dialectical reduction readily makes possible." [7]

That is well said; and it contains the gist of Burke's views on mysticism as a solution to the artist's problem. Its uses cannot be denied. The questions which emerge are of a different order. While this appropriation of mysticism as a *means* is fruitful beyond a doubt, it is also beyond question that mysticism as an *end* results always in a contemplative mode: its mode is in identity, as Plotinus says. Whether an art so founded can escape this stratification is dubious. Perhaps it will not wish to—Dante's rose of fire and love being its highest artistic expression, a reach of identification to which Eliot's *Four Quartets* also aspires. But if so, will its strategies not be limited to such evocative uses as will fall within the mode—to poetry of ideation rather than of action (drama), to adapt a distinction used elsewhere by Burke? [8] But this may be a serious limitation. It may suggest that a poetry of mysticism, for all its contemplative uses, may, from the religious or the existentialist points of view, be the subtlest of all romanticisms. It may be, that is, the fundamental escape from reality

---

[6] "Little Gidding," *Four Quartets*, V, p. 39.

[7] *A Rhetoric of Motives, op. cit.,* p. 323.

[8] See *A Grammar of Motives, op. cit.,* Appendix D, p. 512.

as "engagement," as meeting, as reconciliation in the dynamic context of personal relations.

II

Appendix

by

Kenneth Burke

Rhetorically considered, Mystery is a major resource of persuasion. Endow a person, an institution, a thing with the glow or resonance of the Mystical, and you have set up a motivational appeal to which people spontaneously ("instinctively," "intuitively") respond. In this respect, an ounce of "Mystery" is worth a ton of "argument." Indeed, where Mystery is, we can be assured that the arguments will profusely follow, as *intellectus* flows from *fides*.

The conditions for the sense of Mystery are present when there is communication between different kinds of beings. Not just communication, nor difference—but communication across the gulf of difference. The difference may be real or imaginary, or something of both. Racist theories build on imaginary differences; with persons living under widely different conditions, the differences are real (cf. the widely different ways of king and peasant); sexual Mystery is grounded in a real biological difference that is transformed by social institutions into a vast "ideological" complexity of differences both real and imaginary. Mysticism in religion involves communication across the widest conceivable difference in kind: Communication between an infinitesimally weak Creature and an infinitely powerful Creator. Courtship, politeness, diplomacy, embarrassment, "stage fright," and the like are attenuated secular manifestations of a similar disproportion, or communion across division.

Mystery, as so considered, is seen to be in essence hierarchal. Technically, it ranges all the way from the sense of Divine Radiance to the dingy glamor of Hollywooden sex fiction. Within its compass fall any given society's notions of "success," "prestige," "power," and the like.

But what of Poetry here? Poetry deals, above all, with the language of sensation, of the concrete and positive, whereas Mystery is of the spirit.

Mysticism arises in Poetry in so far as the "things" of the poet's sensory experience are felt to be infused by a hierarchal spirit. Empirically, things just *are;* but mystically, things *stand for.* Mystical poetry is thus forever using the language of things to point beyond things, to the ultimate invisible, intangible order (the realm of hierarchy) by which they are infused.

In the crudest social sense, there is the "radiance" of the material commodity, the possession of which (we are persuaded by the priesthood of advertising) will attest to our "belonging" in a more reputable status. There is a subtler area, more sheerly cultural, where we may "commune" by the "appreciation" of things deemed rare or superior (roughly: "Beauty"). And finally, there is the area of the "anagogic," according to which the things of the natural order are taken to stand for entities of the supernatural order.

A figure like the Roman Emperor, as *pontifex maximus* combining his role as a divinity with his distinction as titular head of the social pyramid, suggests that, for some peoples at least, "religious" and "social" divinity can become subtly interchangeable terms. Such an ambiguity would obviously have great rhetorical possibilities, for it would supply the transition whereby purely social distinctions could enjoy the sanction of Mystery in the theological sense. Particularly when analyzing Henry James's concern with the radiance of "things" in his *The Spoils of Poynton,* we tried to show how James had been concerned with such purely "social divinity," in its role as the motive of the action in this novel.

In so far as natural objects furtively take on the hierarchal nature of the social order with which they are associated, the naturalist's attack upon supernaturalism was a remarkable unconscious swindle. For the naturalist, in his criticism of the supernatural, directed our attention to the respects in which the given society's version of the design in the supernatural order duplicated the design of the social order. He thereby led us and himself to believe that he, on the other hand, was dealing purely and simply with things of the senses, starting from scratch, asking without prepossessions, "Now just what do I see when I look at this object?" The naturalist cult of sensationism, empiricism, by focusing our attention upon the design of social hierarchy reflected in any given version of supernatural hierarchy, thus used the dialectics of opposition to keep us from asking about the possible social hierarchy that might be lurking in his "purely sensationalist" version of nature. (Grass on a college campus, for instance, is not just a "sensory" thing. At the very least, it bodies forth certain principles of order, with related claims, obligations, and promises. It is not merely "empirical." It is "mythic," "ritualistic"; it not just *is,* it *stands for.* And to "begin" by merely asking what one "sees" there, to begin by ignoring the possibility of its hierarchal implications, is to miss the point. Or, when these implications are considered, they are thought to prevail *only* when the grass is considered as an embellishment. The possible presence of a covert hierarchal motive even in grass *qua* grass, is not discussed. And such programmatic omission is the poorest guaranty of all that the assumption is correct.)

Psychologistic doctrines arose in response to this oversight. We are referring in general to the idealistic theories of "empathy," that look upon the poet's imagery as a duplicate, in objective terms, of purely subjective attitudes (states of mind expressed as corresponding states of nature).

This was a step in the right direction. (As Miss Josephine Miles has shown, poetry exploited the "pathetic fallacy" most extremely during the period when the current "scientific" view of nature strove most emphatically to depersonalize nature.)

But the whole stress upon the "objective correlative" can be, in turn, a means for concealing the full reach of the hierarchal motive, unless we deliberately change the terms of the investigation. Then personal motives, in the individualistic sense, would be treated in terms of personal motives in the broader, hierarchal sense (where the individual is seen as an individual sensibility through which the hierarchal motives are expressed and coordinated, while the problems to do with them are imagined and imaginally solved).

I tried to show (both in my address and in my *Rhetoric of Motives*) how this matter comes to a head in what I called "the range of mountings." That is: the pyramidal structure could be variously expressed in a series of modes which (I assume) exhaust the field. They are:

(1) The "kinesthetic." Imagery of height, depth, and the like, as such.

(2) "Alpinism." Mountain climbing (flight, etc.) experienced as "answer to a call."

(3) Sexual ambiguities: "mounting" in the sexual sense.

(4) Improvement of status, in the sense of the social "climber."

(5) The ethical striving upward (as with Dante's *Purgatorio*).

(6) The pyramidal dung heap (Egypt's pyramids as stylized replica of this).

(7) The dialectical Upward Way (toward Oneness, through "higher levels of generalization").

There are many possible combinations of such relations between "higher" and "lower," or rises from lower to higher, or paradoxes whereby a descent from higher to lower in one respect is a rise from lower to higher in another respect (and *vice versa*). Such resources can be studied in their particularity when we center our attention upon one particular poet's work, considered as a "mystical strategy" for responding imaginally to the hierarchal motive. I have analyzed a few such "strategies" in the closing pages of my *Rhetoric* (notably, Eliot, Hopkins, Yeats).

No matter how "supernatural" the source of a poet's inspiration may be, his actual lines must perforce utilize the imagery of social hierarchy. Hence it is the critic's function, as analyst of poetry, to study the terminology as such (viewing language as a social product, and viewing the individual poet's language as a partially general, partially unique manipulation of such resources).

Addendum

by

Kenneth Burke

In general, I would agree with Dr. Hopper's statement (including his introductory remarks about the problem of artistic communication in times of terminological confusion, though this was not an aspect of the subject I was concerned with in my talk).

In my *Grammar of Motives,* I equated mysticism, *philosophically,* with a featuring of the term, "purpose." And I noted that "art for art's sake" doctrines equate "agency" with "purpose" (in defining the medium as its own ultimate end). The *Rhetoric* (material from which I used in my talk) gets us into other motives, because of the relation between rhetoric and dialectic. (Aristotle calls rhetoric the "counterpart," *antistrophos,* of dialectic.) And I have thought that, since Dr. Hopper has so well reconstructed the main lines of the original talk (my copy of which got lost), I might here add some remarks reviewing the question largely in the light of things written later. Thus to summarize:

Rhetoric is designed for appeal (persuasion). The ultimately most appealing design (as regards form) is the pyramidal. Since the pyramidal is the dialectical (with its technique of Upward and Downward way for going from fragmentary to unitary, and thereafter infusing the fragmentary with the unitary), there is a point at which rhetoric in its perfection transcends itself or "abolishes itself" by becoming sheerly dialectical. Instead of being but one of the voices, it becomes the vision arising from them all as they work in cooperative competition. But every human statement is partial, hence even the most "universal" of dialectical manipulations will disclose partisan motives, willy nilly, whereat we are brought back into the realm of rhetorical partisanship.

Such partisanship involves the "universalizing" of some *particular* order. Hence, speculations on the "supernatural" will be more or less overtly couched in the terms of some given temporal order. And "nature" will be understood after the same fashion. The poet's terms for "sensation," "beauty," and the like, will be quasi-natural images secretly infused with the spirit of the social hierarchy through which they are perceived. Here will be the "mystery" in such images. This "mystery" will have class-motivations, since social hierarchy involves the ordering of classes. Hence, we have mystery as "communication between different kinds of beings."

But the ultimate of such a communicative gap is the uniting of opposites (the principle of the oxymoron). And mysticism, in its capacity for going to the end of the line, will attain its completion in this figure (and in the various roundabout ways of embodying the principle of this figure). Hence, as regards "mysticism" in poetry:

If you track down the principle of the oxymoron, as regards the "estheticizing" of *moral* quandaries, you are prompted to look for stylistic devices whereby descent and ascent become subtly interchangeable. So likewise with problem and solution, guilt and exoneration, yielding-to temptation and freedom-from temptation, transcendence upwards and transcendence downwards. In brief, yes and no, like lion and lamb, can by the subterfuges of mystico-literary style be made (for the moment at least) to lie down together. And in times of much social conflict, any such moment is indeed medicinal.

Spotting it, we can next note minor devices whereby such curative mergings occur often, not only in poetry, but in linguistic resources generally. We salute these as "fragments" of the mystical motive. And there is also the menace in the fragment made total, as with "mysticism" of crime, sex, war, and the like (instrumental aspects of life here being treated as universal, all-embracing purposes, as "teleologies," *means* being extolled as ends). And, finally, since the body social is an aggregate of many physical bodies, and since the disrelations of society, being felt as "guilt," are also translated by the poet into bodily terms, we watch to see how "the thinking of the body" figures in such mystic paradoxes. Hence, we get to problems of catharsis: purification by the kill, by association with things ritually clean, by imagery of physical giving-off. Hence even, finally, we may watch for alchemy whereby excrement is made golden, or for ways of defining essence whereby the freeing from an evil spirit is like the transforming of flatus into fragrance. Or thoughts of "fluency" may reveal affinities with the diuretic. Accordingly, our search here may seem to be dismal. The Beauty Boys will object, in so far as they would be parlor-pretty. However, as we have observed before, true beauty must be not mere decoration, but an *ecclesia super cloacam*—and in the thorough poets, it always is so.

The theme of the "reflexive" (the circling back upon the self), also keeps turning up here, in the problems of mystical poetry. In its simplest stylistic form, the "reflexive" is seen in such "atop the atop" or "within the within" designs as with Coleridge's expression, "snowdrop on a tuft of snow," or Donne's, "Death, thou shalt die." It probably gets its most symmetrical visual representation in the design of the snake, with its own tail in its mouth. It is grandly "cosmologized," perhaps, in doctrines of "eternal recurrence." Another variant is that mythic monster, the amphisbaena, a kind of primal worm, each end of which is head or tail.

(In an analysis of the Oresteia, to be published elsewhere, I have dealt with this. Cassandra calls Clytemnaestra an amphisbaena. And since, in her role as true prophetess, she is correctly naming the essences of motivation, I take it that, when Orestes finally slays Clytemnaestra, no less a thing than this ultimate "pre-logical," dreaming labyrinth of the ambiguously vegetating body is among the problems he hopes to solve by the ways of the kill, as sacrificial mode of vindication.)

Oxymoron in its stylistic simplicity is a figure in which a word is modified by an epithet of contrary significance. (Our dictionary gives "cruel kindness," and "laborious idleness.") By the "principle" of the oxymoron, we have in mind such coexistence of conflicting orders as may sometimes reveal themselves in this rhetorical device, which in itself is easily contrived, and can be used mechanically, prettily, without the implication of any profound conflict in the poet's psychic economy. "Black brilliance" would be an oxymoron. But when we come to the notion of the sun as "God's shadow," where are we? The two orders are united. In imagination, quite as with "black brilliance," we may think of the blinding that takes place when we look squarely at the sun, and of the black spots that follow as an after-image. But as regards idea, we glimpse another relation here: an *hierarchal* one, *radiance* in one order being joined with *darkness* in another order. The clash of coexistent images thus stands for a duality of ratings.

Interchangeability of acceptance and rejection, an oxymoronlike transcending of their relation as "logical opposites," would be reducible, in "fundamental" bodily imaging of cathartic problems, to analogous interchangeabilities of "oral" and "anal" motives. "Essence," stated in bodily terms, is either of the breath-fragrance-spirit set or of the flatus-stench-demon set. Hence, since mysticism will be radical in its use of body-imagery, we take it for granted that our concerns with poetry at this point must encounter the resentment of the Beauty Boys.

Such bepuzzlements as we are here considering are reduced to easily viable forms by the deliberate incongruities of comedy, as when loathesome things are treated in terms belonging to the category of food. Thus, if "zaggel" were an accepted name for some substance generally deemed disgusting, one might set up a flurry of comic appreciation by referring to a *spoonful* of zaggel.

At one time, we analyzed the appeal of comedy by stressing its use of incongruity. But one should also note a more complex motive here. The stressing of the incongruity must also reaffirm some "channel of affinity," so that the incongruity is but a roundabout way of confirming some principle of order.

Often the motive thus complexly reaffirmed is relatively superficial (as with an incongruity that confirms the auditor's prejudice against some religious, political, or social group). But by "channels of affinity" we have in mind a more universal order of motives. For instance, jokes are often formed by incongruously relating ideas of food with ideas of sex. And such jokes would derive their appeal not from the incongruity alone, but from the fact that there is a real sense in which both such orders of motivation are different species of a single genus, since both food and sex are kinds of appetition, or desire. Such "channels of affinity" reach an extreme form in jokes based on the interchangeability of oral and anal motives. And we have been suggesting that, beneath these incongruities, may lurk primal ambiguities of the biological cell, a stage at which the distinctions between yes and no, individual and environment, in and out, etc., are absolutely transcended, in being prior to all such distinctions. And in so far as such undifferentiated conditions would form the biological ground above which the many differentiations of human discourse ("reason") are constructed, we might find here a "channel of affinity" confirmed in any picturesquely conflicting merger of "logical opposites." Here, beneath the devices of "comic catharsis," would be a motive solemnly grotesque.

We believe that the oxymoron often comes to operate in neurotic mental states by this route: Imagine, let us say, a subject who was obsessed by some snatch of melody. Imagine that it did not disturb him merely by its refusal to let up (though such a condition in itself would make for considerable disturbance). But, further, there was the feeling that the melody pursued him like an accuser. Digging into the situation, one might disclose that some unlawful desire was expressed in the unremitting nag of this melody. There was something the subject wanted to take place; he could not bring himself to acknowledge this desire; and since the melody happened, by accidents of association, secretly to stand for the essence of this desire, the persistence of the melody would be, in effect, a roundabout affirming of the very thing which the patient refused to admit outright.

Up to this point, there is no "principle of the oxymoron" involved. And, if this were the correct gauging of the motives, the obsessive nature of the melody might be at least weakened, and maybe even completely dissolved.

The "principle of the oxymoron" would figure if there were a further factor involved. That is: Suppose this melody to have been in form like some other melody (as though both melodies were variations on a single theme). And suppose that this other melody had wholly *acceptable* connotations for the patient, representing some period in his life when he was essentially at peace. As regards attitude, then, these two melodies would be *contradictory* species of a single genus. And behind the loathesomeness of the "sinful" melody there would be the undisclosed operations of its counterpart, the "virtuous" melody. The "virtuous" motive (its essence represented by the earlier melody) was in effect acting as a sanction for the "sinful" motive (its essence represented by the later melody, which was formally related to the earlier one as a "variation on a single theme"). This more ingenious form of neurosis would come closer to the ways of the "mystic oxymoron." And we may doubt whether the nag of the "sinful" memory could be quieted until its secret kinship with the "virtuous" melody had been disclosed.

However, given the ingenuities of self-torture, it is not beyond possibility that, were one to penetrate explicitly to the earlier melody, it might, as thus approached in retrospect, come to take on the essence of the later melody. That is, it might cease to be a "virtuous" melody, being felt instead as the furtive, fumbling annunciation of the second melody, the devilish one, that had first appeared in the deceptive form of an angel.

These remarks on the principle of the oxymoron can be viewed as a gloss on Dr. Hopper's statement: "The sinking-down is succeeded by a raising-up."

Unquestionably, there are many "rational" devices, in art, and thought generally, whereby a dualistic moment composed of contradictory motives can be changed into a development in which one part *succeeds* the other. The breakdown of a unitary radiance into such a spectrum of successive parts (the translation of an essence into a temporary series) can take many forms. And primary among these would be the step *from* a sinking-down *to* a raising-up.

The critic could interpret such forms on their face. Or he might view them as varying "rational subterfuges" for translating a self-contradictory nodus into a structure wherein the contradiction seems to be removed. For while yes-no is a contradictory nodus, there would be no such embarrassments in a plot that developed from yes to no, or *vice versa*.

We might then take such a sequence at face value. Or we might say that, underlying it, there is a "mystic oxymoron" in which the contradictory elements exist simultaneously, as parts of a single essence, persons of a single unity (consubstantial moments of one primal motive).

But by our notions, the principle of the oxymoron fully prevails only when contradictory motives are fused in one set of symbols, not analyzed into a temporal succession. And the "radiance" would be in the pure light of the momentary merger. (Tiny "twinklings" of such a resource come easy in language, as the term, "distance," includes "near" and "far," or "rate of progress" includes "fast" and "slow." Upheavals occur only when vast clusters of motives have gathered about contradictory poles, so that tremendous inventiveness is needed to discover and maintain a symbol-system capable of "transcending" the conflict by devices that give expression to both members of the otherwise self-annihilating pair.)

We believe that, in thoroughly analyzing moments of mystic imagery, the critic of such poetry must find himself ultimately confronting problems and processes of this sort. The mystic poet's terminology will reveal terms from three basic orders of motives: (1) the "thinking of the body," that involves "catharsis" by the covert or overt use of terms conceived after the analogy of bodily catharsis or unburdening; (2) the personal, terms for the affections as such; (3) the civic, involving relations to the social pyramid, and headed in such somewhat abstract words as "fate," "destiny," "justice," "vindication," "vengeance," etc. Elsewhere, we have proposed to call them "the Great Persecutional Words," and have tried to show how the logic of them plays a part in the forms of great drama, thus in a sense interweaving formal necessity and moral quandary, thereby even making "perfect form" in art indistinguishable from the compulsions of ethical pursuit by "conscience." [9]

[9] In a given language, though a "good" word and a "bad" word happened to be identical or nearly alike in consonantal structure, they might nonetheless be sufficiently distinguished, for logical purposes, by a difference of vowels. Thus, suppose that *zaggel* were a "bad" word and *ziggel* a "good" word (the one denoting something loathsome, the other denoting something admirable, or at least attitudinally neutral). Obviously, the distinction by *ablaut* (between *a* and *i*) would be quite sufficient for logical purposes. But as regards the ambiguities of tonal imagery that operate in poetry, might not the design of the "good" word furtively embrace the connotations in the analogous design of the "bad" word? Here would be a tiny, but appreciable, stylistic transcendence.

IX

THE USE OF MYTH IN KAFKA AND MANN

BY

HARRY SLOCHOWER

A study of the great literary classics shows that their themes are organically interwoven with mythic and religious motifs. The interconnection is more intimate in the eastern and primitive myths, in the mythopoesis of Greece and Rome, and, of course, in the Catholic myth of Dante. But myth and religion also find their way into modern classics, such as Racine's *Phèdre,* Rabelais's *Gargantua,* Goethe's *Faust,* Wagner's *Ring,* Melville's *Moby Dick,* and the poetry of William Blake. Even in our secular twentieth century, we find that the outstanding writers are preoccupied with them. To mention some: André Malraux, James Joyce, the Danish writer Nexö, and, above all, the two men with whom we are concerned in this chapter, Franz Kafka and Thomas Mann.

I

Myth and religion, along with other cultural forms, are at one in their common attempt to get at basic reality seen in symbolic transformation. However, what differentiates myth and religion, particularly from science and philosophy, is their anthropomorphic approach. Whereas science and philosophy focus on the cosmos as a whole, the special interest of myth and religion is the subject of *man*. A second element which unites the two is their *normative* perspective. Both approach the problem of man, not in terms of neutral objectivity, but apply selected value judgments.

Another feature which connects myth and religion is their view of the human drama as having a *communal* origin and destiny. And these are seen as undergoing a *dramatistic* process: the primary communal stage is followed by a mediate phase, in which the individual loosens himself from his social matrix. This defection is called his crime or sin. It results in his "Cain"-journey, in his suffering and crucifixion. However, in the course of the dramatic development, the crime may become transfigured into "the blessing." This becomes possible to the extent that the individual recognizes the supra-individual element within his ego, and seeks to reintegrate it with his commune on a higher level.

Both myth and religion are concerned with ultimate reality. But myth is distinguished from religion in that it presents reality as an *immanent* mode. The form of the myth is the story or picture—that is, its universal prototypes are presented through concrete, particularized imagery, and are embodied in individual characters and specific situations. Moreover, its sensuous presentation of reality also takes account of the temporal historic situation in which man is placed.

As a result of its stress on the immanent and the particular, the myth can do greater justice to the *mediate* stage of individual defection or revolt. In the myth, the crime of the hero appears as a *necessary* act, *through* which he can become transformed. And while the hero comes to recognize that his revolt has been in excess, and experiences fear and trembling, he never fully surrenders or recants. It follows that in the mythic process, there is no complete redemption as in religion—no eschatology or paradise. Even as the individual is reintegrated with his commune, the element of individuation, of experience, and of revolt, continues as a moment calling for a new revolt aiming at a higher re-recreation.

In sum, the myth contains two basic categories: *Creation,* which relates to the pattern, the prototype, the beginnings and ends of things; and the *Quest,* which refers to the critical questioning of the old tradition aiming at a *futuristic* tradition. In Aristotle's *Rhetoric,* we have the three categories of Logos, Ethos, and Pathos. Generally speaking, we might say that the myth of Creation is concerned with Logos, the myth of the Quest with Pathos or emotion and with Ethos or the character of the individual—always seeking a new Logos whenever the existing law takes on a closed hierarchical form.

We have observed that myth and religion offer a communal standard of behavior. This standard is conditioned by social and political historic factors. Even as history and culture live by the myth, they, in turn, affect the form, content, and direction of the myth. It follows that the all human standard inherent in the myth may be distorted by the "ideology" of the myth, serving partisan and special interests. This opens the way toward the misuse of the myth. And, in the course of history, the myth has been often employed toward inhuman purposes. In our own twentieth century—the era of Kafka and Mann—we are confronted with a plethora of false and manufactured myths. Let me mention two in particular which are relevant to Kafka and Mann: the racial "folk," masquerading as a human commune, and the technological "one world," giving the illusion that the power of mechanical gadgets, such as the atomic bomb, can replace the power of man.

The works of Franz Kafka and Thomas Mann present the menace in the false and dead myth. But they also suggest—Kafka somewhat hesitantly, Mann more confidently—the possibility of a "breakthrough" and the reemergence of the living myth, of one human world.

II

When we look over the life and works of Franz Kafka, we are impressed with the fact that they reveal fear, fear and loneliness, alienation from the world, from the public commune in which he lived. He was a Jew, an alien, in an alienating world, Kafka's commercialized world, the semi-feudal, semi-bourgeois bureaucracy of the old Austro-Hungarian Empire. And we find that he also felt estranged from his father and even partly from his mother, estranged from his country, estranged from his profession, estranged from women, and in fear of marriage. Finally, there is his fear and alienation from his potential reading public, as manifested in his request to his friend Max Brod that Kafka's manuscripts be burned.

Franz Kafka, a Jew and an alien, had a particularly difficult problem in finding the mythic reference in the past. Job could do it. He was near enough to his God, and Sophocles has a certain mythic reference in Moira. The difficulties became greater with Hamlet, Faust, and Ahab. By the twentieth century, especially for those such as Kafka who were Jews in name only, there is an even greater difficulty of finding a reference backwards.

What has become of Job's God in Kafka's world? What has become of the Mosaic Law? What has become of the Judges? They are reduced to bookkeepers. God and the Judges are readers of legal briefs and manuscripts. And the Prophet, the Klamm, this "all" figure has become a fat, middle-aged bureaucrat. This is the form in which Logos and God now appear. This is the communal reference which Kafka finds in his world. Documents which cover lives and aspirations, documents and numbers, have replaced the idea of the law.

We have here the Evil One in modern form. The Devil is Society, this particular Society, Society characterized by impersonality. It is the Fiend, whom you cannot see, a faceless, dehumanized something which accuses you and does not tell you what you are accused of, a kind of bureaucratic version of original sin.

This is the one Devil. The other resides within the individual who has been reduced to this facelessness himself and who remains indifferent to the outrage of evil. This "hero" is not a protesting, passionate, fiery Job, or a Prometheus, or an Oedipus, or even a Dante; he is an orphan, a bachelor, vermin—in the story, "Metamorphosis," a cockroach. And the only way in which he revolts, in Kafka's *The Trial,* is simply by a kind of passive, non-conscious self-arrest. More than that, he is guilty even over this "revolt," guilty because he does not feel the power in him to replace the commune, to replace the father—an echo of Hamlet. Yet, Hamlet is still quite active in his inaction. But Joseph K.'s inactivity, in comparison, is nearer to a man such as Swann in Proust's work or Castorp in *The Magic Mountain.*

And so we find that Kafka's heroes do not reenact the Oedipus theme. They do not revolt against their fathers. Rather, they reverse the Oedipus pattern and the sons sacrifice themselves for the fathers.

In the story, "The Judgment," the son commits suicide, whereupon the energy and vitality of the father's house are enhanced. In the story, "Metamorphosis," the hero wakes up one morning and finds he is a cockroach, whereupon the father's fortunes begin to increase.

Yet Kafka's work contains the suggestion of a third stage, the stage of reintegration. But in Kafka, this phase which we find in *The Castle*, the *Great Wall of China*, is much more of a prayer than a hope. *The Castle* is the omnipotent structure of judges and lawyers that become more remote, the more you try to approach it. As such it reminds one of Socrates's saying, "The more I know, the more I find out that I don't know"; of Dante's theology, that knowledge leads to the realization of man's deep ignorance; and of the idea of the Law which shows man to be utterly corrupt.

The Castle is omnipotent, on the one hand, a taboo not to be violated; on the other hand, it is decadent, as was the Austro-Hungarian castle of Kafka's time. Yet, we have here a more positive attempt to reach the Law. In *The Trial*, Joseph K. begins with a certain militance, but, as the novel proceeds, his revolt is nearly crushed. In *The Castle*, "K." demands a job as a surveyor, holding that he has *a right* to work. And even though he does not get entrance into the Castle, there is a suggestion which Kafka sketched that in time he was to be permitted at least to live in the village.

In this novel, Kafka rejects two approaches; the approach of Amalia, the anarchic rebel, the individual who will have nothing to do with the judges; and the alternative way of the Pepis (in the last part of *The Castle*, which is not translated, unfortunately, in the Knopf edition), who live huddled together in the underground. This way of submerging the ego, K. cannot accept either. When Pepi begs of K.: "Just stay with us until Springtime," the only answer K. makes is, "When does Springtime come?" Yet the feeling we get is that the individual K.'s must first go underground to the Mothers, to the Pepis, to start at the bottom, and work their way through.

But the greater promise lies in man's insatiability and rebellious quest, as suggested in the sermon in *The Trial*. It is the sermon about the legend of the gatekeeper who stands at the gates and will not allow the individuals to pass through. In the end, Joseph K. learns that the gate was kept open only for him. He alone could go through, but Joseph K. is a simpleton. He is called, in German, *"Ein Mann vom Lande."* In other words, he was too simpleminded to try to go through, to defy the gatekeeper.

This defiance is necessary. It is the duty of the individual to defy the gatekeeper, and, having done so, he might be allowed to pass through. We can say, then, about Kafka, that in the main his is the myth of the quest, with very little confidence and hope in the myth of creation; but this quest, this seeking, this critique, is also a certainty which the K.'s cannot give up.

To be sure, the negative elements seem to abound in Kafka's work. It abounds in metaphors, such as air which stifles, incurable wounds, castration symbols (injuries to knees and thighs), the cage, etc.— metaphors which suggest the closed circle. Yet, Kafka is to be distinguished from most of his followers who have taken up these negative aspects and erected them into a system of negativism and of critique, for there remains in Kafka a consuming yearning for the law and the truth. He does not end in a Kierkegaardian "either/or," and he does not end with submission or surrender. The quest in Kafka is also an inevitable and persisting feature of man's way. In its persistence lies the promise of the quest.

III

When we turn to Thomas Mann, we have a man who lacks many of the personal burdens from which Kafka suffered. In Mann's case we, therefore, have a more positive voice, possibly also because he has taken a longer and deeper look backward toward a mythic reference. In him we do find the preoccupation with and the emphasis on the myth of creation. Myths abound in all of Thomas Mann's works, Egyptian, Hebraic, Christian, and Germanic.

But this positive voice in Thomas Mann is not one which ignores the ideology of the myth mentioned before. As a matter of fact, in most of his works we find a warning against two kinds of myth: against the dead myth—the dual symbol for that is the Egyptian mummy—and the German Magic Mountain *Kultur,* an inactive idealism or romanticism. That is the myth as stasis, disporting itself in music, philosophy, and dreams.

The other danger, equally great, and bound up with the first, is the myth as uprooting dynamics, the myth as the devouring father and mother. It, too, appears in two forms. It may be *Kultur* itself, where the transcendent dynamic, while confined to the realm of the idea or the spirit, is a form of imperialism, an esthetic imperialism which may—as shown in *Doctor Faustus* and suggested in earlier works—be translated into the imperialism of the body, the cannibalism of Lidice and Auschwitz.

These are the dangerous myths. Mann encountered them by a living myth which has its roots in a living God, a God Who combines both creation and the quest, the God Who *calls for* the individual quest, as Job's God Who condones Job, at least partly because Job has rebelled against Him, whereas He does not condone the three friends who did not show this critical quest.

The earlier Mann was only groping for this living God and this living myth. In his works through *The Magic Mountain,* we find the presentation of a false creativeness. It is conditioned by the German and European commercialized commune, similar to that in which Kafka's characters were entangled. This false communal base necessarily shapes the false quest of the hero.

When we think of *The Magic Mountain*—and we might also, at this point, think of Mann's much later work, *Doctor Faustus*—our story, in terms of the three stages, unfolds somewhat like this: in both cases, you might say with Hamlet, "The time is out of joint." The flatland of Castorp and the birthplace of Leverkuehn, the hero of *Doctor Faustus,* embody a commercialized collective which they consciously or unconsciously reject. The two heroes then proceed to disport themselves in aloneness, Doctor Faustus much more so than Castorp. Both secede from this commune, Castorp seven years above the flatland to the mountain, Leverkuehn to the valley—his Nietzschean Sils Maria. And here they practice transcendence, ideological, musical transcendence.

But even as they think they have freed themselves from the compulsion of the material base, we find that their ideology is a counterpart, the spiritual counterpart of their mephitic, commercialized collective. To be sure, it is not identical with it. Something is saved, but the vapors from below invade the heights above, or descend to the depths below, so that when Castorp goes to his tertiary stage, at the end of the seven years, and realigns himself with his "comrades," it is not the high commune of Job or Oedipus or Dante, it is Germany in the First World War. Castorp thinks it is Schubert he is fighting for, but we know, and Mann knows by 1924, that Castorp is fighting for Thyssen and Krupp. Similarly, the reintegration of the work of Leverkuehn at the end turns out to be in continuity with the Esau collective of Nazism.

Between *The Magic Mountain* and *Doctor Faustus,* with their false myth, we have the human myth of living creation, the Joseph story, where Mann leaves the bourgeois world to penetrate deep into the human—a kind of international folk song and an attempted answer to the nationalistic howling of the time. It was begun approximately with the ascent of Nazism. Its origin-reference is a God Who appears in the threefold form of the spirit of Abraham, the physics of Isaac, and the human father, Jacob, who combines the two; in psychological terms, the super-ego of Abraham, the id of Isaac, and the integrated ego of Jacob. Joseph would reconcile his three fathers, would unite them all. Not only them. He also reenacts Osiris, Tammuz, Adonis. His is the mediating function of the artist—he is a "between" character, and the word "between," in Hebrew, I understand, has the same root as the words, "knowing" and "insight." Knowledge and insight appear as mediating categories. Joseph's "blessing" consists in the mediation between beauty and wisdom and in his *Geist,* the questing, seeking spirit, but always with reference to his commune, Jacob, the Father—God.

But his is also the hybris of individual revolt, in his notion that all must love him, and more than they love themselves. However, in the third stage, when he comes to Egypt, he returns to his father-brother collective. Yet the story also contains the epilogue of the myth, which prevents a final redemption. For the Egypt-comn.une is a eunuch civilization. There is a question as to whether Joseph's social reforms are a public or a private collectivism. Hence, he loses the blessing, which is given over to Judah, the suffering man. The blessing is taken away from Joseph, whose figure has developed from the Adonis to the Hermes figure, that is, to the worldly leader, the businessman.

Let me now turn to Mann's work of 1948, on which I touched before. In 1924, as we saw, Castorp rejoins a false commune. The Joseph story would correct Castorp's error, which led to the Fascist commune in the nineteen hundred and thirties. The Joseph story deals with the potentialities and possibilities of man in the future. But, in the meantime, the world was in the death grip of Fascism. Hence the story of Doctor Faustus with the background of the Hitler-band, on the one hand—an echo of the earliest Hun barbarism—and, on the other hand, the alternative commune of Bach and Duerer, which also gave birth to the Faust figure. Leverkuehn leaves his heights for the valley, but he is much more esthetic than Castorp ever was. Castorp at least met one human personality, Peeperkorn, and associated with lesser figures as well. Leverkuehn disports himself in complete isolation to practice transcendence. He transcends by indulging himself in theology and music. This esthetic imperialism is his pact with the Devil.

The pact with the Devil has a dual aspect. It is the pact of the German intellectual with pure spirit which is divorced from politics, from society, from the people. This apartness means that it cannot have love or warmth, but only coldness or heat. The embrace of the pure spirit leads to the embrace of the impure body—the Esmeralda episode in Leverkuehn's story, this promiscuous *"Freudenmaedchen"* to whom the most solitary is drawn.

Mann is saying here that we must not separate the good from the bad Germany. There is only one Germany, and the good Germany has contributed toward the bad Germany, although they are not identical. The pact has taken place long before Hitler. Hell means the inability to love, somewhat in the manner in which Zossima defines it in *The Brothers Karamazov*. The price Leverkuehn pays for his creation is precisely the price of removal from women and people and from friends and the world. At the end he calls the commune to him, and makes his confession. He confesses that his work has been the product of the Demon, and should be rejected. But Mann, the writer, the historian, the Appolonian observer of the German Dionysian personality, would partly redeem Leverkuehn's musical effort. Music has been the pact with the Devil, but music is the most universal language. The problem, however, is to bring music back to the folk, to make it communal without making it common. The cancer in the German *Kultur* music of Leverkuehn is that it was produced in isolation, away from people.

IV

Let me, in conclusion, state that Kafka and Mann show us that the choice we face is that between the individual ego, on the one hand, lost in an anonymous public collective which today we think of as "the East." The other danger is that the ego might be choked by the Western private power collective. It is too late to go back to the Eastern primitive collective; but it would be myopic to disregard the Eastern momentum, calling for a supraracial, supranational, supra-individual fraternity. We cannot and must not choose between the Western ego and the Eastern commune. This, it seems to me, is what Mann, in particular, is saying. While both warn against the danger within the existing commune, they both know that the idea of man is not exhausted by historical coordinates. Through him flow eternal currents, prototypes, recurrent motifs, which give meaning to the words, "man" and "one world." There is the possibility of the ego to fulfil itself, not to be choked or destroyed, but to fulfil itself in a public collective, confined to the material realm, and allowing for cultural, for ego differentiations.

This is the promise of the human myth. The fulfilment of this promise depends, to be sure, on a human historic situation, one which might be created by the awakened powers which slumber in man.

X

METAPHOR AND THE FUNCTION OF CRITICISM

BY

CLEANTH BROOKS

There are few subjects on which our own age is more thoroughly confused than it is on that of the function of literature. Moreover, to this confusion has been added a spirit of acrimonious controversy. This, therefore, is hardly a propitious time to write on a pattern of belief in contemporary criticism, though I grant that the very eagerness and bitterness with which the debate over the nature of literature and of criticism has been carried on in recent months argues the need for clarification. But it would be disingenuous for me to pretend to be the cool and moderate honest broker, adjusting conflicting claims and resolving contested problems. I hope that I am honest. I shall try to be moderate, but on this topic I am definitely marked as a man with a *parti pris*. I can do no more than attempt to state a personal position as forcibly and clearly as I can.

I reflect, however, that this kind of procedure is not worthless, even to the non-partisan hearer who desires primarily a clarification of the issues. At any rate, I think that it is just for me to begin with this general warning: that much that I am going to state has recently been challenged. I am thinking particularly of the controversy that raged in *The Saturday Review of Literature* during the autumn of 1949. The position that I shall maintain continues to be challenged—sometimes with solid argument, and sometimes with cat calls. I shall at least attempt to avoid jibes and cat calls in my own statement.

I am tempted to begin with a quotation from the preface of Allen Tate's recent collection of critical essays entitled *On the Limits of*

Poetry. Tate concludes his preface with a reference to the title of his book:

> If the title of this book recalls Lessing, the reader is warned that he will find little Lessing in it, beyond a few references to the relation of poetry and painting. On reading my essays over, I found that I was talking most of the time about what poetry cannot be expected to do to save mankind from the disasters in which poetry itself must be involved: that, I suppose, is a "limit" of poetry. Lessing says that poetry is not painting or sculpture; I am saying in this book, with very little systematic argument, that it is neither religion nor social engineering.[1]

I should like to repeat the last statement: "Poetry"—and here Tate is using the term as Aristotle used it, to mean literature generally—"is neither religion nor social engineering." It is a thesis which in our own day can hardly be regarded as obvious, and in a world terrified of the atomic bomb it can easily be interpreted as implying an intolerable disdain for the world of serious affairs or a cowardly skulking away from reality itself.

Tate's concluding statement, however, is the most succinct summary of the position which I shall maintain in this paper, and perhaps the most illuminating statement about the critical controversy now going on. But I shall perhaps do best to begin with the source of our problem in the nineteenth century. The nineteenth century, it seems to me, was incredibly confused on the relation of art to religion, of art to science, and of science to religion. Matthew Arnold typifies this confusion very well indeed, though it would be unfair to suggest that Arnold alone was confused, or that Arnold did not attempt clarification and redefinition. At any rate, Matthew Arnold's characteristic attempt at a solution provides an admirable startingpoint for a discussion of the status of literature today.

I

For Arnold, the triumph of science had removed the basis for religious belief: fact had exposed religion's grounding in myth, and

[1] Allen Tate, *On the Limits of Poetry, Selected Essays: 1928–1948*, Swallow Press and William Morrow & Company, Inc., New York, 1948.

religion was thus destroyed as the vehicle for values. Religion, in short, had been reduced to art. But mankind needs values—cannot live without them—and Arnold's solution of the problem was admirably neat. Let us, he said in effect, clearly distinguish between science and art, and let art assume the burden of transmitting values. Literature, in short, was to serve as a substitute for religion, for literature, requiring no grounding in fact, and as an imaginative construct, could survive alongside science, as religion itself could not. No wonder that Arnold felt that the future of literature was immense, for in terms of Arnold's insight, literature took over the province of religion and was to serve as a copartner with science.

Arnold's sanguine hopes for literature have hardly been fulfilled. The more aggressive positivists have put art under the thumb of science itself, with art frankly becoming the propaganda office for naturalistic values. But I should like to illustrate the instability of Arnold's position from Arnold's own poetry. You will remember, I am sure, the poem, "Dover Beach." After the speaker's melancholy reflections upon the ebbing tide of faith which now goes out with its long withdrawing roar, leaving bare the naked shingles of the world, the speaker turns to the woman at his side to exclaim in effect: "Let us, therefore, be true to each other as our universe is now seen to be a world without value and can give no support to our own private values."

The exclamation is dramatically motivated, and in terms of the situation which the point portrays, it is an understandable one. But in terms of Arnold's more general theory, is the speaker in "Dover Beach" entitled to his commitment to the value of love? For if science had knocked out religion, had not science also disposed of the value of romantic love? If the geologist had removed the basis for traditional religion, was not the biologist standing ready to reduce the love affair to the biological exercise of a pair of mammals? Aldous Huxley's two lovers quietly sweating palm to palm are quite properly the spiritual descendants of the lovers in "Dover Beach." And if, on the other hand, the biological account of lovemaking did leave the spiritual love intact, then had the geologist really destroyed the public values which Arnold bewailed as having been lost?

For the moment I am not concerned with the proper answer to these questions. I am concerned with Arnold's confusion of the realms of science and religion and esthetics. I am even more particularly concerned with his confusion about the nature of literature and more especially still with that confusion as it has proliferated in our own time. For if it is relatively easy to forgive Arnold, it is not quite so easy, several generations later, to forgive the heirs of his theories.

I have doubtless oversimplified Matthew Arnold's handling of the problem, but I have a purpose in this. The account given may furnish us a convenient scheme for categorizing the modern critics. We might begin by differentiating between those who are aware of the problem raised by Arnold, and those who continue to write in happy ignorance that a problem exists. I refer to the horde of complacent English professors, book reviewers, and popular critics, who object to any more strenuous concern with literature than the assembling of footnotes and the culling out of charming little anecdotes about the foibles of authors. Again, we may take those who are aware of the problem and divide them into those who reject Arnold's view that science has disposed of religion, and those who accept it. This latter subgroup would include, of course, a great variety of critics: sociological critics, psychological critics, Marxist critics, etc. These various subgroups share in common the belief that literature is finally the rhetorical garb for truthful propositions which are to be derived from science or philosophy. At their most consistent, they are compelled to see the literary artist as a specialist in making plain, or else making palatable and attractive, the truths which are given him to express.

I hasten to add that few of these critics would state the matter in terms so crude as those I have used, but I think that their position compels them finally to see the artist as a kind of super advertising man—a specialist at arousing sympathetic emotions for the propositions which he elects to present. In this scheme of things, poetics disappears into rhetoric, and it may be significant that such critics, by and large, not only have displayed no interest in poetics, but find any concern with poetics, as such, incomprehensible.

My own sympathies, I think it is quite evident, are with the group who reject Matthew Arnold's view that science has disposed of religion. In making a more careful differentiation between science and art, these critics have pointed up the limitations of science as the purveyor of all truth; or, if we argue that truth is one, their differentiation has suggested the possibility of other modes of truth and other means for apprehending truth. Thus their analyses of Arnold's characteristic confusion have served not only to rehabilitate art, but concomitantly have also served to rehabilitate religion.

II

It is no accident that many of these critics are communicants of the church, or sympathetic with orthodox religion. But it is only just to observe that the rehabilitation of religion is not a necessary concomitant of the critical position that I have described. In this matter there is the widest variety of position, and I have no wish here to huddle all the formalist critics (or the "New" Critics, or the critics of the School of Eliot, or the critics denominated by whatever name you choose to apply) into one narrow and restricted religious position.

There is a further point even more important. Curiously enough, it is precisely this group of critics who have been concerned not to reduce literature to the role of handmaiden to religion. If I may refer to the statement from Allen Tate with which I began, literature is not only not social engineering, it is not religion either. Thus we get a curious paradox: that it is precisely those critics who, by and large, manifest a deep concern for religion, who are also concerned to maintain the independence of literature and its distinction from religion.

Robert Hillyer's bitter attacks on the so-called New Critics during the summer of 1949 in *The Saturday Review of Literature* accuse them of being mere esthetes, indifferent to moral values or to any values. Yet it is just the writers whom he attacks, whether they be Anglo-Catholics like T. S. Eliot, or stern moralists of the persuasion of Ivor Winters, who probably, more than any comparable group now writing, have put on record their intense concern for moral and social problems. Perhaps it is their concern for the seriousness of these problems which has made them refuse to find in literature a kind of ersatz religion, just as I think that it is their stricter concern for the work of art which has made them draw distinctions between the work of art as such, and the work of art as a document manifesting the time spirit or a personal myth or a set of regional mores or the revelation of a particular author's personality. But the example of Matthew Arnold may most of all help us here. If Arnold's muddling of distinctions has got us into our trouble, the critics most aware of the muddlement will be precisely the critics one would expect to have a renewed sense of the importance of the distinctions which Arnold confused, and the critics who feel the necessity for reviving and maintaining these distinctions.

Seen in these terms, the Hillyer–*Saturday Review* attack on modern poetry and modern criticism, actually reverses the pattern which Hillyer attempted to establish. Hillyer presented on the one side as the good critics those men who have positive convictions, who believe in America and affirm life with a capital *L*. He pointed scornfully, on the other side, to a group of niggling esthetes, snobbish obscurantists, and negative souls, who do not believe in America and quite probably do believe secretly in Fascism. I should accept Hillyer's general sorting out of the two groups, but I would describe them in very different terms. On the one hand, I see a group of muddled and confused writers and critics who wish painfully, though vaguely, to affirm what they find around them, who are uneasy with anything but conventional literary forms and nervously apprehensive when presented with anything more than transparent salestalk for democracy. In the group to which Hillyer gives the back of his hand, I find, however, the true conservatives and traditionalists, though they are to be described as radical, not conventional, conservatives. They are deeply concerned about the decay of our culture; they are very much interested in literature, whether it take the form of Dante or that of e. e. cummings, but they are men who, in their devotion to literature, refuse to make literature support a burden which it cannot support. This is doubtless a biased reading that I have just given, and I have already confessed that I am not an unprejudiced witness, but I am prepared to document my reading of the situation. I am convinced that Hillyer cannot convincingly document his.

III

It may be well, however, to approach the topic of belief in contemporary criticism in quite another way and from quite a different direction. I should be glad to approach it, for example, through a consideration of one poetic device, metaphor, and I should be willing to describe the development of what I find to be the most fruitful modern criticism as a rediscovery and recovery of the importance of metaphor. The poetry of Robert Frost is frequently presented as conservative and traditional poetry, and Hillyer, though he has failed to produce any substantiation of his charges, has claimed that the wicked school of Eliot and its allies have tried to undermine the reputation of this fine and solid American poet. But Frost himself, in his admirable introduction to the Modern Library volume of his *Collected Poems,* has said in so many words, "Poetry is metaphor."

What does he mean—what do the rest of us mean who have argued for the centrality of metaphor in poetry? To see this fully, it is convenient to take the account of metaphor as given by most eighteenth and nineteenth century critics, a view which stubbornly survives today. The function of metaphor so described is to illustrate and to decorate. That is, the metaphor says more concretely and, therefore, more persuasively what could be said otherwise more directly and more abstractly; or else metaphor provides a pleasant way of saying what can otherwise be said directly and bluntly. But notice that in either one of these accounts there is the implication that metaphor is a mere surrogate, an alternate way of saying something, not the necessary and inevitable way. Metaphor becomes not the essence of poetry but a kind of rhetorical gilding.

As A. E. Housman put it in his *Name and Nature of Poetry,* "Metaphor and simile . . . [are] things inessential to poetry." [2] One may point out that Housman's own best poetry cannot be subsumed under this false and glib account. But I have cited Housman to indicate how far astray even the poets had gone—how far they had themselves

---

[2] A. E. Housman, *The Name and Nature of Poetry,* The Macmillan Company, New York, 1933. Used with the permission of the Cambridge University Press.

played into the hands of the scientists and the prose expositors, in implying that their real function was to garnish and dress out propositions which could be stated more directly and more economically in abstract propositions.

On the other hand, if metaphor is the necessary and inevitable means for saying what the poet has to say, the implications for poetry are considerable. The poet becomes no rhetorician glozing the truth found in some process external to poetry. His truth—which I grant is not scientific truth—is arrived at through his own instruments, and his essential instrument, metaphor, becomes itself a mode of apprehension and a method of discovery.

I think that it is no accident that T. E. Hulme, that remarkable figure of the early twentieth century, insists, in his discussion of esthetics, on the centrality of metaphor, and, in his discussion of religion, on the importance of the doctrine of original sin. Nor is it an accident that so many of the modern critics who have been influenced by Hulme or who have taken a position sympathetic to Hulme in making metaphor the essence of poetry, have gone on, either to avow an orthodox religious position, or else to affirm the possibility and necessity for metaphysics as a science. I mention such names as those of T. S. Eliot, W. H. Auden, Allen Tate, J. C. Ransom, R. P. Blackmur, Ivor Winters, Austin Warren, and could mention many more. But by stating the matter negatively, I can be even more emphatic. No critics of positivist persuasion, so far as I know, see metaphor as anything more, finally, than a pleasing or delightful or rhetorically effective mode of expression. I think that it is impossible, indeed, for a thoroughgoing positivist to take a position other than this.

With this rediscovery and rehabilitation of metaphor, I might add that there has been concomitantly among the critics a renewed interest in myth as a mode for apprehension, the apprehension of reality. Ransom, indeed, goes so far as to refer to myths as great radical metaphors. The great myths are not mere fairy tales, that is, mere fanciful elaborations of principles, which might otherwise be abstractly stated. The great myths, on the contrary, like the successful metaphors in a good poem, embody unique insights and are inexhaustible, not susceptible to being reduced to paraphrase.

I. A. Richards, who has powerfully influenced the group of modern critics that I have mentioned, speaks on myth much to the same purpose. I turn to him the more gladly because Richards's literary criticism began with a position very sympathetic to positivism. But in his *Coleridge on Imagination,* he writes:

The saner and greater mythologies are not fancies; they are the utterance of the whole soul of man, and as such inexhaustible to meditation. Without his mythologies man is only a cruel animal without a soul—for a soul is a central part of his governing mythology—he is a congeries of possibilities without order and without aim.[3]

IV

But even in so brief a paper as this, I think that it may be valuable to use still a third approach to the problem of belief, as it manifests itself in modern criticism. I suggest that the interested reader here may find it useful to consult a copy of a recent anthology of modern criticism edited by R. W. Stallman and entitled *Critiques and Essays in Criticism, 1920–1948.* The last item in this volume is an essay written by Stallman himself and entitled "The New Critics." I shall quote his opening paragraph:

There is one basic theme in modern criticism; it is the dissociation of modern sensibility. The loss of a spiritual order and of integrity in the modern consciousness is T. S. Eliot's major premise. The issue of our glorification of the scientific vision at the expense of the esthetic vision, is the central theme in both the poetry and the criticism of the Southern poet-critics. It is this theme of spiritual disorder which the late Paul Valéry exploited. It reveals itself in the critical writings of I. A. Richards, F. R. Leavis, Ivor Winters, R. P. Blackmur, and the Southern critics. The New Critics, while differing among one another in theory or in practice, are as one through the unifying relation of this obsessive burden.[4]

[3] I. A. Richards, *Coleridge on Imagination,* Harcourt, Brace & Company, New York, 1935.

[4] Robert W. Stallman, "The New Critics," *Critiques and Essays in Criticism, 1920–1948,* edited by Robert W. Stallman, copyright by The Ronald Press Company, New York, 1949.

It might be useful at this point to summarize the motifs which Stallman finds to be discussed throughout modern criticism: (1) loss of tradition, (2) loss of a fixed convention, (3) loss of belief, (4) loss of a world order. These phrases tell their own story, and should serve to put at rest any view that these critics, though insisting on the autonomy of the esthetic realm and upon the necessity for dealing with the work of art as a work of art, are actually irresponsible with regard to the world in which they live and careless of the problems of modern civilization.

I am not in complete agreement with all the details of Stallman's essay. I think, on the other hand, that it is a very good essay, and can recommend it to anyone interested in this subject who would like to get the quickest and a not inaccurate over-all view of what this important group of critics has been saying.

I want to make one more brief quotation from Stallman's essay. He says: "Hulme defined the mood and perspective of our age; and this is his importance, almost exclusively. He is important not because he was an original thinker, but because of his influence upon those who have dominated and largely directed the course of contemporary criticism." [5] And then he goes on to say, "The affinity of several critics," whom he names, "and Hulme lies in their common claim that our present disunity has been created by the confusion of two categories: the esthetic vision, which is concerned with quality, and the scientific vision, which is concerned with quantity." [6]

Stallman, I think, is quite right in claiming that Hulme has defined the mood and perspective of our age. He has been much more than an influence. He has been something of a prototype—so much so that many of us who came to Hulme's writings actually very late have been surprised again and again to find how many anticipations he has made; and I can think of no better way of closing these notes than by a quotation from Hulme. For though the critical position which he set forth has been elaborated, extended, refined, and, in many respects, heavily qualified, a characteristic passage from Hulme can suggest very vividly something of the mood of the typical modern

[5] *Ibid.*
[6] *Ibid.*

critic, particularly toward the problem of religion and belief. The contrast between the modern critic and Matthew Arnold on this point is decisive. If Arnold was interested in preserving the general aura and flavor of religion, if he felt that literature could suggest the fluffier and more peripheral aspects of religion, Hulme is emphatically not so interested. Hulme's emphasis is on belief as such, on theology, not at all on the byproducts of religion, either upon good works as such or on a vague religious mood. The Hulme passage is, as follows:

I hold the religious conception of ultimate values to be right, the humanist wrong. From the nature of things, these categories are not inevitable, like the categories of time and space, but are *equally objective*. In speaking of religion, it is to this level of abstraction that I wish to refer. I have none of the feelings of *nostalgia,* the reverence for tradition, the desire to recapture the sentiment of Fra Angelico, which seems to animate most modern defenders of religion. All that seems to me to be bosh. What is important is what nobody seems to realize—the dogmas like that of Original Sin, which are the closest expression of the categories of the religious attitude. That man is in no sense perfect, but a wretched creature, who can yet apprehend perfection. It is not, then, that I put up with the dogma for the sake of the sentiment, but that I may possibly swallow the sentiment for the sake of the dogma.[7]

[7] T. E. Hulme, "Humanism and the Religious Attitude," *Speculations: Essays on Humanism and the Philosophy of Art,* edited by Herbert Read, Harcourt, Brace & Company, New York, 1936, pp. 70 f.

XI

EXISTENTIALISM AS A SYMPTOM OF MAN'S CONTEMPORARY CRISIS

WILLIAM BARRETT

Nowadays we speak quite easily and naturally of the crisis through which our civilization is passing. Without questioning the assumption that we are in the midst of a crisis, I should like to ask whether this feeling of crisis is not something inseparable from human life in any historical period. The more closely we examine the past, the more we find that it, too, is uneasy with its own sense of historical crisis and urgency. Sometimes, in retrospect, these crises look illusory, for mankind has survived some of its worst apprehensions; and then we have to remind ourselves that these men and women of the past felt that bygone crisis in their bones, with the same intimate uneasiness with which we feel ours. We begin to suspect that to live itself is to exist in crisis (more or less actual at any moment), and that only in periods of real historic somnolence and lethargy—real decadence, in short—has mankind been without a sense of crisis. No doubt, there are important differences of degree, and one age may be more plainly a period of breakdown than another; it would be folly to neglect such differences of degree, but the thought that crisis, or the sense of it is a permanent part of human life, does fortify us to see our own contemporary crisis in a much broader light—as a total human condition.

This thought will explain why I prefer to discuss existential philosophy as a symptom, rather than a solution, of our present crisis. For to the degree that we see our crisis as a total and concrete condition, to that degree we shall doubt that any philosophy, no matter how ambitious, can propose itself as the unique path of salvation. Anyone who has had any personal experience of a spiritual crisis will know that recovery does not come through the acquisition of any new abstract ideas. The progress from health to sickness is a change of being, rather than a change in thought. So, if we agree that our civilization is spiritually sick, we should also expect that the recovery will not come through any single set of ideas, or philosophy, but only through a transformation of our whole existence—thus requiring social, economic, and religious change. A new philosophy would be only a necessary *part* of this total change.

Moreover, it is the very characteristic of Existentialism as a philosophy that it must look with irony upon any system of thought that proposes itself as *the* solution for all of life's crises. Let us remember that Kierkegaard, the founder of Existentialism, began to philosophize with the purpose of discovering difficulties, rather than offering easy and readymade solutions. Existentialism as a philosophy attempts to make man aware of certain basic realities of his life. In this sense it seeks to increase, rather than minimize, our human difficulties. The business of finding solutions must come only after a man is aware of the whole depth, import, and, therefore, difficulty, of his human life.

I

This preliminary definition of existential philosophy will be understood better, if we contrast it with the usual kinds of philosophy now taught in our academies. The various schools of philosophy are distinguished from each other by different beliefs. Thus it comes about that a philosophy is understood as a set of beliefs, or propositions, to which a man gives intellectual assent. A man is said to have a philosophy, then, if he has a system of propositions which he holds to be true on purely intellectual or rational grounds. This is the understanding of philosophy that has prevailed particularly in our period of the departmentalization of all human knowledge. But Existentialism seeks to restore a much more primitive sense of the word, "philosophy," than this: namely, the ancient sense of philosophy as a concrete way of life, rather than an abstract set of propositions. Nietzsche, also an Existentialist, pointed out that for ancient man, and even the modern Oriental, the business of achieving a philosophy is one that engaged the whole man, his total being, and was not pursued simply as one specialized department of knowledge among others. Kierkegaard attacked the Hegelian professors of his time as being philosophers without any real philosophic existence: they had a system of propositions to teach, but the system itself was a means of forgetting the concrete realities of human life. For us in America today the philosopher is merely a "professional" savant among many others.

Existentialism, on the contrary, understands philosophy as a thing that is to be lived, and not merely a body of knowledge to be taught to pupils. I have said that Existentialism attempts to bring to human consciousness the basic, even banal, realities of human life: realities such as death, anxiety, choice, love, freedom, guilt, conscience, the willing acceptance of anxiety, etc., etc. In American academic philosophy today these are not the prevailing concepts: philosophers discuss concepts relating to science, knowledge, logic. Existential concepts are thought to belong to literature, perhaps to poetry. This rejection is an evidence of how far one particular tradition among the intellectual elite of our society has tended to set knowledge above life. If the philosopher exists professionally as a member of a department in a university, and if he accepts his role as one that deals with one special department of knowledge among others, then he is inevitably drawn to devote himself to those very special and technical problems that seem to be the peculiar province of the "expert." Our technological civilization has tended more and more to worship the expert, and the philosopher, assimilated to his civilization, strives more and more to justify his own professional existence by a high technical competence in the special problems of logic and philosophical analysis. The result is that a great deal of modern philosophy has tended to become divorced from life. Hence it is only natural that Existentialism, which struggles against this tendency, is looked on somewhat askance by a great many American philosophers.

All this has been by way of explaining why it seemed preferable to discuss Existentialism as a symptom, rather than a solution, of our contemporary crisis. But there has also been in the background of my remarks another, and much more drastic point, which will be substantiated by my further discussion, but can be announced now: the point, quite simply, that there is never a solution to any of life's crises. This is one of the cardinal points in existential philosophy itself. The word, "solution," belongs to the vocabulary of science and engineering, suggesting some kind of blueprint that would immediately deliver us from the pain and muddle of suffering, when, in fact, we know that our really deep crises in life are precisely those that we have to live through. Our deepest personal problems do not in the least resemble any problem of engineering, and it is the same, we suggest, with the sickness of civilization, even though the "cure" of a sick civilization might require vast exploits of engineering.

II

That movement in thought should be a symptom of its time, is not in the least a condemnation of this movement as a wild or trivial aberration. I am using the word, "symptom," in its simple and unprejudiced sense of a sign—something that instructs us about the state of the organism from which it arises. Thus Existentialism has a great deal to teach us—which we might otherwise not know—about the condition of the Western civilization that has brought it to birth.

Most Americans connect Existentialism with the current French movement, and particularly with the name of its most brilliant publicist, Jean Paul Sartre. Sartre's is an agile and energetic mind, but his doctrine represents, I believe, a dilution of existential philosophy, and in any case does not take us back to its original sources. These lie in the nineteenth century, and the great innovators are Kierkegaard and Nietzsche—though the latter, unlike Kierkegaard, is not fully aware of his existential point of departure. Existential themes are treated in the fiction of Tolstoi and Dostoievski. In this century the two most important existential philosophers have been the German professors, Martin Heidegger and Karl Jaspers. To these names we might add the considerable figure of the Spanish philosopher, José Ortega y Gasset, who has described his philosophy as one of "vital reason," though it is fundamentally existential in its directions. These names should indicate that Existentialism is not a momentary intellectual fad, derived from the French, but a much wider and deeper movement in Western thought, having roots indeed in the profound upheavals of this civilization during the past two centuries. To see what these roots are, we may find it more convenient to turn, not to an abstruse text in philosophy, but to a work of literature that takes a simpler and more direct grasp of the issues involved: Tolstoi's great story, "The Death of Ivan Ilyich," which by this time has become something of a basic scripture for existential thought.

The plot of Tolstoi's story is slight and almost negligible. Ivan Ilyich is an amiable and undistinguished bourgeois, who has spent his whole life trying to be like everyone else in his social class: a successful and happy man, where happiness means only the absence of suffering. But one day Ivan Ilyich feels a pain in his side, which resists all treatment by doctors, and as his illness progresses, he suddenly realizes that he is going to die. For the first time in his life death becomes a reality for him. In the face of this awful presence, all his disguises fall away: confronting death for the first time in his life, he is also confronting himself for the first time. Hitherto in his life he had hid from himself amid the routine mechanisms of all his social, official, and familial functions. Now, as he is about to die, he asks himself the questions: Who am I? What has been the meaning of my life? In the end Ivan Ilyich dies content, because he has reached the point of knowing that the life he lived was empty, futile, and meaningless.

What Tolstoi is saying here, to put it now as a general thesis, is that modern life has alienated the individual from himself. The materialistic and rationalistic nineteenth century, with its emphasis upon all the bourgeois routines of life, has so externalized the individual that he has lost the feeling and the passion for his own personal existence. Modern man, Tolstoi is saying, has lost the meaning of life, and, as with Ivan Ilyich, it will take nothing less than the presence of death to restore this sense of life.

The sense of decadence haunts the nineteenth century, even at the moments of its most splendid optimism. There is a widespread uneasiness that life has lost its passion, intensity, and meaning; that there has been some secret decline in human vitality. Kierkegaard puts it as eloquently and compactly as one could wish:

Let others complain that times are bad; I complain that they are petty because they lack passion. Men's thoughts are as flimsy as thin ice and men themselves as insignificant as the thin snow that covers it. Their thoughts are too petty to be sinful. A worm might consider such thoughts to be sinful, but not a man created in the image of God. Their pleasures are circumspect and boring; their passions, sleep; these materialistic souls fulfill their duties, but they collect their usury for it; they believe that although our Lord keeps His accounts in good order, they can hand Him counterfeit. Out with them! This is why my soul always hearkens back to Shakespeare and the Old Testament. There one feels that those who speak are men; there they hate; there they love; there they kill the enemy, curse their descendants for generations to come, there they sin.

This passage might almost have been written by Nietzsche, who launches his plea from the diametrically opposite anti-christian pole. Modern man, says Nietzsche, lacks a goal, and his existence is, therefore, purposeless and nihilistic. Similar themes appear also in such diverse writers as Stendhal and Burckhardt.

The twentieth century has no reason to forget these fears. Our technological civilization has become even more involved with elaborate apparatus to catch and smother the individual. We have gone beyond the nineteenth century in the development of a fantastic mass culture—in radio, movies, and television—that stamps out all individual differences. Modern society has become more and more a mass society. Cities grow larger, crowds become more and more potent factors, and the individual threatened more than ever by anonymity in the mass. The image of modern man lies in T. S. Eliot's line: "Men and bits of paper, whirled by the cold wind." [1] These fears of the nineteenth century turn out to be prophetic for us: amid this general purposelessness of life, this mass drifting, we set ourselves the task of recapturing the sense and the meaning of life.

[1] T. S. Eliot, "Burnt Norton," *Collected Poems of T. S. Eliot, 1909–1935*, Harcourt, Brace & Company, New York, 1936, p. 217.

III

When Tolstoi speaks of a loss of the meaning of life, he is not referring to a loss of some rational explanation. Nor is the meaning that is to be restored an intellectual one, some new fact or discovery of the mind. On the contrary, the disorder in modern man that Tolstoi's story speaks of is a disorder in the more primitive and irrational, or non-rational, parts of man's being. Existentialism as a philosophy seeks to deal with these irrational parts of our existence in a way that philosophy has never done before, and by so doing gives reason itself a new place in the human hierarchy.

This is why existential philosophy has been frequently—and, I think, unjustly—criticized as anti-rational. One is not against reason, if one insists that the irrational is an inseparable part of life, and that it is precisely with the irrational parts of our being that modern civilization fails to deal adequately. This so-called "anti-rational" tendency in modern philosophy has now had a long history, from Rousseau to Bergson, Whitehead, and Heidegger in our century, and it embraces too many great names to be dismissed out of hand. Any future rationalism worth its salt will have to assimilate a great deal from these thinkers, and we ourselves would be less than rational, if we did not make an earnest effort to understand in detail how the irrational enters human life.

We gain some idea of the irrational character of life, if we turn back again to Tolstoi's "Ivan Ilyich." As death appears to Ivan Ilyich, it presents itself as something altogether unreasonable and incomprehensible. Immersed in the comfortable structure of his life, he sees this strange and dark intruder creep in to destroy everything. Yes, death is a banal fact, and we know that all men have to die; Ivan Ilyich knows all this with his head, but his heart cannot grasp the incomprehensible fact that he, Ivan Ilyich, should have to die. This bewilderment may strike us as childish, but it is Tolstoi's means of showing us how the irrational, like death, may fall upon us in the most incalculable and unpredictable way, upsetting all our plans for life.

Kierkegaard has expounded the presence of the irrational in another area of human life—in the act of choice or decision. We do not doubt that some decisions are more rational than others, and we may even speak of a decision as being the only rational choice under the circumstances. But is a rational choice one from which the irrational is ever completely excluded? Is any choice, however rational it be, free from the uncertain contingencies of risk and adventure? Of course, there are certain trivial choices that we make every day, and that we may reverse the next day, if we are proved wrong. But these are choices that do not commit us deeply, that leave us relatively disengaged from the consequences. As soon, however, as a choice cuts deeply; as soon as it commits our whole life in a certain direction; so soon, then, do the immense difficulties appear, the balance of probabilities becomes harder, and each alternative appears, however we may canvass its possibilities, as a leap into the unknown.

The choice that personally involved Kierkegaard happened to be the question whether or not to marry. Engaged to a young woman in Copenhagen, he desired marriage intensely, but he felt in himself also a certain religious mission that would prevent him from giving himself completely in marriage. The particular psychological facts involved here are important for an understanding of Kierkegaard's biography, but the peculiarly personal difficulties should not obscure for us the fact that the pathos of choice Kierkegaard faced is universal. There are, in short, choices in life that are irreversible. Kierkegaard could not have made an *experimental* choice of marriage, in the expectation that if it "did not work out"—to use the expression that has become common among us these days—he could return to his religious vocation and its tasks, for the vocation might have been lost through his marriage. On the other hand, if he renounced marriage experimentally, he could not hope to return to the young lady, should the other alternative not work out. She might not be there (as in fact she was not) when he returned. Love has to be seized at the moment it is offered; our indecision pollutes and destroys it.

All of this points to the fact that the situation of human choice is not at all a situation of scientific experiment. A situation is experimental in science when certain scientific controls have been established, so that through these controls we can repeat the experiment at any time and place we choose, and indeed repeat it indefinitely. The more precisely scientific the experiment becomes, the more its features of accidental particularity become refined away, and the easier it becomes to repeat it in all its detail. But our fundamental choices in life do not permit us this degree of control, because they do not permit us this degree of detachment. We have to choose here and now, and for the rest of our life, and the alternative we renounce is lost forever. We could be completely experimental about our own lives only if we were immortal, and so could repeat any situation or choice indefinitely.

But as death is real and our lives finite, every choice is also a renunciation, and this is why Kierkegaard speaks of the *pathos* of human choice. It was this sacrificial and pathetic aspect of choice that led Kierkegaard to his great polemic against the excessively rational philosophy of Hegel. The old adage puts the matter quite simply and adequately, "You cannot eat your cake and have it, too"; but Hegel devised a sophisticated dialectic by which it was possible to bring together two conflicting alternatives, thesis and antithesis, into a higher synthesis, so that the speculative philosopher, triumphing over life, could both have his cake and eat it, too. Such a reconciling of opposites is indeed possible in knowledge, where a more inclusive theory may embrace two conflicting alternatives; but it is not possible in life, where the suffering of renunciation cannot be altogether eliminated by reason. This opposition between knowledge and life has been one of the chief themes of Existentialism, as well as of a great deal of modern philosophy and literature.

IV

These two brief illustrations of the irrational—death and human choice—which cannot be altogether expunged from our existence, also illustrate that science, and scientific experiment, cannot take over the whole of life. The fear that science might devour the whole of human life has been a very powerful current of thought in the West, from William Blake onward. Indeed, from the Enlightenment in the eighteenth century to the present day, two deeply opposed attitudes toward science have dominated Western thinking: along with the great hope in science and its possibilities of human liberation, there has developed a great fear that science would somehow mechanize and impoverish human life. This fear of science cannot be dismissed simply as a crude popular superstition, for it embraces too many great names of our culture: Blake, Wordsworth, Kierkegaard, Nietzsche, Dostoievski, Tolstoi, Bergson. Our task, rather, should be to disengage the philosophical traits that characterize this fear of science at its deepest level.

One of the best expressions of the fear of science is found in the first part of Dostoievski's great novel, *Notes from Underground*. The hero is afraid of the scientific society of the future, in which human life can be rationally controlled and ordered, down to the very last detail. When human life is so scientifically precise and predictable, nobody would want to live it. Dostoievski's hero would prefer to smash this machine that would seek to contain him—out of sheer spite, as he puts it—to show that his human will in its liberty transcends the mathematically predictable, even if he has to show this in a destructive way. We come back thus to our principal point: what Dostoievski is saying, through his tormented and oppressed little hero, is that human life must be more than pure reason, and to attempt to reduce it to the latter is to destroy it, even if we make that reduction in the name of universal enlightenment.

It would be a mistake to consider the Underground Man as merely a sick and neurotic individual produced by the stresses of modern society. He is that, of course, but he is also a universal human character. We are all the Underground Man, to some degree or other. He is that dark side of our being, with which we must try to live in peace, and if we take lightly his fulminations against a human regime completely controlled by science and reason, we do so at our own risk.

As he is thus universal, the Underground Man reappears, and perhaps I may drive home my point by turning to the rather extraordinary position advanced in the nineteen hundred and twenties by I. A. Richards, the British critic and psychologist—a position that seems to me to express the extreme of hope that science will master life. (In justice to Richards, however, we must point out that at the time he was much more enamored of the possibilities of psychology than he is today.) Richards contended nothing less than this: that we can anticipate the time when psychological science will have advanced to the point where we can have, if we choose, whatever minds we desire. In the perfectly scientific utopia, in short, you could order your personality at a psychological laboratory the way you might order a prescription at a druggist's. Select your label, follow the prescription carefully, and you will have the personality, or the mind, that you want. Science which has performed so many miracles in the transformation of matter, and has found synthetic substitutes for almost everything, would here have found at last a substitute for life itself. In this psychological utopia it would be possible for a man to have a certain character without living through the risks, anxieties, and uncertain struggles that make it. We need not live to become a certain kind of being; science would provide it readymade.

We notice that this possibility that once inspired Richards with such hopes, is precisely the possibility against which Dostoievski's Underground Man rebels. Sick and resentful though he may be, the Underground Man at least insists upon having his own human life, rather than some mechanized substitute for it. The science of psychology has gone on developing since Richards's remark, but it is now further from maintaining any such utopian claims as once enchanted him. Among some circles in America, psychoanalysis may be regarded as a kind of magic, but not by the analysts themselves. Some people tend to think of psychoanalysis as a process in which the analyst, somewhat like a mechanic, overhauls the patient and gives him a new engine or set of works. But the serious analyst, while hoping to transform the neurotic patient's fundamental orientations toward life, insists that the patient can solve his problems only in actual life and not in the psychoanalytic session. Life has to be lived, there is no substitute for living—not even psychoanalysis.

Existential philosophy, in its insistence that the categories of life cannot be reduced to science, carries this point further. It may seem a rather trivial platitude to say that there can be no substitute for living, but the saying may not strike us as so platitudinous when we reflect upon the vast mechanized passivity that our civilization imposes upon so many of its members. In such circumstances the living rediscovery of certain banalities may represent an immense task and an immense triumph. Some of the greatest chapters in the history of philosophy are its discoveries of what lay obvious, but unnoticed, before every man's eyes. We may recall the great saying of Heraclitus, at the very dawn of philosophy in the sixth century B.C.: "Man is estranged from that with which he is most familiar, and he must continuously seek to rediscover it." This saying might serve as a very good motto for Existentialism. Among other things, it may make clear why the modern Existentialist, Heidegger, finds these early pre-Socratic Greeks his real forebears in the effort to confront human life and the whole life of nature with a primitive directness. The ancestry of existential philosophy thus turns out to be very ancient. I come back thus to a point made at the beginning, which should now be considerably clearer in its import: Existentialism, a modern movement in philosophy, is, in fact, an effort to recapture an old and very primitive sense of philosophy. Philosophy, here, is not the mere putting together of certain abstract propositions into a system; it is rather the concrete effort of the living individual to relate himself to his own life and the life of others around him. Quite literally, philosophy is a task that each individual has to perform for himself.

V

In this search for the primitive, Existentialism is in line with the most considerable movements in art and literature in this century. The word, "primitive," here is bound to arouse misunderstandings, if it is associated with the life of savages, barbarians, or big game hunters. Primitivism suggests to some the beat of tom-toms, Tahiti, maidens in sarongs, Gauguin; in short, an escape from modern civilization into the illusory simplicities of some South Sea island. These forms of primitivism have abounded, but they have always ended in a blind alley, because the desire for escape is itself a very non-primitive state of being. I am using the word, "primitive," in a much more basic—I almost wrote primitive—sense: the primitive is the primary; and the valid search for the primitive is a search for the sources of our being which a too routinized civilization tends to obscure. In this sense, nearly all the art and literature that matter in the past half century have been primitive.

Modern painting and sculpture, for example, have really succeeded in creating a new kind of vision. In these works we stand in a new and more direct relation to colors, shapes, and forms. It is a vision of things at once simpler and more complex than the Western art of the past. In its distorting simplifications, bold arbitrary forms, it often resembles primitive art, from which indeed it has consciously drawn inspiration in certain cases, though it could not exist without the whole tradition of Western art. Moreover, the artist himself seems to stand in a new and direct relation to the very materials of his art: he seeks naively to assert the presence of his paint, stone, or metal, and his art is no longer a device to conceal or transcend this presence.

In literature, in writers such as D. H. Lawrence, James Joyce, and Thomas Mann, we find similar and diverging efforts to deal with the primitive. In his Joseph stories, Mann seeks to restore the primitive mythic consciousness to literature. James Joyce, in his last work, uses the most sophisticated literary technique, drawing upon the whole past of Western literature for its resources, in order to render the most unconscious, inarticulate, and primitive parts of human experience. Of these writers perhaps Lawrence is the most explicitly programmatic in his search for the primitive simplicities that he believes modern life to have lost. The organic unity of being that Lawrence seeks through sexual experience, is something that existential philosophers have sought in other directions. As T. S. Eliot reminds us, Lawrence was a man with an intense spiritual vocation, and his interest in sex was not at all a message of sex-for-sex's sake. Nevertheless, his proposed solution to the sickness of modern civilization seems to us today to be rather onesided. His perception of the sickness was real enough, but his prescription for cure represents a kind of impatient rush toward a solution. We are reminded, again, that when a sickness is total, the recovery can come only through development along many avenues of being at once.

This list could be swelled indefinitely to show that this struggle for rebirth is one of the great themes of modern culture. I have appended these brief indications to my main discussion only to point to the total historical context in which we must try to see the development of modern existential philosophy; and to suggest that this philosophy is not an eccentric movement, but lies in the main stream of modern culture. Existentialism makes clearer the human tasks that our epoch confronts. Unless we realize what the tasks are, we can hardly work significantly toward any solution at all.

XII

THE PROBLEM OF MORAL ISOLATION IN CONTEMPORARY LITERATURE

BY

STANLEY ROMAINE HOPPER

The long standing feud between morals and esthetics has today reached a new, and unanticipated, phase. It is a phase arising out of the artist's need to find systems of reference, acceptable to the experience of our time, by means of which he can give order and unity to his work; and it is a phase arising out of his need to understand the nature of his calling. Both questions drive him in upon himself —the conventions of meaning having broken away, and the primary presuppositions of our culture being no longer adequate to sustain us in their classical or traditional forms. The artist must speak today, therefore, directly into the vacuums created by the recession of our former patterns of belief and seek his meanings there. This is contradictory, of course—to seek for meanings where meaning has ceased to be. Nevertheless, we must seek for meaning where we are; and what we observe outwardly as a cultural phenomenon of our time is experienced inwardly as alienation, abandonment, isolation, and solitariness. The poet's calling today is one of alienation and return —if he can make it. And on the journey he must encounter all the dragons of the inner life, including those let loose by the breaking of the chains of custom. "I have learnt," quotes Jean Paul Sartre from Brice Parain, "after much spiritual abandon, that the mediating forces exist to prevent us from escaping from ourselves, and raise against our excesses barriers beyond which we are threatened with destruction." [1]

[1] *Essays on Language and Literature,* edited by J. L. Hevesi, Alan Wingate, London, 1947, p. 143.

But the mediating forces no longer constrain us, or sustain us, and so the artist of today enters, like Childe Roland, "the ominous tract which, all agree, hides the Dark Tower." Or, since the problems of order and of calling are not merely psychological, but also ethical and religious, it would perhaps be better to say that modern literature, like St. George, has gone out to capture dragons—with its wreath of roses.

I

The pattern of this quest may be documented almost at will from contemporary literature. It is evident even in the very titles and themes of the relevant writers: Baudelaire's *Flowers of Evil,* Rimbaud's *Season in Hell,* Valéry's *The Serpent,* Joyce's *Ulysses,* the *Hamlets* of Jules Laforgue and Archibald MacLeish, the movement of Eliot from *The Waste Land* through *Ash Wednesday* to the perpetual descent of the Dove in *Little Gidding, The Double Man* of Auden, or Pound's *Cantos,* his abstract for a contemporary hell. The devious contours of the contemporary novel from Dostoievski's *Letters from the Underworld* and Proust's *La Recherche du Temps Perdu* through Gide's Manicheeism to François Mauriac's Pascalism illustrate the same quest. It is evident in the pit-motif of Thomas Mann's Joseph cycle as it is in Malraux's speculation upon *Man's Fate.*

The quest is not outward, but inward. It is a descent into the void of contemporary lostness: a descent in which the moment in time is our only possession, but a time in which there is no fullness . . . only a time which annuls, and in which

> Time, the serpent, retrieves the telescope,
> Constricts it to its primal nest of vertigos,
> The labyrinth, compressible, of our own egos.[2]

The descent is the more terrible in that the ego's descent into itself has really neither the myth-structure of Orpheus to support the climb (as in Rilke), nor the Purgatorial cornices of Dante's Underworld from

[2] Hart Crane, *Cape Hatteras,* early draft, *Poets at Work,* edited by Rudolf Arnheim and others, Harcourt, Brace & Company, New York, 1948, p. 113.

which to peer (as in Eliot): it goes this way alone. And it chooses to go because it must, and it must because it has already chosen. It is the raw descent of the ego into itself. It is negation seeking negatively to negate itself. And it is awesome: "I am filled with awe," as Thomas Mann exclaims, "in presence of the religious greatness of the damned." [3]

Contemporary literature, where highly serious, has this greatness. It is both a moral and a religious greatness. It is perhaps the more austerely religious in that it is not prejudiced by religious belief! But its greatness is that of the lost—not the damned. It is the acknowledgment and exploitation of a Moment in which we stand, a Moment in which we are still permitted to cry out, "Peer Gynt salutes you, Brother Star! To shine,—to be quenched, and lost in the void." But the Gyntian self has reached the last crossroad, and the whole of our literature recoils on the question, "Is there no one in the universe— nor in the abyss, nor yet in heaven?"

One has only to explore a little the border territories of this serious- ness to see how farreaching and how penetrating the moral conscious- ness of contemporary poet or writer has become. Tiutchev's poem, entitled significantly, "The Abyss," is one of the most summary:

> Behold man, without home,
> orphaned, alone, impotent,
> facing the dark abyss; . . .
> And in this strange mysteriousness night
> he sees and knows a fatal heritage.[4]

The sense of solitariness, of lostness, or of being "unravelled, alien" (as another translation has it) is but barely relieved by the suggestion that we experience today the "dark night of the soul." For the abyss is not sustaining, and "in the dim depths of his soul (man) sinks." It is interesting to compare the concluding lines of this poem—

> The flood waxes and bears us on
> to a dark immensity . . .

[3] Introduction to *Short Novels of Dostoievsky*, Dial Press, New York, 1945, p. viii.
[4] Quoted by Nicholas Berdyaev in *The End of Our Time*, Sheed & Ward, New York, 1933, p. 72.

whilst we sail encircled
by the flaming abyss.[5]

with the following from Archibald Fleming:

It is the moment of the whirpool, moment
Of the abyss where all things stream.

(*The Destroyers*) [6]

We note the close, though fortuitous, approximation of mood and idea between two poets, the one Russian and the other American, who have otherwise but little in common. "The Pilgrim Way," as Auden says, "has led to the Abyss."

A relatively naive unfolding of this quest is traceable in the passage of Thomas Wolfe from the nostalgic longing of *Look Homeward, Angel* of 1929 to the more mature realization that *You Can't Go Home Again* of 1940. The following sentences from his account of his own quest (*The Story of a Novel*) will show at once how intimately and how representatively the author is identified with his work:

My conviction is that all serious creative work must be at bottom autobiographical. . . . The fact is that one writes a book not in order to remember it, but in order to forget it. . . . What many of us were doing in those years when we fled from our country and sought refuge abroad was not really looking for a place to work, but looking for a place where we could escape from work; . . . from the necessity of grappling squarely with ourselves and the necessity of finding in ourselves, somehow, the stuff to live by. . . .[7]

What this pursuit led to in this *autarkeia*-centered pilgrimage is sharply indicated in the following passage:

The deepest search in life, it seemed to me, the thing that in one way or another was central to all living was man's search to find a father (Cf. Proust's search for a mother, Kafka's relation to his father, et cetera) . . . not merely the lost father of his youth, but the image of a strength and

---

[5] *Ibid.*, pp. 72–73.

[6] Archibald Fleming, "The Destroyers," *The New Republic*, July 13, 1938, p. 273.

[7] Thomas Wolfe, "The Story of a Novel," from *The Portable Thomas Wolfe*, edited by Maxwell Geismar, The Viking Press, New York, 1946, pp. 572, 570, 577.

wisdom external to his need and superior to his hunger, to which the belief and power of his own life could be united.[8]

This problem which he confesses he but barely comprehends, he tried to meet squarely, "not with reason but with life"—but it led him to "that state of naked need and utter isolation which every artist has got to meet and conquer if he is to survive at all." [9] With Wolfe, this led (on his grounds) to four insoluble contradictions, or existential antinomies, through which he sought courageously to pass. The first (1) was *the dialectical duplicity* of the creative gift: the realization that "in a man's work there are contained not only the seeds of life, but the seeds of death, and that that power of creation which sustains us will also destroy us like a leprosy if we let it rot stillborn in our vitals." [10] Associated closely with this was (2) *the metaphysical duplicity* of time—its Heraclitean dispersion, on the one hand, and, on the other, its "tranquil, muted, and unchanging light," forever present "above the universe of dreams." This was his "dream of time," and tied in with it was his "dream of Guilt"—his awareness (a) that he had allowed his own life "to waste and rot in the slothful and degrading surfeits of Circean time," and (b) that "man's inhumanity to his fellow man" was so bleak a picture as to have left an ineffaceable scar upon his life. This led to (3) the feeling of *moral duplicity* in his own sense of guilt. "There dwelt forever the fatal knowledge of my own inexpiable guilt. I did not know what I had done. . . ." (Cf. Franz Kafka, *The Trial*.) And, finally, (4) there was the *spiritual duplicity* in man himself:

For what is man? First, a child, soft-boned unable to support itself on its rubbery legs. . . .

After that, a boy, hoarse and loud before his companions, but afraid of the dark. . . .

Then the youth: goes after girls . . . , hints at a hundred seductions, but gets pimples on his face. . . .

Then the man: he is busy, he is full of plans and reasons, he has work. He gets children, buys and sells small packets of everlasting earth, intrigues against his rivals, is exultant when he cheats them. . . .

[8] *Ibid.*, p. 582. Parentheses mine. Ed.
[9] *Ibid.*, p. 590.
[10] *Ibid.*, pp. 590–591.

This is man: a writer of books, a putter-down of words, a painter of pictures, a maker of ten thousand philosophies . . . for the most part a foul, wretched, abominable creature, a packet of decay. . . .

Yes, this is man, and it is impossible to say the worst of him. . . .

Here, then, is man, this moth of time, this dupe of brevity and numbered hours, this travesty of waste and sterile breath. Yet if the gods could come here to a desolate, deserted earth where only a few marks and carvings of his hand were legible upon his broken tablets, where only a wheel lay rusting in the desert sand, a cry would burst out of their hearts and they would say: "He lived, and he was here!" [11]

And though this rhetoric, after so fiery a flight into man's blackness bursts but feebly as compared with Pascal, Wolfe has blundered nonetheless upon the greatness and misery of man without God. We may feel from this that Wolfe is not so much a giant as he is gigantic, and that when the helmet of his volubility and terrors is toppled off there appears within the frightened face of a little boy; nevertheless we must note carefully that even the naive sense of isolation brings him sharply upon the dialectical junctures of our own existential antinomies where decision must be reached.

II

To compare Wolfe with Franz Kafka in these respects would perhaps be unfair; but we may note in passing that the God-consciousness of Kafka aggravates the sense of moral isolation infinitely, for the antinomies are stressed absolutely. Here, too, the Job question is posed—guilt without knowledge of "what I had done." Kafka gives to this consciousness its religious setting. "The original sin," he remarks, "the ancient wrong committed by man, consists in the complaint, which man makes and never ceases making, that a wrong has been done to him, that the original sin was once committed upon him." [12] Again

We are sinful not merely because we have eaten of the Tree of Knowl-

[11] Thomas Wolfe, "You Can't Go Home Again," *ibid.*, pp. 547–552.

[12] Franz Kafka, "Aphorisms," from *The Great Wall of China*, Schocken Books, New York, 1946, p. 270.

edge, but also because we have not eaten of the Tree of Life. The state in which we find ourselves is sinful, quite independent of guilt.[13]

Our "destiny has been altered," and we both pursue and contrive rationalizations and illusions in which to mask from ourselves the moment of the Fall, and we project an ego-self in flight from the true self to fit the illusory world.

Now the question that is raised by Kafka, and the dimension that he supplies, is that of the God-relationship. Correspondingly the resolution of all the *existential antinomies—the dialectical, the metaphysical, the moral, and the spiritual*—depends upon the nature of this relationship. This relationship, for Kafka, is viewed as that of a finite person to an infinite God. The two terms are morally incommensurable, which leaves to fallen man the dialectical options of exploring *negatively* his contradictory condition.

A man was astonished how easily he went the eternal way; he happened to be rushing backwards along it.

There are countless places of refuge, there is only one place of salvation; but the possibilities of salvation, again, are as numerous as all the places of refuge.[14]

But we experience here—at the point of salvation—a void. It is as though the moral incommensurability of the finite and the infinite had become an article of knowledge and had been seduced into metaphysical incommensurability of absolute dualistic stringency: so that the "journey to God" is no more a coming to oneself in the God-relationship. "There is," as Kafka says, "a goal, but no way; what we call the way is only wavering." [15] Frederick Hoffman has noted the derivation of Kafka's views from Kierkegaard's notion of paradox. When measured by the human reason, the God-relationship is essentially paradoxical; but when "qualified by man's mature acceptance of God's will, paradox no longer exists." Paradox is characteristic of the individual who is in process of becoming; but where faith exists the paradox disappears. Kafka was not capable of this faith-

13 *Ibid.*, p. 298.
14 *Ibid.*, pp. 286, 283.
15 *Ibid.*, p. 283.

acquiescence. For him "there was no having, only being, only a being panting for its last breath, panting to be choked out." [16] So the paradox remains with him a contradiction, a contradiction expounded with dialectic and esthetic skill, but a contradiction whose movement returns upon his moral isolation infinitely. Negatively ("what is laid upon us is to accomplish the negative") he may be compared with Pascal:

> We sail within a vast sphere, ever drifting in uncertainty, driven from end to end. . . . Nothing stays for us. This is our natural condition, and yet most contrary to our inclination; we burn with desire to find solid ground and an ultimate sure foundation whereon to build a tower reaching to the Infinite. But our whole groundwork cracks; and the earth opens to abysses.[17]

But Kafka rejected the Christian Mediator who was the saving focus for Pascal's faith. Pascal never committed the blunder of converting spirit into substance to be probed by metaphysical analysis: nor did he prolapse God's world into a moving image of himself. D. S. Savage rightly notes that the action of Kafka's narratives centers around one individual and one alone—Kafka himself: that while he is "an explorer of the human condition" his world is solipsistic; and it is for this reason that "with each succeeding work, the atmosphere of isolation increases" and disintegration takes hold.[18]

It is to the peculiar quality and to the universality of this atmosphere of isolation that we would direct attention. It may begin superficially in the discovery that we are today "waylost, wanderers" (MacLeish); but it becomes in seriousness the journey to the self—which is, as the ancients proclaimed "a journey without return." "Thou lonesome one," exclaimed Zarathustra, "thou goest the way to thyself! . . . Ready must thou be to burn thyself in thine own flame!" But the religious greatness of contemporary literature consists in the courage and the skill with which it has undertaken its quest. It has come

---

[16] *Ibid.,* p. 286.

[17] Blaise Pascal, *Pensées,* Everyman edition, J. M. Dent & Sons, Ltd., London, 1931, # 72.

[18] D. S. Savage, *The Kafka Problem,* edited by Angel Flores, New Directions, New York, 1946, pp. 333 f.

upon the fundamental antinomies of existence; but the antinomies evoke the turn inward, where the ego, in reprisal for its dread of "the infinite" seeks to enthrone false infinites. But the "whole ground-work cracks" and the ego opens to an abyss of solitariness. Thomas Wolfe knows that the way home is the way forward, but he does not know that the way is a narrow way; Kafka knows that the way is narrow, but his reason is not yet "redeemed from incestuous fixation on her own Logic" (Auden). The extremes are infinitized, and we are left gazing into the ego's emptiness, an abyss we had thought well lighted by the candles of the Enlightenment. But these are out now. We are today drawing nearer, as Slochower has noted, to *the moment of recognition.* "It is the moment in which a character comes to understand the meaning of his dilemma and his true rela-tion toward his fellowmen and his world. . . . We are approaching it the hard way, through an unparalleled period of dissidence. . . . The new substance must be reached through the battle-field of alienation." [19] This is the moment of "transfiguration by estrange-ment." It is the moment in which we discover that man "is a creature inevitably stigmatized: either he bears the wounds of the old Adam, or those of the crucified." [20]

III

We may now define more closely the nature of the contemporary quest. Clearly it is not, as in the childhood myths and fairy stories, a quest after dragons which will turn into princesses at the appropri-ate moment—though dragons and monsters are involved. Nor is it the quest for innocence as Auden has noted of the detective story,[21] in which the innocence of all is established through disclosing the guilt of one—though the question of innocence is involved. It is rather the quest of the Prodigal—which is, indeed, a narrative of alienation and return. But it is that moment in the quest just prior to the moment

[19] Harry Slochower, *No Voice is Wholly Lost,* Creative Age Press, New York, 1945, p. 380.

[20] Jacques Maritain, *Réponse à Jean Cocteau,* Librairie Stock, Delamain et Boutel-leau, Paris, 1926.

[21] Cf. W. H. Auden, "K's Quest," in *The Kafka Problem, op. cit.,* pp. 47 ff.

in which the prodigal comes to himself—the moment when the groundwork cracks, when the abyss opens, and "time, the serpent" (changed suddenly from a dalliance of princess into a dreadful *eschatos* of dragon) "retrieves the telescope" of indefinite temporal projection, and "constricts it to its primal nest of vertigos, the labyrinth, compressible, of our own egos." He has reached the nadir of moral isolation: he is lost. And he knows it.

> Anthropos apteros for days
> Walked whistling round and round the Maze,
> Relying happily upon
> His temperament for getting on.
>
> The hundredth time he sighted, though,
> A bush he left an hour ago,
> He halted where four alleys crossed,
> And recognized that he was lost.[22]

Now human kind, as Eliot says, "cannot bear very much reality." *"Nicht dass du Gottes ertruegest die Stimme, bei weitem"* (Rilke). But just as he cannot endure the voice of God, so he cannot endure for long the direct gaze into the black hole of his lostness. The dizziness floods: he recoils from the plunge into his voided interiority. He flies from the moment—into the illusions of relief. "Human life is thus only a perpetual illusion. . . . We are only falsehood, duplicity, contradiction; we both conceal and disguise ourselves from ourselves. . . . We wander in the times which are not ours. . . . But diversion amuses us, and leads us unconsciously to death." [23]

Just here appears the inestimable moral service of esthetics: in holding up the mirror to man's psychic nature, man is enabled to peer into himself as it were at second hand, and to regard himself "for the time being" (as Auden says) refracted into *personae* (masks) of his condition *with the masks removed!* The literary mask of himself, that is, is the unmasked aspect of his own ego—itself an image of his real Self. And he is able so to behold himself *without responsibility.* He

---

[22] W. H. Auden, "The Labyrinth," in *The Collected Poetry of W. H. Auden,* Random House, New York, 1945, p. 9.

[23] Pascal, *op. cit.,* # 100, 377, 172, 171.

dissolves, that is, the moral imperative in the esthetic medium. For this reason, perhaps, the most important confessional writing to-day (*Ash Wednesday,* for example) and the most significant pro-phetic writing (I would *not* include here the so-called novels of the "social consciousness") will be found, chiefly, in the best modern poetry. Direct prophetic communication is vitiated by its inability to gain a foothold in generally accepted conventions of belief, for it is precisely this consciousness that is disintegrated; the poet, however, can take hold within the disintegrated consciousness and exploit the disintegration. Which, paradoxically, reinstates the moral conscious-ness. It reinstates the sense that I must become responsible—for my-self, for the task (my vocation and proper calling in the world), for the bearing of this upon others and upon the world, and for the realization of this single task as *my* mode of response to the imperative demand (command) of reality itself (God Himself). (Auden's *Age of Anxiety* will serve as an example of this moral movement. And here, it will be noted, the prophetic consciousness *can* take hold, as in the poetry of Jeremiah.)

This will become clearer the moment it is observed that most effective modern writing is intrinsically dialectic rather than dramatic. It may be questioned, for example, whether Kafka really wrote "novels." He has *personae* to be sure; but, as Mr. Savage has noted above, his narratives are collapsible, and center around one individual —himself. The fact that Kafka finishes nothing coincides with the fact that Kafka has no solution for his problem. Proust projects two alternate ways of life—*Swann's Way* and *The Guermantes Way* and seeks to mediate between them. Thomas Mann's early preoccupation with the artist and society does not really undergo any great change in Mann's "step . . . from the bourgeois and individual to the mythical and the typical"—for Joseph is collapsible toward Goethe (*The Beloved Returns*) and Goethe, more than any other is "Mann's own prototype." [24] Which means that Mann is still concerned with the artist and his mediatorial task: the subordinate *personae*—the voices of the dialectic—all achieve their focus in Joseph, the "most representative" character—who is both individual and typical. Of

[24] Slochower, *op. cit.,* p. 352.

which two things may be observed: (1) that the artist's concern with his "individual task" is a concern for vocation, as noted above, and contains therein a moral imperative—toward oneself and toward the world; and (2) that turning on the matter—no matter how artistically contrived—all esthetic dialogue—(regardless of its "form") remains essentially dialectical rather than dramatic. "Where the ideas are in action, we have drama," says Kenneth Burke; [25] "where the agents are in ideation, we have dialectic." In all of this the agents are "in ideation."

This dialectic property is still more apparent in modern poetry, where the device of irony is today employed so ingeniously. Through the device of irony we explore and exploit the disjunctions of a disintegrating culture, as well as of the existential antinomies. At the same time we abstract ironically from the contradictions and so remain superior to them.

The exploitation of this device in Eliot's *The Hollow Men* is an obvious example. Here the contradictions of mortality and creaturehood—death *versus* the Kingdom, idea and reality, conception and creation, potency and existence, etc.—are all specified, and at the same time set up as empty affirmations over against the spiritual emptiness of the cultural pattern—"here we go round the prickly pear . . . ," "This is the dead land, this is the cactus land," etc. Yet the ironic knowledge that we are the hollow men, provides us here with the moral advantage of an esthetic superiority to the problem.

Irony also insulates the ego from itself, erecting an impressive egoistic eristic or rhetorical achievement on the precise knife edge of its own collapse. Or, to change the figure, while the ego rides buoyantly in on the breaking wave of its own esthetic achievement in irony, it fails to observe that in the ebb or recession of the esthetic experience it has been quietly beached upon the shoreline of an ethical requirement. It is, therefore, entirely logical (in the existential sense) that *Ash Wednesday,* a poem of religious repentance, should follow upon *The Waste Land* with its ironic denouement. Negatively, this ethical requirement is that a mask must be removed from some ego-

[25] Kenneth Burke, *A Grammar of Motives,* Prentice Hall, Inc., New York, 1945, p. 512.

pretension: disclosing by the abrupt juxtaposition of the two terms of a contradiction the sham property of the term masquerading as the real. And religiously it is the requirement that the mask of ego-pretension understood as self-sufficiency must be removed, leaving us exposed to the requirement of the God-relation. This is a negative achievement, in which the ego is disabused of a supposed fixed knowledge, or of a moral presumption, and released from its bondage. For this reason, it is held that irony is a transitory form, that it derives from an imperfection, from a failure in equilibrium, and that it has no other *raison d'être* than to correct this and to disappear with the correction.[26]

Tate comments upon the seduction scene in *The Waste Land,* in which the "small house agent's clerk," an aggressive young man, betrays the arrogance and pride of conquest which are "the badge of science, bumptious practicality, overweening secular faith. The very success of this conquest witnesses its aimless character; it succeeds as a wheel succeeds in turning; he can only conquer again. His own failure to understand his position is irony, and the poet's insight into it is humility." Whether or not "humility" is the proper term here, it is clear that the poet's insight is superior to the terms juxtaposed: the young clerk's pride and achievement are unmasked in their emptiness when they are revealed as compulsive expressions of a secularized world. This means that the moral superiority of the poetic insight is a (negative) release from an ego-pretense, and renews the context of ethical responsibility. At this point we are abandoned. As I have mentioned elsewhere, irony "confronts the issue without responsibility. It retreats into the esthetic and shuns decision through its art. It refuses its apostleship by escaping into its medium." [27] But its achievement has been a dialectic one.

We may now specify two things: (1) the subject matter of irony is contradiction, and (2) its true ethical correlate is humility; but its temptation, as Burke has put it, is a Pharisaic one—that of "superiority." "True irony, humble irony, is based upon a sense of fundamental

[26] Father Paulhan, *La Morale de L'Ironie,* Librairie Félix Alcan, Paris, 1925, p. 173.
[27] Stanley Romaine Hopper, *The Crisis of Faith,* Abingdon-Cokesbury, Nashville, 1944, p. 125.

kinship with the enemy, as one . . . is not merely outside him as an observer but contains him *within,* being consubstantial with him . . . Dialectic irony (or humility) here . . . provides us with a kind of 'technical equivalent for the doctrine of original sin.' "[28] I am suspicious of any "technical" equivalents for original sin, but an "esthetic" equivalent with a dependent status may surely be allowed: an ironic status, that is, for its function would be to show that any esthetic equivalent for original sin would be a moral sham, just as any esthetic superiority to the terms of the essential human contradiction would be, morally, a signification of the Fall. For within the context of Original Sin the function of irony would surely be to present the human Contradiction absolutely: which should lead to irony's reversal—humility. If it led to the opposite—superiority—it would be the irony of irony, considering that when the nadir of moral isolation is reached *it is just our self-sufficiency as a groundwork that has cracked* and opened into the abyss.

IV

It is, however, the irony of contemporary literature that, just as it has brought us sharply up before the ultimate terms of the human contradiction, assisting the ego to perceive itself (by the ironic but dialectic distribution of itself through its own *personae*), it still seeks to maintain a superiority to the dilemma through converting the ethical requirement (of reversal) into an esthetic world-view. This was the deficiency in Yeats: for, despite his several spiritisms, it is still the old "Platonic tolerance" in one more twist of its neo-Platonic forms, that presides over his aims. The "Galilean turbulence" never quite upset his use of poetry as a magical means, a formula of incantation, a wreath of roses on a lance of rhymes—an esthetic equivalent for original sin. "What theme had Homer but original sin?"

Homer is my example and his unchristianed heart.
The lion and the honeycomb, what has the Scripture said?
So get you gone, Von Huegel, though with blessings on your head.[29]

[28] Burke, *op. cit.,* pp. 514, 515.
[29] William Butler Yeats, "Vacillation," *Collected Poems,* The Macmillan Company, New York, 1951, p. 247.

This was the decisive point for Yeats.

Rilke travelled farther: for he reached the Mountains of Primal Pain—and there he probed the antinomies of lament and praise, of death and life, of love and death, of Orpheus and the Angel. And so the flowers on his lance of steel were thrust into the infinite, and the pathos of his longing rose like solitude about his hope—which was, that "at the last moment, as in all ancient myths, the dragons would turn into princesses."

But Eliot and Auden are the poets in whom the consciousness of the relevance of dogma to esthetic interpretation has become most explicit. Both have been forthright. "I doubt," said Eliot in his *After Strange Gods,*[30] "whether what I am saying can convey very much to anyone for whom the doctrine of Original Sin is not a very real and tremendous thing." And Auden makes, in one instance, the prefatory comment (to his sermon on "Depravity") : "I can only hope that this piece will seem meaningless to those who are not professing Christians." [31] Of the two, Eliot is perhaps the "most ethically orthodox," as he himself remarked of James Joyce; he knows that "the perception of Good and Evil—whatever choice we may make—is the first requisite of spiritual life." But though Eliot is the more ethically orthodox, it is Auden who knows what it means, who gives to the dogma its existentialist content.

This is a discussion we cannot enter into here. Our point is simply that the artist's dilemma today has thrust him inward upon himself in such a way that his journey has brought him round to the ultimate mysteries, where ethical and religious understandings take hold.

We may, however, note two important references to this problem appearing in Eliot's poetry as he emerges from the ironic catharsis of *The Waste Land* and passes beyond the repentance and prayer of *Ash Wednesday.* In the *Choruses from "The Rock"* he notes that "the Mystery of Iniquity is a pit too deep for mortal eyes to plumb" [32]

[30] T. S. Eliot, *After Strange Gods,* Harcourt, Brace & Company, New York, 1934, pp. 61–62.
[31] *Op. cit.,* p. 242.
[32] T. S. Eliot, *Choruses from "The Rock,"* in *Collected Poems,* Harcourt, Brace & Company, New York, 1936, p. 208.

—as indeed it is if he means it cannot be grasped by formal analysis; and he advises,

> Take
> Your way and be ye separate.
> . . . be ye satisfied that you have light
> Enough to take your step and find your foothold.[33]

It is possible that there lies in this advice a very subtly concealed (perhaps unconsciously concealed) reluctance to face the Mystery in its existential form—that is, within us, most deeply within us, where, though we do not formally comprehend it, it is nevertheless recognized as our true condition and our responsibility. It is here precisely that the neo-Platonic symbol of Light (as in Dante, or in Eliot) becomes a moral and dialectic fallacy: for until I discover that I have no light (in terms of ego-self-sufficiency) and that I have no foothold, it is certain that I shall never have a foothold and shall never experience true light. As Auden puts it:

> As long as the self can say "I," it is impossible not to rebel;
> As long as there is an accidental virtue, there is a necessary vice;
> And the garden cannot exist, the miracle cannot occur . . .[34]

Or again, in the *Four Quartets,* Eliot's reference to this same Mystery takes an unusual and impressive form:

> The backward look behind the assurance
> Of recorded history, the backward half-look
> Over the shoulder, towards the primitive terror.[35]

Since he puts this in the form of personal affirmation—"I have said before . . ."—are we perhaps justified in noting here a positive reluctance to take more than a backward half-look at this Mystery, over the shoulder, while our effort is creatively in flight from it? In short, is there an evidence here (slight though it be) of the subtlest of all moral equivocations: that, namely, of acknowledging the Mystery and of escaping into a theology which, though containing it formally,

[33] *Ibid.,* pp. 208–209.
[34] "For the Time Being," *op. cit.,* p. 412.
[35] T. S. Eliot, *Four Quartets,* Harcourt, Brace & Company, New York, 1943, p. 24.

avoids meeting it actually? If we take the view of Auden, that "Hell
is the being of a lie"; or of Nicolas Berdyaev, that "eternal perdition
means that personality remains self-contained, indissoluble and absolutely isolated . . . that Hell is nothing other than complete separa-
tion from God" [36]—if we take these views (and it would appear that
we must so far as the testimony of contemporary literature is concerned), then a distinction of farreaching ethical and religious significance must be made. As Berdyaev puts it: "The justification of hell
on the grounds of justice, such as we find in St. Thomas Aquinas
and Dante, is particularly revolting and lacking in spiritual depth.
It is the idea of freedom and not of justice that dialectically pre-
supposes hell." [37]

Concerning this we must limit ourselves to one observation only.
It is that the myth or dogma of Original Sin, which has become so
central in literary discussion today, implies as its dialectical opposite
not the notion of Original Righteousness (with its intellectualistic
ethic implied), but the fact of Original Freedom, which has to do
with the existential relationship to God (with its ethics of love implied). This is both the mythical and doctrinal implication of the condition of lostness to which so much modern literature testifies, and
which we are experiencing in its negative form:

> your existence is indeed free at last to choose
> its own meaning, that is, to plunge headlong into
> despair and fall through silence fathomless and dry,
> all fact your single drop, all value your pure alas.[38]

Or again, in terms of the *Genesis* narrative:

> Since Adam, being free to choose,
> Chose to imagine he was free
> To choose his own necessity,
> Lost in his freedom, Man pursues
> The shadow of his images . . .[39]

---

[36] Nicolas Berdyaev, *The Destiny of Man,* Charles Scribner's Sons, New York, 1937,
p. 340.

[37] *Ibid.,* p. 340.

[38] W. H. Auden, "The Sea and the Mirror," *op. cit.,* p. 395.

[39] "For the Time Being," *ibid.,* p. 420.

This is the paradox of the "dreadful freedom" that our literature is probing so relentlessly and so courageously today.

Therefore, the esthetic exploration of our lostness in these days becomes ironical in its first motion to rescue itself without modifying centrally the inmost cause of our trouble. But the irony which momentarily protects us from the ethical dilemma only aggravates the negative awareness and thrusts us upon the necessity for a new decision. But this is to be thrust essentially upon our freedom which renews, in its primary form, the religious question. Which is the curious point of contact between letters and the tradition at the present time. We are experiencing the paradox that just at the moment when these two had appeared to be farthest removed from one another, and just when the causes of both seemed most nearly lost, they encounter each other in the one form whereby they are both renewed—at the point that is, where moral isolation, having wandered far, concedes that it is lost, comes to itself, and remembers its Father. This, too, is a "mystery": for, as Berdyaev puts it, "The Good appears in a new aspect: it does not condemn 'the wicked' to eternal torments but suffers upon the cross." [40] Therein is the love of God made manifest. For it is the very essence of religion that He should come to seek and to save those who are lost.

[40] Berdyaev, *The Destiny of Man, op. cit.,* p. 371.

RELIGION AND THE ARTIST'S BELIEFS

Grace is insidious, it twists and is full of surprises. . . . This people will finish a way they never began. This age, this world, this people will get there along a road they never set out on.

Charles Peguy, in "Clio"

XIII

RELIGION AND THE MISSION OF THE ARTIST

BY

DENIS DE ROUGEMONT

Recently I was asked to speak on "The Mission of Art as a Creative Expression of the Human Spirit." I would not have agreed, but for the bearing of the subject upon a conference of ecumenical study, bringing together some artists and writers, and some Protestant, Anglican, and orthodox theologians.[1] It seemed to me that this title, as it was proposed specifically by Christians, and not by vague or hazy humanists, merited a serious *mise au point*.

To me, the expression, "Mission of Art," rings false. Art, with a capital letter, is one of those official allegories which we have inherited from the nineteenth century and from Romanticism (with its admiration for Wagner and Baudelaire), who were condemned and fined by our forebears. This allegory marks the existence of a sort of "religion of Art," born of the romantic sects and brotherhoods— the preRaphaelites, the symbolists, etc.—which in our time has lost its sacred vigor; but which subsists nevertheless under the form of a very widespread prejudice, amongst the Philistines, the middle class (la bourgeoisie), in Hollywood, and in inaugural addresses. Art, with a capital letter, is something ideal, something distinguished, vaguely *en rapport* with the Infinite, not useful for anything; respectable, interesting women more than men; the business of certain specialists allowing escape from the too real cares of daily life, elevating souls and softening mores—in short, resembling closely the con-

---

[1] International Conference on Christianity and Art, convened at the Ecumenical Institute, Chateau de Bossey, Celigny, Switzerland, May, 1950. Translated, with the author's permission, by the editor.

ception which most of our contemporaries have of the Christian religion. It is not serious if we admit with Talleyrand that "whatever is exaggerated is lacking in seriousness." No serious artist says that he makes "Art," unless it is to defend himself against the tax collector or the suspicious policeman.

On the other hand, the word, "art," is a serviceable term, which denotes the ensemble of artistic activities and the objects which result from them.

In either case, whether it is a question of romantic exaggeration or of a generic term, it is evident that Art, with or without the capital, cannot have any "mission." Neither a false god, nor a word, can have a mission. Only a man is capable of receiving one.

In the next place, I have some doubt about the adjective, "creative," as it appears in the title as proposed.

The use of the verb, "to create," in relation to human activity is, I believe, rather recent. This manner of speaking of the human act, by comparing it, or even equaling it, to the divine act, not only comes from a synergist doctrine which demands examination, but coincides historically with the impoverishment or loss in the modern epoch of the belief in a Creator God. I am not at all sure that man is capable of creating, in the true sense of this term: that is, of producing an absolute mutation, an absolute novelty in the universe. That which is currently called today a "creation" is in reality only a slightly different arrangement of elements already known according to laws known or knowable. Therefore it is a *composition*. Before Romanticism, we were content to say that a musician composed an opera, that a painter composed a picture. But today, we say that he "creates" a symphony, that he "creates" forms. No one can prove that a man creates something, because no one can know the totality of existent things with their structures and their rapports. We shall limit ourselves, therefore, to the classical term, "composition," when speaking of works of art.

So much having been said, let us consider now what is the mission —if there be one—of the men who compose books, pictures, scores, statues, pleasure grounds, poems; and, first of all, what is the nature of their activity, and what are its proper ends.

I

All sorts of people make things, objects, and instruments. *Homo faber* designates a great part of humanity: workers, artists, scholars, legislators, and craftsmen.

Let us ask what difference there is between the man who makes a poem, a score of music, a picture, a façade, and the man who makes a machine, an equation, a law, a shoe, a chemical product, or a photo.

For about two centuries now, we have become accustomed to answering this question in an apparently simple manner. We think that artists make useless objects (or, as we say in French, *gratuits*), and that others make objects necessary to our daily lives, genuinely useful, such as automobiles, statistics, tools. We cannot do without razors, says the modern man, but if necessary we can—and even without much sacrifice—do without pictures, or statues. Art products are a luxury, and the other products are necessities. All our education leads us to believe this, and if we are required to justify this habitual belief, our professors have recourse to certain interpretations of Kant, according to which an object of art would have its end in itself, and would serve no end, therefore, but that of being contemplated— which is to say, honored with a glance on the way to the dining room.

But these criteria of utility or necessity, on the one hand, and of gratuitousness or uselessness, on the other, are inconsistent and absolutely superficial. They teach us nothing concerning the nature of the work of art. But they do teach us something about the nature and attitude of the society which accepts them: the knowledge that this society has lost the sense of the sacred. Many civilizations have existed, and perhaps will exist, for which a stone or a piece of wood, sculptured or painted in a certain manner, have been infinitely more "useful" than an electric razor is for us. These objects have been regarded as eminently useful, because they contained a power, an exalting or terrifying quality, a meaning. They were taken seriously by the peoples who believed that the meaning of life, the fear of death, the sense of dread before the sacred power, are serious things. Whereas we consider as serious, and, therefore, useful, whatever permits us, for example, to go more swiftly, though it matters little from what motive or toward what end.

The fact that even in theory we hold the work of art to be destitute of direct utility, proves simply that art does not respond to the most potent desire of modern man; that modern man should be able, therefore, to dispense with it; that he has in truth no need of it (as we call useful that which we need); and that he believes he should respect it only by virtue of a kind of prejudice. From which, it may be said in passing, we should be able to deduce the utter vanity of the actual attempts made to vulgarize art to give it publicity. It is the need for art which should be awakened. To this end, we should change the total attitude, the entire orientation of modern man—before setting out to distribute reproductions of Van Gogh!

If therefore I set aside the criterion of utility, or lack of utility, as being relative, variable, and subject to change in meaning according to the religious condition of a society, I find myself once more before the initial question—in what respect does artistic activity distinguish itself from the other activities of man?

I would venture the following answer: that, as distinct from all other products of human action, *the work of art is an object of which the raison d'être necessary and sufficient, is TO SIGNIFY, organically, and by means of its own structure.*

Whether it consists in a structure of meanings, or forms, or sounds, or ideas, the work of art has for its specific function the bribing of the attention, the magnetizing of the sensibility, the fascinating of the meditation, the ensnaring—and at the same time it must orient existence toward something which transcends sounds and forms, or the words so assembled. It is a trap, but an oriented trap.

It is true, of course, that an equation is an object which has no function other than that of signifying. Nevertheless, its structure remains entirely analyzable and reducible to its elements which are susceptible of being grouped in other ways—as the equal sign shows —without destroying the signification: which is not the case with the work of art.

It is true that a machine may very well fascinate us, or even a face, or a waterfall. However, these objects were not made for this purpose—for this alone, by the deliberate act of man.

But if, in searching for the nature of the work of art, I define it as a *calculated trap for meditation,* we see that the understanding of its nature is tied up with that of its end: a trap is made in order to capture something. In the work of art, nature and aim, essence and end, are inseparable. It is a question of a single and identical function, which is, to signify something by sensible means.

II

It will perhaps be thought that I am holding beauty rather cheaply in all this, and that my definitions will run counter to some classical definitions in much the same way as they run counter to our current and commonplace ideas. In fact, there are those who insist that beauty should be the aim of art, and that the proper function of the artist should be that of "creating beauty," as it is said. I confess that I am not at all sure about this. And I will make, on this point, three remarks of unequal importance.

The first is a simple statement of fact that I throw into the discussion without presuming to judge it. *The principal artists of our epoch,* such as Picasso or Braque, Joyce or Kafka, Stravinsky, T. S. Eliot or André Breton, *do not try to make beauty,* and without any doubt they will refuse to say that beauty is the aim of their work. Whether the work be beautiful or ugly, charming or odious, for sense and spirit it matters little: their aim is to express or to describe realities at any cost, and even at the price of ugliness, if necessary. The academic artists alone, the false artists, still try to make something "beautiful or flattering."

My second remark is of a much more serious nature. It seems to me that "beauty" *is not a biblical notion or term.* The Scriptures speak to us of truth, justice, freedom, and love, but very little or not at all of beauty. They do not tell us that God is Beauty, but that God is Love. Neither does Christ say that He is the Beauty, but that He is the Way, the Truth, and the Life. This way is not beautiful, but rough and painful. This truth is not beautiful, but liberating. This life does not open into beautiful harmonies, but passes by the narrow gate of death.

Is it necessary to think, as one has written, that in the Bible there is a question of a "terrible lacuna"? A lacuna which the Greek ideal would have filled through amalgamating itself into the Christian tradition, then distinguishing itself anew at the time of the Renaissance? Or must we, on the contrary, ask ourselves whether our notion of beauty is not subject to serious revision?

Finally, my third remark, which is entirely independent of the first two, will take the form of a confession. I find myself incapable of making any use of the *concept* of beauty in itself. Obviously, it happens that as frequently as anyone else I exclaim, "How beautiful it is!"—before the most varied things, such as a landscape or a building, a human being or a work of art, an airplane, a sporting exploit, a fruit, an heroic act, a sentiment. . . . But this enumeration, by virtue of its heteroclitic character, shows that beauty is not a specific property of the work of art. We can describe anything as beautiful. It is a subjective qualification, a term convenient but vague, an exclamation. If I exclaim that a work is beautiful, it is easy to see that this "beauty" which I attribute to it resolves itself upon analysis into very diverse realities. In saying, "how beautiful it is!" I wish to say, I ought to say, "How well it is made!" "How true are its proportions!" "How much more free or strong one feels for having seen this!" "How it excites the passions, or is of inexhaustible interest!" or simply, "How I love it!" because one calls, "beautiful," whatever one loves with intensity. Thus, after all, behind the word, "beauty," we find again justice, or truth, or freedom, or love.

To put by the Greek concept of beauty, is not, therefore, to deny art. To declare that the Bible scarcely speaks of beauty, is not for a single instant to say that the Bible excludes art; and, similarly, to state that the modern artists do not seek beauty in itself and primarily, does not signify that they are bad artists. Very much to the contrary, all this is tantamount to saying that art is something other than a search for beauty, and that those who make a work of art assign to themselves a very different aim.

I believe that the aim (conscious or not) of all true art is to make objects which signify; therefore, it is to make one attentive to the meaning of the world and of life.

Naturally, what the artist succeeds in signifying does not need to be understood by him prior to the work itself. There is not first of all a certain meaning, and then afterward a determination to illustrate it by a work. But rather it is by the work, and in it alone, that a certain meaning manifests or reveals itself. The critics or the public, or sometimes the artist himself, will try afterward to "disengage" this sense, and to isolate it from the work by an effort of translation or abstraction. But in reality the meaning is tied to each detail, just as it is tied to the work as a whole—if it is good—and it truly exists only within it. If it were possible to express this meaning by some other means, the work would lose its *raison d'être*.

We will qualify, therefore, as a "great work," that work which commands attention the most imperiously and for the longest time, that which carries farthest man's meditation upon his destiny and upon the order of things. And we shall call "lasting," that work which will play its role as a trap most efficaciously for many generations and peoples. The current expressions, "I have been captured by this work," or "It is very taking," appear to me accurate and revealing, from this point of view.

III

If such, then, is the nature and end of the work of art, we may now consider under what conditions an artist is able to fulfil his particular mission.

There are two things that I should like to indicate at the outset and in the simplest manner possible: the artist fulfils his mission

(1) in so far as he is a good *craftsman*

(2) in so far as his works *signify* in an efficacious manner.

Which calls, naturally, for some explication.

The good craftsman is he who has a mastery over his means, who follows well the rules of his particular game, who, in short, constructs, exactly and craftily, his traps for the sensibility, reflection, and imagination. Let us call all this—that is, the ensemble of the processes of the craft and the rules of composition—*rhetoric*. This is the part of the "artificer," artificial *and* skillful at the same time. But it is precisely respect for the skills, the love of their proper uses and their laws, which from the outset distinguishes the true artist from the amateur—any person who feels himself inspired or moved, and thinks he can replace rhetoric with sincerity. I am not certain whether it is Laforgue or Valéry who has written: "The bourgeois are those who believe that there is something in the world more important than a convention." Or let us cite Baudelaire: "It is clear that the rhetorics and the prosodies are not arbitrarily contrived tyrannies, but a collection of rules required by the organization of spiritual being itself, and at no time have the prosodies and rhetorics prevented originality from putting itself forward distinctly. On the contrary, to understand how they helped in the hatching of originality would be infinitely more true."

Sincerity has scarcely any import in art. It certainly has none when it is a question of the craft of the artist, because this craft is, by definition, made up of artifices. On this point the moderns have committed a strange error, when, after Romanticism and some of its byproducts, they have believed that they must betake themselves, as they say, "to the school of Nature," and so accept no longer any guide other than sincerity, or even naïveté. I put it as a fact, that a man possessed by the need to express himself, or to express something by means of a work of art, is absolutely incapable of expressing sincerely what he wants to express, unless he has first of all mastered his rhetoric. When Jean Paul Sartre gives his disciples the precept of not "writing," that is to say, of explaining oneself it matters not how and without trying to "write well," he gives the formula for modern philistinism, and deprives his disciples all the more of the means for really expressing their message. Let us remark also, *à propos* of this term, "message," which we especially abuse—and not only in Christian surroundings— that it is impossible "to deliver a message," in so far as we have not mastered its means of expression to the point of being able to adapt them, to make them serve, to orient them—and this even unto the least detail—in the direction and according to the *sense* of that which we wish to communicate. To express a message of truth, but "no matter how," is almost certain to express something altogether different from the message in question—*i.e.,* the disorder of language, the absence of inner coherence, and finally, non-truth itself. It is to forget that what we first of all perceive in the work of art are the means —the words, the colors, or the forms, the sounds and their rapports or groupings. To be sure, even if one knew all the rules of the game and if one applied them with care, one could never be sure of winning; in other words, the artist is never *sure* that the public perceives truly what he has wished to say—but at least it is necessary to make the odds in his favor.

Of course it is possible to object that the public perceives in a work, first of all, not the technical means in themselves, but rather the author's style. If I have not mentioned style as the third condition whereby the artist fulfils his mission, it is because in my view the style is born of the conflict between the first condition—the craft, the means—and the second—that which the artist wishes to signify, the message. If there is no style in a work, it is because there is no drama between the means of expression and that which one wishes to express, between technique and signification, between rhetoric and message. And if there is no drama, it is because one of the two terms is strongly deficient, or even absent. In the latter case there would then be no *art* properly so-called. There is only an almost empty form—and that is academicism—or a formless message, and that is the daily communication, without art, precisely. Or further: if the means are not put in question (or to the question) by a very exacting signification, one will fall into what we call "pure rhetoric," into eloquence and formalism. If, on the other hand, the signification that one wishes to express is too intense and imperious for the means at our command, we shall fall into obscurity, or into an inarticulate cry.

Let us come then to the second condition—the signification, or the message.

On this point I will be brief and will limit myself to a few formulas. I think that an artist (it being granted that he is a good craftsman) fulfils his mission, in proportion as his work elicits in the spectators, readers, or hearers, a sense of liberation; manifests the true, that is to say, renders a truth sensible; evokes the order of the world of the laws of man's destiny; builds or reveals the structures in the sensations, imagination, ideas; and finally, induces to greater love.

A single remark upon this point; it is evident that a classical work of art, a work of Bach, for example, creates order in man, evokes the order of the world, renders its laws comprehensible and even lovable. But some entirely different works, which seem to have no purpose other than that of evoking the present disorder, chaos, and absurdity, the "sound and fury" of a tale "signifying nothing"—I am thinking of certain parts of Joyce's work, or *The Waste Land* of T. S. Eliot, or the stories of Faulkner, the painting of Picasso—these works, dialectically, nostalgically, in revolt and defiance, carry still a witness to the lost order of the world—because art, all art worthy of the name, never has had and never can have any other object.

Such being the two conditions which an artist must fulfil to be equal to his mission, it becomes clear that criticism, the evaluation of the works of art, ought, on the one hand, to bear upon the skill and the means, and, on the other, upon the meaning and the value of the realities bribed and revealed by those means. That is to say, criticism ought to be at one and the same time *technical,* on the one hand, and on the other metaphysical or ethical—which is to say, in the end, *theological.*

IV

I realize full well that in speaking of a theological criticism of the works of art, I shall shock not only the great majority of my contemporaries, on the public side, and some artists, but also the theologians. The latter will say that it is not their business, that they must occupy themselves with the dogmas of the Church. With that I agree. Note that I do not say that this theological criticism would necessarily be the business of the theologians. They are often badly prepared by a strongly didactic turn of mind—most of them are saddled with some teaching obligation—and in that particular case it is a question of developing first of all a power of comprehension, and of nourishing it with a living experience of art. But perhaps one may propose that those who devote themselves to the criticism of art —and every artist more or less is of this number—might at least make an effort to go beyond the stage of a total lack of theological culture where we see them today.

It is within this perspective that I am going to run the risk of suggesting neither a scale of judgment, nor a doctrine, nor a canon for the arts, but a theme for meditation which perhaps would be of such a nature as better to sustain and to justify the judgments which one brings to bear upon works of art—and this, through making ourselves more attentive to the spiritual situation of the artist.

What does the artist really do, after all? In the exaggerated language which we have inherited from Romanticism, without reflecting at all upon the import of the words, we customarily say in the twentieth century

(1) that the artist *creates*

(2) that he *incarnates* in his works certain realities

(3) that he is *inspired*.

I say again, these three verbs are used improperly, and deserve justly the greatest severity on the part of the theologians. But the exorbitant misuse itself suggests a possibility of faithful and sober usage. The three everyday verbs that I have just cited—to create, to incarnate, to inspire—irresistibly evoke the attributes of the Holy Trinity.

If we are able to say of the artist that he creates, it is not merely the consequence of a Promethean or Luciferian overestimate of the human powers. In composing with what he had learned from the world and with that which he is internally, a work external to himself, man imitates symbolically the act of the Creator forming the world and forming Adam. And certainly we must question whether this human work adds anything to the world, in spite of the fact that it is something which was not here before. Man is only able to rearrange that which God has created *ex nihilo*. But in the artist's love for the work which he detaches from himself—not in the work in itself—there is a parable of the fatherly action, an attempt to love the creation as the Father has loved it.

Why has God separated the world from Himself? Why and how does He love it? In what way is this object of His love distinct from Him, and what autonomy does it enjoy? These questions and many analogous ones arise and fix themselves in the mind which pauses before the mystery of the First Person. Thus, to meditate upon the mystery of the Father, would be to lead at one and the same time to the best understanding of the act of the artist, and to its limits or its relativity.

In the second place, we have seen that the artist, in composing a work of art, tends to signify something which would not be perceptible otherwise. Let us not say that he incarnates a reality, for it is not a question of the flesh. But he renders this reality intelligible, legible, audible, by physical means. What takes place then, from the side of the spectator, the reader, the auditor? It happens that the expression veils that which is expressed, while manifesting it at the same time to our senses. Because that which is expressed is not separable from the means of expression, or is so by abuse only. That which reveals is at the same time that which conceals. The meaning of a picture, for example, is not distinct from the colors, forms, proportions, and style, by which, but also in which, it exists. It is possible, therefore, to see them and not to see it. In the eyes of reason the means remain essentially heterogeneous to the reality which they express— why those and not some others?—and yet we would know nothing of it without them. . . . I do not press the matter. I am obliged here to limit myself to indicating the possible point of departure of a dialectic which would find its model, and perhaps its norms, in the doctrine of the Second Person of the Trinity, and in a meditation on its mystery.

In the third place, the artist is currently credited with being inspired. The most determined adversaries of Romanticism, such as Valéry, have never denied that the primitive impulsion of a work of art might be a "gift of the gods"—a single verse, for example, or the vision of a form, on which the operations of the technique afterward develop themselves. The inspiration, whether it operates at each moment or whether it intervenes only at the start and in a single instant, is an undeniable fact of experience. But from whence does it come? What Paul Valéry calls "the gods," without compromising himself, would be for certain other people the Holy Spirit, and for others still a message from the unconscious. So netimes, we imagine that this instantaneous vision has revealed in a lightning flash the existence of a secret way, which it remains only to follow; and sometimes we have the impression that we invent the way while advancing upon it. This problem, let us observe, torments not only the artist, but also, and more consciously still, the physicist of today. Do I invent, he says to himself, or is it rather that I discover a reality? Do I project into the cosmos the forms of my spirit, or is it rather that I espouse by the spirit some of the objective forms of the real? And the man who receives a call sometimes subsists in this doubt to the point of anguish. Do I surrender to some obscure determination of my desire, or is it rather that I really respond to a summons received from somewhere else? Where does the voice come from? Who speaks? Myself, or the Other? Such is the predicament which the intervention of the Holy Spirit creates in man.

Once again it is my purpose here merely to suggest some possible direction for thought. I limit myself to submitting this notion: that Christian meditation upon the act and the work of the artist can deepen, inform, and instruct itself within the framework of a meditation upon the doctrine and mystery of the Trinity; and that Christian meditation will find in the vocabulary and dialectical arguments employed for nearly twenty centuries by trinitarian theologians the whole of a theory which introduces us better than any other to the human mysteries of the act of art.

I will add one last suggestion. We know that the greater part of the heresies have resulted in interpretations sometimes excessive and sometimes deficient in some particular point of trinitarian doctrine. May we believe that the deviations or excesses represented by such or such an artistic school reflect these heresies, or perhaps come from them, unknown even to those who represent them? And would we not have there the principle for a theological critique of the development of the arts? It is certain that if this were the case, we should be able at last to go beyond the stage of arbitrary judgments upon tastes and colors, or upon the import, moral or not, of the works of art, judgments which are based ordinarily upon the mode of the day before yesterday, or upon bourgeois prudence, or upon a revolt against them. It seems to me that some attempts along this line would be worth the labor of the risk—and by laymen first of all.

V

By way of conclusion, I shall try to summarize in two sentences the conception of art which I hold and upon which the preceding pages are based.

Art is an exercise of the whole being of man, not to compete with God, but to coincide better with the order of Creation, to love it better, and to reestablish ourselves in it. Thus art would appear to be like an invocation (more often than not unconscious) to the lost harmony, like a prayer (more often than not confused), corresponding to the second petition of the Lord's prayer—"Thy Kingdom come."

XIV

PATTERNS OF BELIEF IN CONTEMPORARY DRAMA

BY

GEORGE R. KERNODLE

The most difficult problem of modern belief appears at the beginning of the twentieth century, not in terms of man's relation to God but in terms of man's relation to nature. The heritage of the nineteenth century was an alienation of living man from a dead, soulless nature. The twentieth century was born with a millstone around its neck—a millstone of heavy, dead, cold matter—a millstone that would crush any effort to achieve anything and permit man only his illusions and daydreams. His daydreams might amuse him and he frantically held on to them, but he could not possibly imagine that they had any relevance to reality. Just let him try to live by his dreams, let him try to escape from his millstone, go against nature, and he quickly found that he was caught, caught by external nature, or—it did not matter which—by his own nature. But escape he could not.

In 1893, Thomas Huxley was lecturing on Evolution and Ethics, and saw man as constantly at strife with nature. He reminded himself that of course man is as much a part of nature as the humblest weed. But his view of the long ages of rocks and plants, and the short span of man's civilization, made him consider man's mind and works as artificial as a little garden that man struggles to protect—against the cosmic nature, against the jungle of the struggle for existence outside. A garden Huxley thought completely antithetic to the cosmic process.

In 1897, Conrad wrote to Cunninghame Graham, comparing nature to a machine that evolved itself "out of a chaos of scraps of iron, and behold!—it knits. I am horrified at the horrible work and stand appalled. I feel it ought to embroider—but it goes on knitting. . . . The infamous thing has made itself; made itself without thought, without conscience, without foresight . . . without heart. It is tragic accident—and it has happened. You can't interfere with it. . . . It knits us in and it knits us out. It has knitted time, space, pain, death, corruption, despair, and all the illusions—and nothing matters." [1] Such was the characteristic attitude of many thinkers at the beginning of the century. As late as 1929, Joseph Wood Krutch could describe that concept of nature as one of the basic realities of *The Modern Temper,* and 1929 is in many ways the low point in modern despair. Krutch wrote, "But Nature's purpose, if purpose she can be said to have, is no purpose of his [man's] and is not understandable in his terms. Her desire merely to live and to propagate in innumerable forms, her ruthless indifference to his values, and the blindness of her irresistible will strike terror to his soul, and he comes in the fullness of his experience to realize that the ends which he proposes to himself—happiness and order and reason—are ends which he must achieve, if he achieves them at all, in her despite." [2]

The belief that man and nature are enemies has had enormous consequences. It has split man's personality wide open. It has set the part of him that dreams, that yearns for higher things, at war with the baser drives which he can identify with nature. It has set man at constant conflict with his environment. It has turned his eyes all the more inward, because the dreams, the subconscious, the illusions, are all the more cherished, if they are constantly battered and thwarted by the harsh outer world. It is no wonder that the most frequent theme in realistic modern drama is the theme of escape, and that dreams, illusions, and fantasies have sent the theater off in a dozen different experiments away from realism. For the theater, more than poetry or the novel, expresses and shapes the central fears, tensions, and wishes of an age. Because it is a public institution rather than a private expression, the public participates in a group sanction of the ritual

[1] William York Tindall, *Forces in Modern British Literature, 1885–1946,* Alfred A. Knopf, New York, 1947, pp. 170 f.

[2] Joseph Wood Krutch, *The Modern Temper,* Harcourt, Brace & Company, New York, 1929.

action on the stage. Because characters are often simpler and clearer than in the novel, the visible actor on the stage is a far better projection of the dream images of the public than most of the complex characters on the printed page of the novel.

I

The modern dramatic myth of escape is more than the nineteenth century romantic plot of an adolescent escaping from an unhappy home. It is man's helpless struggle against the trammels of nature. A few plays dealing with a particular narrow Victorian background show a happy, successful escape. Elizabeth Barrett in *The Barretts of Wimpole Street* does throw off the sickening influence of her father. Many people in our century have escaped from small towns and narrow families into the wider freedom of the cities. In *The Silver Cord,* in *The Petrified Forest,* in *The Glass Menagerie,* in *Death of a Salesman,* one person does escape from the strangling arms of home and family.

But by far the largest number of escape plays have shown the impossibility of escape. The old sea captain had sent Anna Christie to the country to escape the sins of the seaports, but human weakness found her even in Minnesota. Play after play of Galsworthy shows a person caught in a web of circumstance, but none of the others in the web is flexible enough or has sympathy enough to help him escape. In one play named *Escape,* one person after another does help him evade the law—until he realizes it is himself he can never escape. Galsworthy was fond of quoting the phrase, "Character is Fate."

Many dramatists showed that the attempt to escape only left man in far worse condition than before. The novel, *Ethan Frome,* written in 1911, has a typical pattern. Ethan and Mattie, in love but unable to leave because of Ethan's invalid wife, try the romantic escape of suicide, but their bob-sleigh sideswipes the tree, and they both live, maimed and tortured, far worse off than before. The family of *Juno and the Paycock* expect a legacy to take them out of their neighborhood and their responsibilities, but their hope betrays them and destroys the family, leaving only the agonized cry for compassion of Juno and the drunken clowning of Boyle, who indeed realizes "the whole worl's in a terrible state of chassis." O'Neill's last produced play, *The Iceman Cometh,* belongs at the beginning of the century. Indeed, O'Neill set it in 1912, and denied that a dramatist could write anything based on his own day. It shows that same desperate belief that nature, the world, man's own inner nature, dooms him to defeat, and that, although he may live in a fool's paradise of illusion, any attempt to escape will only destroy his little dream. The scientists tell man to face the facts—to see the world as it is. But the vision of the world that the nineteenth century left him is a vision of a nature either cold or completely at strife with all he would desire or will.

Such is the concept of nature that is tacitly assumed in many modern plays. Yet, just as the physicists have not been satisfied with the world view of absolute determinism, so many of the dramatists have forced out of the depths of deterministic pessimism some plants of hope and belief. And just as it is the physicists themselves, more than the critics of science, who have found the new belief in the complexity of nature, so it is those dramatists who have plumbed the most abject depths of natural and human degradation who are able to build the first foundations for modern belief. It is no easy view of man and the universe that the playwrights have discerned. They gain their hope after long grappling with the full revelations of modern science and scientific observation. I believe we can say that one of the characteristics of the vital plays of the twentieth century is that they do carry the audience through a *purgatorio,* they do face the possibility that nature is cold and indifferent and that man must find his own values, his own relation to the universe, without a warm and friendly earth around him. Even the most assured religious plays gain that assurance after a desperate struggle. "Out of the depths, I cry out to Thee, oh Lord."

Let us look at two naturalistic plays more closely, to see how they diagnose the modern problems of the spirit. *The Lower Depths* and *Tobacco Road* show some very significant changes in man's attitude toward nature. Gorki was writing *The Lower Depths* in 1902, at the very time some of the first mathematicians and physicists were suggesting new formulas different from the exact deterministic "truth" of nineteenth century physics. The play shows the basic assumption that man is caught by nature, but at the same time indicates several new insights that have led to later developments perhaps as momentous as the insights of the atomic physicists. The basic pattern of the play is the same as O'Neill's *The Iceman Cometh:* a group of down-and-outers, the very dregs of society, are stirred up by their hopes and illusions, their desire for something better. But their hopes are all doomed to defeat. In the course of the play a dying woman dreams of peace, one person reads novels, a couple dream of getting far away and starting life over again, a down-at-heels baron dreams of his former importance. A drunken actor hears of a beautiful friendly sanitarium where alcoholics are cured. The pilgrim, Luka, who encourages all these hopes and illusions, is himself a wanderer in search of a new religion. But the play ends in a murder and the arrest of the couple hoping to escape, the pilgrim has disappeared leaving only a cry for compassion and pity, and the drunken actor hangs himself.

Here man is facing the truth—the facts of life as they fit into a vision of man at strife with nature. The play assumes the truth of nature's cruelty, but there is something that rebels at such truth. Kletch, the old locksmith, is so outraged when he hears someone mention truth that he jumps up screaming, "What truth? Where is there truth? (tearing at his ragged clothes) Here's truth for you! No work! No strength! That's the only truth! Shelter—there's no shelter! You die—that's the truth! Hell, what do I want with the truth?—To live —Christ Almighty—they won't let you live—and that's another truth!" The plight of these lost souls is shown to be universal. The streetwalker is sick of her own life, and sick of watching others fighting and dying around her. "I'll go away from here," she cries. "I'll find another lodging house." The quiet capmaker, Bubnoff, merely asks, "Why? Where?" She goes on, "I'm sick of this—I'm not wanted here!" But gets the calm reply, "You're not wanted anywhere—and anyway, all people on earth are superfluous." When the baron asks the pilgrim, "Are you a tramp?" he gets the answer, "We're all of us tramps—why—I've heard said that the very earth we walk on is nothing but a tramp in the universe."

Yet out of this pit of agony and hopelessness two positive characters stand out. Both see that there is a difference between this external truth of a mechanical view of nature and the inner truth of the human spirit. Luka, the pilgrim, turns from the external view of truth, in favor of the subjective values of love and compassion. When the lonely old Anna has died, Luka says, "But all the same, how can you neglect a human being like that? No matter who, or what, every human life has its worth."

When Pepel says, "I don't like corpses," Luka replies, "Why should you like them? It's the living who demand our love—the living." The streetwalker cries out, "God, if they'd only a little pity—if only someone would say a kindly word." Luka leaves unchallenged the view of the external world, and hence encourages all the illusion the mind can invent. He makes faith itself a subjective act. When someone asks, "Is there a God, tell me?" he quietly answers, "if you have faith there is, if you haven't, there isn't—whatever you believe in, exists."

The other character, Satine, goes further than Luka to a more enfolding concept of truth that includes the external world as well as the subjective, a truth based on a desperate humanism, a rediscovery of the idea of man—universal man—over and above the mechanical concept of nature. At the end he declares, "The weakling and the . . . parasite—they both need lies—lies are their support, their shield, their armor! But the man who is strong, who is his own master . . . needs no lies! . . . Truth is the religion of the free man." When he sees the Mohammedan Tartar praying, he gets a vision of all men, alone, yet united, man centrally important, free, not subordinate to nature or in need of illusions. "He prays? That's fine! A man may believe or not—that's his own affair—a man is free—he pays for everything himself—belief or unbelief—love—wisdom—a man pays for everything—and that's just why he is free! Man is—truth! and what is man? It's neither you nor I nor they—ah no—it's you and they and I and the old man—and Napoleon—Mohammed—all in one! Do you understand? It's tremendous! It contains the beginning and the end of everything—everything is in man—and everything exists for him! Man alone exists—everything else is the creation of his hands and his brains! Man! It is glorious! It sounds—oh, so big! Man must be respected—not degraded with pity—but respected, respected." The audience might notice that Satine is gloriously drunk, and Gorki ended the play with news that the actor has hanged himself. But still by touching the depths, the lower depths, some new sources of belief are discovered that would never have been found by the conventional small town churchgoers of the nineteenth century.

II

In play after play the pattern continued—man against nature: man striving to get free from small towns, repressive parents, narrow environments, but caught by circumstances, or defeated by his own nature. O'Neill's young dreamer had a chance to find what lay beyond the horizon, but was tricked by love and saw his dream and his love both turned to gall. The young man in O'Neill's *Dynamo* escaped from the narrow religion of his parents, but found himself caught by old habits of devotion, and electrocuted by the blind power of nature.

Of course, many people were never convinced that nature was man's enemy. No farmer could ever believe it, no one who took part in seasonal ceremonies of spring and harvest could ever believe it. In some casual comedies the opposite attitude began to appear. For instance, in *Front Page* the young reporter tries throughout the play to get away from his job, which holds him and allows him no time for his own free life. At the end he does not escape. But we know that down deep he does not want to escape—that man and his environment can be congenial.

By 1933, when *Tobacco Road* began its amazing run on Broadway, man had discovered new terrors of erosion and drought in nature, and for more than three years the whole social and economic system had broken down. *Tobacco Road* presented a new *purgatorio*—a new lower depths, with images of human erosion far worse than the erosion of soil, and rural degradation worse than the urban.

The play has been misunderstood and much maligned by the intelligentsia, who dismissed its popularity as due to the bad taste of the public. For one thing, it shocked the seriousminded that the audiences laughed at the plight of hungry human beings. Looking back, I suspect the instinct of the public was sounder than that of the social reformers. The play is cast in the form of comedy—the comedy of the hillbilly cartoons, where all normal human emotions and relations are absent or reversed. Jeeter is only amused at his wife's infidelity, and irritated at her death. But comedy has always affirmed the ideal, by laughing at those who do not live up to it. The audience got real satisfaction out of seeing that man can survive, even if all the fabric of material civilization is removed. Here is a family down to the last shreds of decency that separate human beings from animals. Here is man ready to start over on a new basis with nature.

In its treatment of the theme of escape, the play shows that we have come a long way from the attitude of the beginning of the century. The main happening of the play is the escape of the daughter. Her mother gives her own life, in a ritual sacrifice, for the daughter to escape from the coarse husband her father was selling her to. We are still willing to see people run to a more favorable environment. Yet on the other side, Jeeter, after all his degradation, shows the persistence of one of man's deepest and oldest insights—Jeeter believes that man and nature are partners. The health of man is in planting the crops—as a loving partner of the warm and friendly soil. At the end of the play, completely defeated in every attempt to get seed or backing as a farmer, Jeeter sits and lets the beloved soil run through his fingers. This is one play that goes back to earlier intuitions to combat the theory that man and nature are enemies. Much of the satisfaction it gave must have been due to that.

The boldest, the most modern pattern of belief has grown up in the midst of naturalism. Not so much a protest at the revelations of science, but indeed based on some of the concepts of science itself. Several biologists have seen the sequence of matter—to life—to mind as the emergence of new qualities, not from the outside but from what is within nature. Henri Bergson, Samuel Alexander, and C. Lloyd Morgan have gone a step further, and have presented a view of God not as a complete assumption from the beginning, but as an inherent possibility latent but gradually realizing itself. Just as man's strongest aspiration is to create something higher than himself, so the Life Force has been struggling for countless ages to become conscious of itself. It has made innumerable experiments and mistakes, and has discarded many forms. From inert matter to the amoeba on and on to man, who is only a stage in evolution, it will go on and on to super-man, angels, archangels, and last of all, an omnipotent and omniscient God. Here, as in so many other things, Bernard Shaw, though nobody would take him seriously, was ahead of the biologists and ahead of the philosophers. In the "Don Juan in Hell" episode of *Man and Superman,* he has a character say:

Life is a force which has made innumerable experiments in organizing itself; that the mammoth and the man, the mouse and the magatherium, the flies and fleas and the fathers of the church, are all more or less successful attempts to build up that raw force into higher and higher individuals, the ideal individual being omnipotent, omniscient, infallible, and withal completely, unilludedly self-conscious; in short a god.[3]

That deep belief in the sacredness of the Life Force is implied in many of Shaw's plays. He gave the fullest expression to the religion of emergent evolution in the play (or rather the series of plays) called *Back to Methuselah.* In a scene set in our day, he has his characters explicitly call for the doctrine of Creative Evolution. They say, "[Creative Evolution] is going to be the religion of the twentieth century: a religion that has its intellectual roots in philosophy and science, just as medieval Christianity had its intellectual roots in Aristotle." [4] To illustrate his thesis, Shaw writes a series of historical scenes from the Garden of Eden to the time thousands of years from now, when men have almost cast off flesh and matter, to dwell in pure spirit. The scenes of Adam and Eve form one of the most charming poems in modern literature. Adam, and especially Eve, listen to the Voice and to the Serpent, but themselves decide to create both birth and death. At first they have two impossible alternatives: either to face living forever or total extinction by accidental death. Shaw is certain that both theories of endless life and total extinction are wrong, and life could have no meaning under such conditions. But when Eve invents birth, and that permits Adam to set a finite limit to individual life, then the processes of will, life, and conception are started. The serpent

[3] George Bernard Shaw, *Man and Superman,* Brentano's, New York, 1928.
[4] George Bernard Shaw, *Back to Methuselah,* Brentano's, New York, 1922.

whispers to Eve, "Imagination is the beginning of creation. You imagine what you desire: you will what you imagine: and at last you create what you will." [5] Thus Shaw puts mind, will, purpose, at the very center of the universe, in sharp contrast to the Darwinians who wanted a dead, cold nature without mind or heart.

Maxwell Anderson was the next dramatist to express the religion of emergent evolution. He did not have the rich philosophical and scientific resources of Shaw. He belonged to the generation of Joseph Wood Krutch that still took seriously the belief that nature was cold and indifferent to man. Yet in the face of that desperate thought, he had, from the belief in evolution and the belief in the power and importance of man's inner vision, a strong and bold hope. In 1935, he showed the disillusioned old father in *Winterset* finding proof of man's spirit in the bravery and love of the young couple. He expresses a religious belief, similar to the belief of Luka in *The Lower Depths,* but even more definitely stated in terms of an evolutionary view of the universe. Notice that he still views the outer world as dark and cold. The old father says:

On this star, in this hard star-adventure, knowing not what the fires mean to right and left, nor whether a meaning was intended or presumed, man can stand up and look out blind, and say: in all these turning lights I find no clue, only a masterless night, and in my blood no certain answer, yet is my mind my own, yet is my heart a cry toward something dim in distance, which is higher than I am and makes me emperor of the endless dark even in seeking.[6]

Even more in 1939, after Spain had gone down before Franco, Anderson felt the spirit of man was lonely in the cold, empty spaces under the moon. Still he finds in man's choice, in man's ability to fight and die for his beliefs, a basis for hope. "Now that the sky's found empty," one character in *Key Largo* says, "a man has to be his own god for himself." [7] At the end of the play, the American deserter from Spain finds that he must stop compromising, and the blind old father of

[5] *Ibid.*
[6] Maxwell Anderson, "Winterset," *Eleven Verse Plays, 1929–1939,* Harcourt, Brace & Company, New York, 1940, copyright by Maxwell Anderson.
[7] *Ibid.,* "Key Largo."

the girl proclaims his belief in the future and in the destiny of man
to move upward toward a view of God, no matter how frightening
the cold wind from off the dead stars. The blind father says:

> Where this voyage started
> we don't know, nor where it will end, nor whether
> it has a meaning, nor whether there is good
> or evil, whether man has a destiny
> or happened here by chemical accident—
> all this we never know. And that's our challenge—
> to find ourselves in this desert of dead light-years,
> blind, all of us, in a kingdom of the blind,
> living by appetite in a fragile shell
> of dust and water; yet to take this dust
> and water and our range of appetites
> and build them toward some vision of a god
> of beauty and unselfishness and truth—
> could we ask better of the mud we are
> than to accept the challenge, and look up
> and search for god-head?
>
> . . . .
>
> Over and over again the human race
> climbs up out of the mud, and looks around,
> and finds that it's alone here; and the knowledge
> hits it like a blight—and down it goes
> into the mud again.
> Over and over again we have a hope
> and make a religion of it—and follow it up
> till we're out on the topmost limb of the tallest tree
> alone with our stars—and we don't dare to be there,
> and climb back down again.
> It may be that the blight's on the race once more—
> that they're all afraid—and fight their way to the ground.
> But it won't end in the dark. Our destiny's
> the other way. There'll be a race of men
> who can face even the stars without despair,
> and think without going mad.[8]

[8] *Ibid.*

If Anderson cannot reach as cheerful and warm a vision of the evolutionary religion as Bernard Shaw, it is because Anderson still holds the old view that separates nature from man. If man is totally apart from nature, and nature a cold, blind, purposeless force, then man's dreams and illusions are either completely irrelevant and doomed to defeat, or at most desperate means by which man finds his own purpose.

III

Yet modern drama has not left the matter there. While only a few have set about building a new view of nature, others have discovered there is another way out—an excellent way out, or rather a way in. If man is driven back to his inner self by the thought that external nature shows no sign of God, a number of dramatists of the past twelve or thirteen years have gone on from there and in man's inner life have found a basis for belief. If man finds only the empty sky when he looks at external nature, he has found deep channels to God by looking into his own soul.

There may be many reasons for the enormous popularity of fantasy, dreams, and illusions in the drama of the past ten or eleven years. We do have more insanity and do read far more about psychological states than we used to. But I am convinced also that audiences are eager to explore patterns of faith, illusion, and belief, that suggest an idealism not present in the popular scientific picture of the world. Saroyan's comic pinball machines and horse races are challenges to belief. The bell in the novel and play *A Bell for Adano* is a focus for the hopes and belief in a rebirth of an old tradition of folk and democracy. Even the colossal rabbit, Harvey, is proof that man can believe.

Perhaps the most crucial play in this new turn to images of the inner mind is Philip Barry's *Here Come the Clowns*. It celebrates in 1938 the coming together of religion and psychoanalysis—a coming together that already threatens to become as potent as a mixture of alcohol and gasoline. Barry had already written an easy fantasy of psychoanalysis in *Hotel Universe* and an easy comedy of religious influence in *Joyous Season*. But now he did not feel either one was so easy. He wanted to face all the destructive possibilities of the release of the subconscious—to pull the last mask of illusion off the surface of reality and find at the rock bottom of the human mind the inextinguishable will toward God. He presents a stagehand who believes he is to meet God in a drinking dive where the vaudeville artists— all masters of illusion—gather after the performance. The magician, or the illusionist, as he insists on being called, is an amateur psychoanalyst. He strips off the illusion from several performers by putting the vaudeville dwarf on his knee and letting him echo people's thoughts. But instead of curing them, as the fantasy scenes in *Hotel Universe* had done, this process leaves them far worse off than before. Clancy, the stagehand, has the most painful time of all. His former wife tells him that the little girl he had loved—his fondest memory —was not even his own daughter. The illusionist tricks him out of his hope of finding a visible form of God, but still, as he is dying, he proclaims the indomitable will of man to believe in God.

As though that play had won the full right for the spirit of man to speak directly to God and ignore the statistical external world, there immediately appeared that young Lochinvar from the West, William Saroyan. I am well aware that Saroyan is much too sentimental and sweet for some tastes. His plays are exasperatingly diffuse. He ignores the expected logic of the stage. He definitely does not seem to win his belief the hard way; he usually creates no *purgatorio* at all, but exudes happiness and belief and gay fantasy from every pore. But still I am convinced that the plays and some of the short stories of William Saroyan are of great historical importance. Let Barry's *Here Come the Clowns* serve as the *purgatorio* for Saroyan, for Saroyan takes off from that subjective basis and carries it to its full conclusion. Through the insight of the human imagination he discovers the goodness of God, and from that the mystic unity and goodness of all nature and all men. There, the dead external world crumbles, and the universe is filled with the love and oneness of God. While we are waiting for the scientists and philosophers to demonstrate that it was all a mistake, that nature is a friendly partner to man, Saroyan takes the short cut and discovers it in his own soul.

The basic assumption of Saroyan [9] is the love of God and in that the wholeness of life and the oneness of all being. Saroyan creates mainly two kinds of characters, or rather two dream symbols which he merely repeats in all his characters. One of them is the man who loves God, and hence has faith and creates self-faith in others. The other image is the man who learns to love God, and is converted from doubt to belief and joy. Those who love God are constantly merging their identity. In several plays father and son are one. In the play *Jim Dandy*, Jim Dandy, Jim Crow the colored boy, and Jim the Maharajah who is a Cherokee Indian, are all one. When Fishkin, the doubter, is converted, then he also is Jim Dandy. In *Decent Birth, Happy Funeral*, there are three Hughmans. One is named Joseph and the others have a father named Joseph and a mother named Mary. All three are the same. When news of the death of one comes, the other takes his place in the coffin for the happy funeral. He jumps up every few minutes expecting news of the birth of his son, while the clown goes on with his funeral sermon, "The man gone may be the one who's arriving, while the one coming may be the one who is leaving."

The wholeness of life includes all opposites: inhale and exhale, aloneness and oneness, life and death, sadness and joy, sentiment and comedy, philosophy and horseplay. Many people dismiss Saroyan, because the horseplay seems imbedded in the whole fabric of his vision. They have missed the philosophy, but it is there. Saroyan would say that if you discover God through the inner dream, if you discover your kinship with all things through the *aloneness* of the inner dream, then the whole of God's world will be lit up with joy. Read the following passage from *The Beautiful People* and you will see that Saroyan is proclaiming a new view of the universe—a view that echoes Plato and Whitman, but one that completely overturns the popular scientific view at the beginning of the century. Jonah is the character who is speaking:

My church is the whole blooming universe and mice are as much a part of its magnificence as men, if they only knew. We are alive with all other

[9] Here I am indebted to the unpublished Master's thesis of Bedford Thurman, *The Dream World of Religious Mysticism in the Plays of William Saroyan*, State University of Iowa, 1948.

things alive, from the mite to the whale. Pole star and pyramid, man . . . The image of the pyramid to the human mind is the image of our grace as men. The slaves who built the pyramid—the thousands of them, over the hundreds of years—did not know the majesty of the thing being made. But the *image* of that thing began where it ended—in the living human mind. The line goes from one to the other: from the heart to the star, and from the star to the pyramid and from the pyramid back to the heart. From *one* thing to *all* things. They're all *one,* to be seen as a whole majesty, or not to be seen at all. I choose to see, since I am by nature a religious man. . . . It's not enough to make a record of the world—it's necessary to change it! And you cannot begin to change it from the *outside*. The image of the good must first be real to the *mind* before it can inhabit substance and occupy space. My world is myself and my kinship with all other things—and my delight is my children.[10]

Saroyan is as much interested in dreams as any of the surrealists— indeed all his plays have a dreamlike quality. He is constantly playing with illusion and fantasy. But how radically different his use of dreams is from the surrealists'! They use dreams as a therapeutic device—the stream of consciousness, or dream painting—to reduce the agony of a mind sick from beating against a dead world of matter. Saroyan uses dreams to release the spontaneous creative power of a soul that has discovered God. Further, his plays are constantly concerned with how the dreams become reality. Kitty in *The Time of Your Life* looks like a cheap helpless streetwalker in the eyes of the cynical detective. But Joe, the man who believes, makes her listen to her own dreams of herself, and by his faith she becomes what she dreams. In the beginning is the dream. It is the dream which creates the outer world. Joe says, "I believe dreams sooner than statistics." [11]

IV

In 1940, a very similar religious development appeared in a play of Clifford Odets. Just five years before, Odets had appeared suddenly with three strong plays, all looking toward the reorganization of

[10] William Saroyan, *The Beautiful People, Three Plays By Saroyan,* Harcourt, Brace & Company, New York, 1941.

[11] William Saroyan, *The Time of Your Life,* Harcourt, Brace & Company, New York, 1939.

man's social and economic systems. Man had only himself to depend on, and when he saw his way, he was ready to act, to change the external world. But by 1940, when Odets writes the play, *Night Music,* he sees man's problem as purely a problem of the inner spirit. Now it is no social scheme that is all to blame. Steve Takis is bitter and tormented as he is trying to come out of the tunnel of the depression. He loses his one chance at a job by a series of accidents. But he regains his belief in himself and his belief in America. It is partly the girl he meets, but even more it is the help of a guardian angel who follows him constantly and rescues him from chance and despair. That guardian angel is an old police detective named Abe Rosenberger. About to die from cancer, he has learned compassion from his own suffering. When he learns that Steve's mother died of cancer, he feels a special bond. He says, "These higher class diseases are international, like music." [12] Here compassion is more than that need for human pity and sympathy voiced in *The Lower Depths* and *Juno and the Paycock.* Here it is become an allegorical concept, a personified force that transforms human beings. The hero is no longer the self-reliant figure of the striker in *Waiting for Lefty.* Here he is a helpless mortal, as dependent on his guardian angel as the faithless characters in Saroyan. Compassion as a guardian angel seems to me definitely a religious concept.

Odets presented very similar characters and a very similar point of view in writing and directing the movie *None But the Lonely Heart,* based on the novel by Richard Llewellyn. The bitter, lonely wanderer stays to help his mother in her secondhand shop, when he learns she is about to die of cancer. Under the pressure of poverty each one gives in to temptation and lands in jail. The pain of the action is given meaning by the bond of sympathy and affection between the helpless, terrified mother and son. Each finds a guardian angel—the mother in a Jewish dealer, the son in an old Cockney who had lost his son in the First World War.

It may have been the coming of the war, or perhaps it would have happened anyway, but a number of people in the early nineteen hun-

---

[12] Clifford Odets, *Night Music,* Random House, New York, 1940.

dred and forties turned from concern with the external social order to concern for the inner man, and that led many thinkers to larger philosophical and religious problems. One strong indication of the new direction was Koestler's novel, *Arrival and Departure*. The psychiatrist in the book can explain all the details of the spiritual crisis of the young man, but she cannot explain them away. Koestler says farewell to the pragmatic concern with external effects, and points to the existence of inner causes. Man's character and ethics and will are far more durable entities than any external symptoms of neuroses.

So, at the same time that Saroyan is talking seriously of grace and oneness with God and oneness with all nature, and Odets is talking about compassion, Robert Emmet Sherwood seriously quotes St. Paul on Tribulation. His doctor in *There Shall Be No Night* had been looking forward, almost like a character in Shaw, to the gradual emergence of enough knowledge and consciousness to control even the violence of human nature, but in the crisis of the war it is to more definite religious concepts he turns. "We glory in tribulations; knowing that tribulation worketh patience; and patience, experience; and experience, hope." [13]

It was also during the war that James Bridie brought out *Mr. Bolfry,* a fantasy of the visit of the devil to the home of a Scotch minister, where the young people are too modern to believe in a personal devil. The existence of Hitler and the war seems full justification for a return to the old belief in the reality of evil—and the positive use of evil as a challenge and trial for the good.

I am including little about the obviously religious plays. I believe their patterns of belief are much easier to discern, while the reader might have failed to notice these other plays that are seriously concerned with man's relation to God, to earth, and to his fellow man.

One can distinguish three main approaches to religious drama in this age. The first way is to dramatize biblical events in the idiom and psychology of the present day. *Tobias and the Angel* and *Family Portrait* have been very effective as religious fantasies, though slightly

[13] Robert Sherwood, *There Shall Be No Night,* Charles Scribner's Sons, New York, 1940.

apocryphal. The masterpiece of this method is, of course, *Green Pastures,* considered by many the finest play of the twentieth century. Notice that it approaches the evolutionary position of Shaw and Anderson, in showing that even deity changes and learns and grows by time and suffering.

The second approach seeks an exaltation in method, as well as subject. It fuses modern poetry and modern stage techniques with the methods of the miracle plays, to dramatize some religious figure of the past. I would mention *Jacob's Dream* of Beer-Hoffman, and two plays of the annual Canterbury Festival, Dorothy Sayers's *Zeal of Thy House* and Eliot's *Murder in the Cathedral.*

The third method is to dramatize a contemporary religious problem. Many readers are doubtless familiar with the delightful *Father Malachy's Miracle,* about a miracle that had to be undone—it caused such embarrassment.

The most widely discussed recent play about religious problems is Eliot's *The Cocktail Party.* For years Eliot had bitterly satirized the dry materialism of the modern world, and in *Murder in the Cathedral* had dramatized the medieval saint who found in martyrdom a spiritual alternative to the ways of the world. His women of Canterbury knew they were capable only of humble living, but looked to their leader for an act, a suffering, to redeem them. Eliot takes up the same alternatives of martyrdom and humility in a modern setting in *The Cocktail Party.* As one of his alternatives is to accept the world, he uses the traditional form of the comedy of manners—since the Restoration one of the strongest traditions of English drama. But what a difference from the Restoration tradition! There one adjusted to the social world with tremendous zest, making an art form, a game of wit, out of man's social activities; Eliot's worldly couple learn to make the best of a bad job, and carry on at a cocktail party, adjusted in humility to a world without spirit or meaning.

Eliot's other character, Celia, chooses the way of Thomas à Becket. Like the characters of Saroyan, she has discovered that everyone is alone. But her other discovery, a sense of sin, leads in the opposite direction. Where Saroyan's characters, from that aloneness, reach a sense of oneness with God and hence can look on the world and find it good, Celia finds an unworthiness in herself and in the world for which she must atone by some desperate choice that will take her outside of herself and outside of the world. News of her martyrdom floats back like a strange mocking echo to the new cocktail party where the others carry on the burden of living. To those who like Saroyan, Eliot's repudiation of the modern world, indeed much of the revival of the concept of sin, may seem like a religious acceptance of Thomas Huxley's vision of a cold dead nature. Indeed Huxley's grandson, Aldous Huxley, has likewise turned from the world and from the self, to seek new religious patterns of dedication and humility. Perhaps these years of worlds in collision seem to prove the nineteenth century vision of a soulless world. *The Cocktail Party* is a very successful mixture of medieval mysticism, nineteenth century science, Restoration comedy, and twentieth century psychiatry, presided over by a charming spirit-medium who can cure you in one sitting.

The best dramatization of a modern problem is undoubtedly Carroll's *Shadow and Substance,* one of the finest plays of the century. It has allegorical meanings on several different levels, but its main vision is of man's fresh, tender faith being crushed between two conflicting forces—one too traditional, too devoted to the old, while the other is too radically striving for the new. The girl of faith loves them both, and through love and compassion they come to understand each other. Here again it is her inner dream that is the beginning of love and faith. Just as with Saroyan or Odets, anyone with the grace of that inner dream can transform the life of anyone she touches.

The best of these religious plays have one thing in common with the other plays I have been talking about. They gain their belief by plumbing all the way to the depths. Modern drama is written indeed *de profundis.* The whole course of modern drama has been a *purgatorio,* facing a world that nineteenth century science and nineteenth century rationalism said was dead and cold, and indifferent to all man's dreams. The scientists and philosophers have in the meantime done much to correct that old view and present the world as a friendly home for man. But the playwrights have already discovered in a subjective idealism that if man starts with the inner dream, as the source for religious faith, he can recreate the outer world in the image of faith.

XV

THE CONTEMPORARY JEW AND HIS JUDAISM

BY

JUDAH GOLDIN

There are two passages in Ignazio Silone's *Bread and Wine* (which had already appeared in English translation in 1936) that I want to quote despite the fact that they are very long. They are a characterization and verdict of, at one and the same time, recent history, moral development, and literary expression.

The first selection has to do with Don Paolo (really the professional revolutionary Spina in disguise) after he has had a long conversation with the girl Cristina. For a while Don Paolo sat and wrote down some thoughts which the conversation during the day now stimulated. But after five sentences:

He stopped writing and thought of the naive illusions with which he had entered his first Socialist group. His real reason for leaving the Church while still so young had been not because he had grown out of it spiritually or criticized it intellectually, but because of the profound disgust with which he reacted to the abyss which he perceived between its practical actions and the words it preached. That disgust had provided his sole impulse for joining the Socialists. He had not been a Marxist then, having only become one after joining the Socialist fold. But now he had been a Marxist for fifteen years, and it had become his profession. Alas for all professions that have for their ultimate aim the salvation of the world! For the sake of saving others, you ended by losing yourself. . . . Don Paolo saw clearly now that his return to Italy had been at heart an attempt to escape from that profession, to get away from the Marxist bureaucracy, to return to the rank-and-file and recapture in action the enthusiasm that had originally led him into the movement. This discovery left him perplexed. What had those fifteen years devoted to the political struggle been worth? He went to bed, but the question would not let him sleep. He got up again, sat down at the table, reopened his notebook, and wrote:

"Is it possible to take part in political life, to devote oneself to the service of a party, and remain sincere?

"Has not truth, for me, become party truth? Has not justice, for me, become party justice?

"Have not party interests ended by deadening all my discrimination between moral values? Do I, too, not despise them as petty-bourgeois prejudices?

"Have I escaped from the opportunism of a decadent Church only to fall into bondage to the opportunism of a party?

"What has become of my enthusiasm of that time? By putting politics before anything else, before all other spiritual needs, have I not impoverished, sterilized my life? Has it not meant that I have neglected deeper interests?

"There are remarkable potentialities in man. . . . These potentialities are now exploited by all the reactionary institutions. If, as in my case, they are directed towards the proletariat, what becomes of them in professional politics? Is it right that they should be stifled? Is it right that they should be combatted? Is a true and lasting revolution possible without them?"

When he came to the end of the page Don Paolo read through what he had written. He noticed that all he had done was to draw up a list of questions to which his divided mind could give no certain answer. He went on sitting for a long time with suspended pen, but he was not able to write anything else.[1]

The second passage, also not a short one, is an account of a meeting Spina the revolutionary has with an old friend, Uliva, a musician, whom Spina has not seen in many years. Uliva, too, has been an enemy of Fascism, and as a result has suffered imprisonment, torture, starvation. Now he is living in a filthy room withdrawn from his former associates, no less than from the enemies. Spina tries to stir him to action once again, and Uliva replies:

"There is something corpse-like even about the dictatorship (*i.e.,*

[1] Ignazio Silone, *Bread and Wine,* translated by Gwenda David and Eric Mosbacher, Harper & Brothers, New York, 1937, chapter IV.

Fascism) that stifles us. For a long time it has not been a movement, even a reactionary movement; all it is is a bureaucracy. But what is the opposition? Another bureaucracy that aspires to totalitarian domination in its turn, in the name of different ideas and on behalf of different interests. If it does conquer, as it probably will, we shall thus pass from one tyranny to another. We shall have a so-called economic revolution, thanks to which we shall have state bread, state boots and shoes, state shirts and pants, state potatoes and state green peas, just as we now have state railways, state quinine, state salt, state matches, and state tobacco. Will that be a technical advance? Certainly it will. But it will be the basis of an official, compulsory doctrine, a totalitarian orthodoxy which will use every means, from the cinema to terrorism, to extirpate heresy and tyrannize over individual thought. A Red inquisition will succeed the present inquisition, a Red censorship the present censorship. Instead of the present deportations there will be Red deportations, of which dissident revolutionaries will be the favorite victims. Our future bureaucracy will identify itself with Labor and Socialism and persecute everyone who goes on thinking with his own head, denouncing him as a paid agent of the industrialists and the landlords, just as the present bureaucracy identifies itself with patriotism and suppresses all its opponents, denouncing them as traitors bought by foreign gold. . . .

"Illusions, illusions. . . . You have already become simply a group of professional revolutionaries. The regenerating passion by which we were animated in the student group has become an ideology, a network of fixed ideas, a cobweb. That is the proof that there is no escape for you, either. . . . That is the destiny of every new idea. It is crystallized in formulas so that it may be propagated. It is intrusted to a body of interpreters so that it may be preserved. That body is prudently recruited, sometimes specifically paid for its task, and is subject to a superior authority whose duty it is to resolve doubts and suppress deviations from the line indicated by the masters. Thus every new idea invariably ends by becoming fixed, inflexible, parasitical, and reactionary. And if it becomes the official doctrine of the state, no more escape is possible. A carpenter or a laborer can perhaps adapt himself even to a regime of totalitarian orthodoxy, and eat, digest, procreate in peace; but for an intellectual there is no escape. He must either bend the knee and enter the ranks of the dominant clerks, or resign himself to hunger and defamation and be killed off at the first favorable opportunity." [2]

[2] *Ibid.*, chapter VIII.

I

These two long quotations had to do with the Italian, the Continental intellectual of Christian upbringing; yet they are as much a vivid and unambiguous account of the journey of many modern Jewish intellectuals and writers—and these amongst the most articulate—a journey not only which they made individually or personally, but to which they have given expression, in other words, a journey of the literature they have produced. Some minor details in Spina's or Uliva's reflections might have to be modified slightly in the case of the Jewish artist—for example, unlike Spina who maintained that he was *not* alienated from the Church on intellectual grounds, many Jewish writers, though they hardly knew very much of Judaism, nevertheless, said at first that in its idiom they could not find a vocabulary for their deepest needs. Except, however, for such minor differences, it was to some Marxist pattern of interpretation and judgment that the young Jewish intellectual was attracted and by it he was guided. Perhaps on *re*reading the stories and novels by Jews of the twenties and thirties this is too sweeping a generalization. The term, "Marxist," perhaps does not apply to quite as many of them as one expects. But if an orthodox Marxism was not what they had adopted, the following at least is true: Marxist insights were appropriated; the principal drama which they thought fit to record, and to use as the point of departure for their major criticisms of society and their essays on Man, was that of social tension. The individual in relation to his immediate environment—where poverty degraded and failure, as well as success, could be seen in a materialist context—was the theme they elaborated at great lengths. The economic, the political, the social protest story, dominated expression. Jews without money or with money or affected by a money economy, were by and large the subject, when the Jewish writer did turn to describe the Jewish world or Jewish character.

Consider, for example, Meyer Levin's *The Old Bunch,* the longest and most earnest and most ambitious novel of the naturalistic-sociological genre about Jews in America. Who and what are the main characters? (There are certainly no heroes, not even chief protagonists.) As individuals they are not Levin's concern. It is the whole bunch, the fate of the whole bunch, he wants to depict and tell. That they are Jews is an important sociological datum for the author—thus their associations with one another are established; thus they constitute a neighborhood, a "section" in a large city, Chicago. Their being thrown together by the fact that they are Jews and by the events in Chicago (strikes, the battles of political parties, the emergence of gangsters, the depression) determines the lines of their lives and careers. But of the more than two dozen characters in a volume close to 1,000 pages, only one attempts to discover a correlation between what he is and the content of the religion or the culture known as Judaism. I do not mean that Levin should have shown the relevance of Judaism to these characters. If Judaism was irrelevant to their thought and feeling, and he was out to describe these people, it would have been worse than dishonest to include what was not in the scene. My point is, however, that just such a scene was the characteristic material or subject for the writer; and undercurrent always moved the suggestion that none of the lives in the novel might have been twisted out of shape if there had been abundance instead of poverty, decent housing instead of slums, if the parents had not been immigrants, if a whole generation could have been spared the demoralizing concomitants of an economic depression. Their problems were problems which grew out of their collision with general social phenomena, not out of an encounter with the tradition of their ancestors; and to the solution of their problems, it was taken for granted that Judaism had nothing to contribute.

I do not want to suggest that Jewish writers alone were caught up in this naturalist-socialist idiom or world view. The very opposite in fact was the case—for in that same period, the decade and a half after the First World War, appeared the works of Hemingway, of Farrell, of Dos Passos. Jewish writers whose theme was Jews simply employed in their task the language and the method adopted by the militant writers generally. Moreover, it would be untrue to say that *all* the writers—or even the same writer all the time—wrote novels or stories of so-called "social significance," ruthlessly reporting the devastations of the working class and the unemployed and the frustrated in capitalist society. Nevertheless, a review of the most influential works of the period reveals that the naturalist-sociological-socialist novel met with a most immediate response and articulated most eloquently what men and women were feeling acutely: to wit, that the moral and theological emphases of the past were meaningless to the contemporary.

Levin's novel, however, appeared just about the time when a turning point had already been reached: and his own novel indeed exemplifies this. By the middle of the thirties, more so at the end of the decade, and quite manifestly as the forties got under way, questions which many of the artists had been asking themselves in their diaries, questions like those Spina had put to himself, became persistent, stubbornly refused to be silenced or tabled, and little by little came to be expressed out loud and in print, until the new tone of voice was unmistakable. In part, no doubt, this questioning arose as a result of the Russian purges, in part because of the Nazi-Soviet pact, in part because the New Deal brought some measure of recovery, in part, too, because the recognition that Nazism-Fascism had to be crushed moderated some of the bitterness toward whatever might be associated with the American way of life (so-called). Surely, however, in part the questioning of their recently held premises was the result of the intellectual's and artist's independent re-examination of their thinking and commitments. Again like Uliva and even Spina, the writers were beginning to discover that their original passion had become an ideology, with a tyranny every bit as thoroughgoing as the tyrannies they were attacking, and an orthodoxy every bit as demanding as the orthodoxies they had rejected.

II

Compare, for example, two stories, one which even in 1935 was included in an anthology [3] of Jewish literature as an expression of "new frontiers," namely, "The Revolution and the Zussmans," by David

---

[3] The anthology referred to is *The Jewish Caravan*, edited by Leo W. Schwarz, Farrar & Rinehart, Inc., New York, 1935.

Bergelson,[4] and a story in 1947, by Jacob Glatstein called "Citizen God." [5] In Bergelson's story we have a description of a middle class, well-to-do Jew whom the Russian revolution has ruined economically —consequently, the whole pattern of his life has been broken by this event. With humor and grace—but no less effectiveness—Bergelson points up the uselessness, the whining emptiness of the Zussman parents and daughter who still long for their former comforts, and refuse (even inability is a refusal!) to cooperate with their neighbors in the collective settlement. The two Zussman sons, ne'er-do-wells formerly, now fling themselves into a peasant and pioneer life, not only come to terms, but actually identify themselves with the hopes and activities of the new regime; and, as a result, alienate themselves entirely from their parents. Before long, the sons and the rest of the family hardly address each other. Never does Bergelson crudely parade his sympathies; but in the portraits he draws of the eternally groaning mother, the fantastical, unworldly planning father, the sullenness of the spoiled daughter, and the down-to-earth, hard working sons, there is no mistaking where *he* finds dignity, with whom *he* identifies the new age.

In the 1947 story, Glatstein likewise takes us to the Soviet Union. This time it is the story of the visit of an elderly Jew (he calls himself Citizen God, no less) to the home of some minor commissar or official, Moissaye Ossipovich. Citizen God's visit is quite an occasion and all sorts of neighbors drop in. Obliquely various kinds of criticism are soon voiced. Says one old maid: "They tell me a new order has arrived. The sun has risen on the common people. I—I am the same. . . . They have built a paradise, a paradise on earth. Me—they try to distract me by giving me work." [6] And what a rush of reminiscences all at once! Looking at Citizen God, our commissar begins to think, not at all unwillingly, of an *ethrog*.[7] There is recollection of the upstanding and charitable human beings the commissar's grandparents

---

[4] David Bergelson, "The Revolution and the Zussmans," *Menorah Journal*, XVII, 3, December, 1929, p. 239.

[5] Jacob Glatstein, "Citizen God," *Commentary*, III, 5, May, 1947.

[6] *Ibid*.

[7] The citron used in the religious observances during *Sukkot*, the Jewish Feast of Booths.

were; and when an occasional scoundrel of the past is remembered, he is no longer a specimen, an inevitable byproduct of a wicked system, but simply a human sinner, you might say—for after all, there are always some bad individuals everywhere, as everyone readily admits. When Citizen God retires for the night with Moissaye's sons —all evening they have been fascinated by the man—he teaches them a verse from Scripture (the first verse of the Bible, "In the beginning God created the heavens and the earth"). The whole story is an almost lyrical commentary on the refreshment, the human and humane feeling, introduced into that collectivized and summer hot community by the pious old man. At one point in the conversation he makes a few remarks that serve as a succinct estimate of and sentence on the Marxist Utopia:

"This is a world?" he asks. "A piece of cobweb! A squeak. A puff. Now —when an Ezriel used to lug his pails of water and fill up a poor man's empty barrel. Or when your Uncle Mendel—not to let a Sabbath be disgraced—used to leave his couple of coins in some poverty stricken home . . . then it would become something like a world. Otherwise? This way? Ah, me . . . call it a world?" [8]

The tables seem to be turned! Wit and irony are now aimed at a target which only recently had been not the target at all, but the position *from* which to shoot one's arrows.

Or another example, which furnishes a splendid coincidence—and will also serve admirably as a transition to the next point worth calling attention to.

In *The Old Bunch* (the date of its appearance, you will recall, is 1937) there is a description of a Passover *Seder* celebration in the apartment of one of the bunch, the second generation Jews in America. Invited to the Passover service and dinner, by the way, is also one non-Jewish couple "who were dying to see a Jewish Passover ceremony"! [9] The evening begins with cocktails and little caviar canapes on *mazzot*. In the center of the table is a layercake, topped with a doll in a long flowing robe, with white cotton for a beard pasted to the doll's chin. Typical of the remarks around the table is the one,

[8] Glatstein, *op. cit.*

[9] Meyer Levin, *The Old Bunch*, The Viking Press, New York, 1937.

"If you can't eat bread, eat cake!" [10] (That is why the host had bought the cake as a centerpiece.) There are placecards with actors' faces, meant to be "cartoons" of biblical personalities. As caps everyone wears party paper hats generally found at New Year's Eve parties. Hot biscuits are served, and the maid carries in an immense, sugar baked ham.

One is suddenly overcome by violent revulsion from the vulgarity (not the author's, I hasten to add, though this should be unnecessary: but Levin was completely misunderstood by the self-appointed custodians of Jewish public relations) and vulgarization of these individuals. Levin has indeed captured a mood, an attitude and mannerism which had become epidemic in certain quarters. And it is in the conclusion of that episode that Levin reveals, perhaps unwittingly (one is, nevertheless, justified in taking this as a symbol, even if Levin was innocent of such intention), the turning point which I have been speaking about. For as one cheap parody of the sacred night is piled on the next, and the horror of the evening becomes unbearable, Sam Eisen (one of the principal characters in the book) rises and moves to the door—even his wife cannot stop him—mumbling in thought: "This is where I get off. This is where I get off." [11]

III

It is not too much to say that this is, in fact, where the modern Jewish artist did get off. He had not given up wit or satire, even iconoclasm; nor, as we shall see shortly, did he reembrace the religious tradition. But the cynicism and the disillusion which had been turned on the tradition now recoiled on cynicism and disillusionment themselves. And as a result, a new willingness to reinspect the religious tradition appeared.

Thus, witness another story on the Passover *Seder,* this time eleven years later by Hamlen Hunt, "Tonight We Eat Leaning." Here, too, is a *Seder* of young Jews who feel far removed—in their immediate interests, in their operating convictions, in their education and associa-

[10] *Ibid.*
[11] *Ibid.*

tions—from religious observances and belief. To this *Seder* also comes a non-Jew who asks, "What is this celebration?" [12] There are cocktails this time also to begin the evening. Even some stupid wit occurs, as when one of the men says, "When haggadah go, haggadah go." [13] And as the service is read, none of the people around the table is at all clear what meaning the ritual can possibly have for him, for all of them. What they have learned from Freud makes what they now enact embarrassing to them, downright disquieting. No, at least one of them, "in the core of his heart," is convinced that "religion is bad." [14] Yet a strange thing happens, despite the resistance of their usual attitude and certainties and rational will. The words they recite weave a spell which they cannot shake off. Memories rise to the surface of their awareness that are amusing, but stinging also. And when the service and dinner are over, "They were slow to depart. For a brief time, no one quite knew why, they had been joined together, around food, and perhaps by words: they had remembered a past, and hoped for a future: and no one wanted to break the spell." [15]

Where Sam Eisen got off, Hamlen Hunt's characters got on. Which is where?

To say that there has been a return to belief, would be absolutely without warrant. Perhaps this is what religious institutions and their caretakers would like to feel, but for such a feeling there is no basis in fact. What is it then that has taken place? Briefly this: a former self-confidence has collapsed; a former aggressiveness toward religious cult and even principle has been tempered. What their ancestors represented was dismissed gaily by the writers in the twenties and thirties. This has not been followed by a readoption of the ancestral tradition, but by a romantic tentativeness toward it, by a reexamination of it, by an esthetic interest, by an attempt to study its meaning in its own framework and in the refraction from recently acquired discoveries and parables. If I may borrow an expression from Leslie Fiedler,[16]

---

[12] Hamlen Hunt, "Tonight We Eat Leaning," *Commentary,* V, 4, April, 1948.

[13] *Ibid.;* the prayerbook with the order of service for the home on Passover eve is called *Haggadah.*

[14] *Ibid.*

[15] *Ibid.*

[16] Leslie Fiedler, *Commentary,* VI, 6, December, 1948, p. 582.

for the modern Jewish intellectual, the ethos of his ancestors is approached not by belief but by the suspension of disbelief. In short, rejection has been succeeded by nostalgia.

An interesting development has, therefore, taken place. A universe with which the *Maskilim* [17] were impatient (to put it mildly), and from which the generation of the twenties and thirties wanted above all to escape, to forget at all costs, has now been dug up, has now become an object of delight, sometimes even of inspiration, has been made into a subject of affectionate and tolerant humor, and has been explored for hints, philosophical, literary, psychoanalytic, theological, ethical, mythological. Lionel Trilling, for example, reflecting recently on the nature of Wordsworth's poetry and the modern uninterest in it, summons up remembrances of his own boyhood when he sat reading a rabbinic text instead of reciting the required prayers. Now, he tells us, through the content and spirit of that text (*Pirke Abot*), to which he has devoted some study of late, an essential element in Wordsworth is made manifest. In Wordsworth and the Synagogue Fathers Trilling discovers a "quietism, which is not in the least a negation of life, but on the contrary an affirmation of life so complete that it needed no saying." [18] Wordsworth made intelligible by the Rabbis! Even more significant. Out of a total of fifty short stories published by *Commentary* from its first appearance in 1945 until the end of 1949—exclusive of straightforward reminiscences from "the American scene"—seventeen (in other words, one third of all the stories published by the journal) have had as their theme or locus, in one form or another, the tradition, or the world and character of Jews still attached to their tradition, or the young Jew, long absent from the tradition, now brought into contact with part of it. And by a combination of introspection, irony, juxtaposition of the sacred and grotesque, reminiscence (twenty-two of *Commentary*'s stories, almost half, are written in the first person), quotation and even misquotation, a new *mystique* has been created. An excellent

---

[17] The anti-traditionalist intellectuals who were eager to bring enlightenment (*Haskala*) into the lives of their fellow Jews, *i.e.*, to Europeanize and secularize Jewish life and letters. Cf. Jacob S. Raisin, *Haskalah Movement in Russia,* The Jewish Publication Society of America, Philadelphia, 1913.

[18] Kenyon Review, Summer, 1950; the quotation is on p. 488.

illustration of this is furnished by Isaac Rosenfeld's story "Bazaar of the Senses." All kinds of transparent Freudianisms are strewn through the paragraphs; the grandfather is a specimen of *"schlepperei"* (Rosenfeld's own word) of whom the boy, Bernie, cannot help feeling ashamed. There are times the old man disgusts him. Nothing told of the grandfather throughout the story is even remotely attractive. Suddenly, however, as we approach the conclusion, a transformation occurs. The old man is with his hasidic cronies, in a corner of the room sit two chess players (plaster cast model of the Jewish thinker!), a hasidic melody rises in the room, and in the ecstasy which follows everyone is caught, the young Bernie as well as the dishevelled and drivelling grandfather, and a transfiguration takes place. "I could see my grandfather transformed into a new person. A look of completeness lay on his face, an expression of gratitude, as if for the ecstatic understanding" [19] to which he had been led. "Though unable to understand, I had shared the experience of that ecstasy, and I, too, felt grateful for it." [20]

Virtually the same outcome in the brilliant story by Paul Goodman, "A Prayer for Dew," the first story published by *Commentary*. A whole assortment of nondescript characters, whose behavior in the synagogue is a parody of what conduct in the synagogue was intended to be, suddenly begin to recite a prayer required by the tradition: a liturgical piece extraordinarily appropriate in its content to these people, and of whose appropriateness the worshippers, amusingly enough, are not even aware: "Renew our days of old, Beloved—uplift our home—Make us like a garden well watered." [21] One catches himself muttering in the end, "How true, how true! How desperately necessary is the need for some reviving shower for regeneration!"

Nor indeed is this all. When Spina and his counterparts discovered the impasse they had reached—that as a result of becoming the servant of a political party, the individual and his discrimination and his normally moral reactions were being submerged, that an ideal become institutionalized was a transubstantiation into political expediency,

[19] Isaac Rosenfeld, "Bazaar of the Senses," *Commentary*, I, 4, February, 1946.
[20] *Ibid.*
[21] Paul Goodman, "A Prayer for Dew," *Commentary*, I, 1, November, 1945.

opportunism, vested interest and tyranny—when the intellectuals made this discovery, there took place a reaction whose effects may well leave a deposit of nihilism behind them.

For what happened as a result of the reaction against what for convenience's sake we have called the literary pattern of the late twenties and thirties? Having once been scalded by total commitment to a philosophy and its institutional agencies, the intellectuals have become extremely reluctant to commit themselves again so completely. Of course this has not always been the case. Witness, for example, some of the contemporary sensational conversions: and Gifford Maxim of Lionel Trilling's *The Middle of the Journey* may serve as an emblem for all these. But far more typical than these has been the detachment from institutional ties, from ritual obligations, and from complete submission to dogmas—whose intellectual consistencies and texture may be studied with appreciation, used, too, as principles of criticism in letters and philosophy, but whose demands may also be resented. For the modern artist cannot, of course, pretend that a century of scholarly research and scientific, psychoanalytic, and anthropological investigation, are as though they had not been. Henceforth, if he is to ally himself with religion—specifically in our case, if the Jewish writer is to ally himself with the Jewish tradition—he can do so, he feels, only to the extent that its doctrines and practices make him more sensitive to the realities and agitations of man and the universe as a whole. In so far as Judaism is capable of doing this for the young writer he will draw upon it; but on the other hand, merely for patriotic reasons, social expediency, group discipline, or abstract piety and exhortation, he will not abandon his independence ("freedom" he knows he has not).

IV

This reluctance to affiliate, this unwillingness to commit oneself wholly or to submit to the Law out of loyalty, has characterized not only the artist as an individual, but also his work. Naturally this is what we would expect, for the dilemmas and certainties of the artist never remain confined to himself. But it is wisest not to leave the fact unstated, lest our study of the works of art be unconsciously deflected into an investigation of the lives of the artists. To come back then to the main point: not only the artist himself, but the literature he has been producing, has become a reflection, a description, an expression—at times it is almost an appeal for understanding and perhaps also sympathy in behalf of the Jew to whom Judaism remains a haunting echo, a source of possible insights, a luggage of folklore not entirely welcome. It is, therefore, a source of inner dialectic and conflict—a fact of existence which one cannot escape, and which, therefore, must be permitted to rise to the surface, must be articulated, must be held under the light and scrutinized: at least thus it will be understood, at least one will not be its ignorant victim (though one may still be helpless against it). The artist's experiences, in short, become typical of his character's. Hence we now begin to meet a new type already in danger of becoming a stereotype. That is the young Jew whose Jewishness or Jewish origin (which he may even try to suppress) achieves a positive function by the very negative nature of his conduct or act (for example, by marriage with a non-Jew)—by the very device, say, that the Jew has chosen as the most effective rupture with his tradition and its commands. As though only through extreme renunciation of what one is will he discover the meaning of what he is.

Thus it turns out in one story ("The Eternal Values" by J. Ayalti [22]) that the only one to respond with piety and an awareness of sanctity to a symbol of the Jewish legacy is the young Christian wife of a refugee—even he, not to speak of his American relations, is bored by the book he has been given in the spirit and as a sign of a great inheritance.

More subtle still is a story by Leslie Fiedler ("Let Nothing You Dismay" [23]), of the little daughter of a young Jew married to a non-Jewish woman. The child has somehow come to suspect that there is an affinity between her father (to her, he looks like Kafka—(!)—whose picture she was once shown) and the word, "Jew." What the word means she does not know, but the sound ("Joo," as she imagines

[22] J. Ayalti, "The Eternal Values," *Commentary*, IV, 6, December, 1947.
[23] Leslie Fiedler, "Let Nothing You Dismay," *Commentary*, V, 3, March, 1948.

the word) has a talismanic quality for her. By means of this word she feels herself especially close to her father and safe from all dangers. And yet the father had been pathetically over eager for the child to be like her mother: that is why he had gone so far as to give the daughter the same name as her mother. The child, however, feels that she is "not a bit like her (mother) really." Of course you may say we have here one more instance of the father-daughter complex. But there is obviously more than that to the story and the relationship. For the child guards the box, on the inside of whose lid she has written the letters "JOO," with the instinct of a conspirator. She never lets the box out of sight; she keeps it under her pillow at night; when by accident it has fallen out of her hands and a visitor picks it up and examines it, the child lets fly at the woman with a truculence which astonishes the father. The Jewishness which has been fastidiously suppressed in this family becomes, then, the source of a kinship, an intimacy which otherwise the father might never have enjoyed.

Or again, there is the story by Ralph Manheim "The Girl Who Loved Seders." Here, too, there is a Jewish husband, Orlansky, and a non-Jewish wife. Has the faith of his fathers become entirely meaningless to the Jewish husband? In a sense certainly, for he is unable to take it literally any longer. But evidently, ever since it left his life—or better still, ever since he turned his back on it, nothing but a nervous intellectuality has taken its place. His wife says to him at one point, after an exasperated moment with him:

"Look at those shabby books. Your intellectual history. The intellectual history of all our friends. Marx, Engels, Lenin, Trotsky. My, what happened then? The Spanish war. The Spanish war brings doubt. Plato. Maybe there's something in academic philosophy after all. The logical positivists turn up in their long overcoats. And don't forget phenomenology. And then Kierkegaard stalks into the room. And Existentialism. And always such passion. Everything changes. Nothing is left of what you used to be. But if you'd been a Jew . . ." [24]

He tries to interrupt her outburst, but she continues:

[24] Ralph Manheim, "The Girl Who Loved Seders," *Commentary*, VII, 3, March, 1949.

"Do you realize . . . that we've had five or six philosophies right here in this room? You'll say it's the fault of the housing shortage. But isn't that too many?" [25]

In the end they go to the Passover *Seder* he had at first refused to attend. So it is once more the non-Jew who has recalled the Jew to the worship of his fathers. Yes, so it would seem. But this is not all—because it is with reluctance, after all, that the Jew is returning, and even that, we discover as we study the story attentively, is only a half way return.

For even after he has agreed to go to the *Seder,* a savage exchange of comments about Jews takes place between them, and for the savageness of the remarks his own attitude toward Judaism and Jews is as much—if not more—responsible as his wife's pitiless words. In a fury he exclaims that he has had enough, he is going to put an end to "it." You cannot be sure you know what he is talking about—very likely he himself does not know. Does he mean that never again will he participate in a *Seder* service, or that he will leave his wife? The answer is anything but a neat alternative. The answer is actually in the song the non-Jewish wife has been humming all evening, a song she had been taught by his pious uncle (the uncle for whom Orlansky "had considerable affection, mingled with considerable animosity"). What is the song—and, in the last analysis, what about the fact, too, that the author is guilty of slovenly quoting—what is the song, if not an epitaph for the self-alienated Jew? "Two hold onto a *tallit:* this one says, I found it; and the other says, I found it." And for all who remember the Talmudic source,[26] the decision is clear—*yahaloḳu,* they divide the *tallit* between them. Neither the uncle nor the wife then will get all of Orlansky; they will have to divide him between them. O, for a Solomon!

And so we come back to our type and to what he seems to say. A full return has for him become impossible—in either direction. Some wounds never heal; some commitments he fears to make, the total ones in particular. In the meantime, too, he has been reading Kafka, and he has not yet recovered from that experience—but that is a story

[25] *Ibid.*
[26] *Mishnah,* edited by Herbert Danby, The Clarendon Press, Oxford, 1933, p. 347.

for some other time. But he no longer believes that it is possible for the tradition of the fathers to be eliminated; nor properly can it be said to be marginal to the life of the Jew. It has become something to be reckoned with, something also to be drawn upon as the Jew tries to understand himself, to understand himself in any context where he occurs, even in a context of withdrawal from the forms and practices of the traditional belief.

V

One word more. The pattern of belief in the past ten or eleven years has certainly changed; but one element has remained constant. It was a moral fervor, a kind of passionate honesty which led the Jewish literary man before and after the First World War to rebel against the tradition and seek the good in a materialist philosophy. He destroyed altars in the conviction that only in this way would injustice vanish, poverty be conquered, society purified, and man regenerated. That philosophy now betrayed him as he witnessed its translation from theory to action. And so he was outraged; because of the same moral fervor he broke with the new creed, and resolved that never again would he give himself over heart and soul to anything, lest he be trapped in its institutional form. An end to expediency at the expense of integrity! *Let this not be underestimated.* The circle has been completed.

XVI

CATHOLIC ORIENTATION IN CONTEMPORARY
FRENCH LITERATURE

BY

WALLACE FOWLIE

The subject of Catholicism and contemporary literature calls up
to mind the especially significant contribution of France. American
literature is quite thoroughly non-Catholic. There has never been in
this country anything that would resemble a Catholic school of letters
or movement in literature. It is true that in 1949 a Catholic magazine
was founded, *Renascence,* concerned with art and literature, but the
title was ill chosen. It is difficult to have a renascence of something
that never existed. Appropriately enough, the first issue of the magazine was given over to a discussion of French Catholic literature.

In American literature of the past there are only a few scattered
names of Catholic writers, such as Louise Guiney and Agnes Rep-
plier. The same state prevails today. Thomas Merton, a convert and
Trappist monk, is an esteemed poet. J. F. Powers, born in 1917, has
distinguished himself with a first volume of short stories, *Prince of
Darkness.* Mr. Powers was discovered in 1943 by *Accent,* a little
magazine published in Illinois. He is a born Catholic who has chosen
for his writing the specialized regionalism of the Minnesota parish
and rectory. Of all the younger Catholic writers of this country,
Powers has achieved, I think, the highest degree of artistic integrity.
His subject matter is specifically Catholic, usually a study of the
American Catholic priest. He is primarily an artist. I find in his writing no trace of the proselytizer or the apologist.

In England, the Catholic influence in literature is felt only slightly
more than in America, although two novelists of today have reached

a high degree of well deserved fame. Graham Greene, a convert, shows in his novels, which are usually in the form of a thriller or a crime story, that theology plays an integral part in his thought about the world and in his feelings for his characters. The adolescent hero, Pinkie, of *Brighton Rock* (1938), has an extraordinary knowledge and understanding of his own evil. He is a murderer who thinks a great deal about the reality of hell and the reality of the terror he feels in himself. Greene is an eschatologist, a writer who is interested in the final things. His books contain an extensive repertory of sinners, many of whom are fugitives from justice, such as the priest in *The Power and the Glory,* also called *The Labyrinthine Way,* of 1940. This pattern of flight is reminiscent of the soul fleeing from God or Satan.

Evelyn Waugh, the other Catholic novelist in England, a convert also, and equally sophisticated, is a penetrating social critic, the recorder of a disintegrating world. By emphasizing the intricately organized modern world and its departmentalized secular culture, he has thrown into relief the emptiness of modern man's inner life. The title of his novel, *A Handful of Dust,* is taken from Eliot's *The Waste Land,* and like the poem, is a document on modern man's conflicting ideologies of positivism, romanticism, and economic liberalism. His, like that of Greene and of other English converts, such as Eric Gill and E. I. Watkin, is no smug Catholicism. He is intensely and alertly self-critical.

But the Catholic literature of France is far more significant than that of England and America. French culture has at all periods of its history brought to Catholicism a very remarkable understanding. It is not exaggerated to say that without a solid understanding of Catholicism, much of French civilization and literature will remain obscure to the foreign student. François Mauriac has recently commented on the art of Graham Greene and particularly on *The Power and the Glory.* Although he recognized all the theological themes of the book, Mauriac said that the religious atmosphere puzzled him. He felt that he was entering upon Christianity through some back door. The French writer, he claims, has a far different approach. His immediate and distant past have given him a familiarity with Catholic problems. His very education taught him, even when he was without firm religious convictions, to take sides with Port Royal or with the Jesuits, with Bossuet or with Fénelon and quietism. Although Mauriac greatly admired the almost secretive way Graham Greene treats the religious problem in his writing, which almost corresponds to the subterranean radiation of grace in the world, he confesses to feeling disoriented and even ill at ease in the world of the English novelist.

I

During the twenty year period between the two world wars, French literature was given over to a very serious self-examination and self-criticism. Catholic critics, especially, had seemed severe in their analyses and reproaches. Henri Massis, as late as 1941, in a book called *Les Idées Restent,* bitterly attacked Gide, Proust, and Valéry for having alienated French intelligence from its real goal, for having undermined the moral precepts of the nation. Claudel has not been sparing of harsh epithets of criticism, in calling the contemporary atmosphere in France morbid and depressing. In time, and in some degree of perspective, such criticism, especially that of Massis, will seem unwarranted and intolerably severe. During the same years, a strong renaissance of Catholic literature and a rehabilitation of Catholic thought were taking place. The study of medieval philosophy, especially St. Thomas, received a new impetus from the teaching of Étienne Gilson, at the Collège de France, and from Jacques Maritain, at the Institut Catholique. Eminent ecclesiastical figures, such as Monseigneur Verdier, participated actively in the Christian Socialist movements. In the art form of the novel, Catholic thought and sensibility were to play an especially important part after 1930.

Georges Bernanos died in 1948 and was at that time claimed by the astute and learned critic, André Rousseaux, as the sole contemporary writer upholding the Catholic tradition in France. It is true that the novels and essays of Bernanos are being read and commented upon more than those of other writers who seem to belong to this tradition. Bernanos was a man of prodigious vitality whose character was marked by opposing traits of violence and tenderness, gaiety and vituperation. Those who approached him saw in him the man of his books. He is remembered especially for his passages of invective and strong polemics. He has often been called the pamphleteer of modern France, the successor of Léon Bloy. The work of Bernanos constitutes a major testimonial of our time. From now on, I imagine that his work will gradually reveal its essential meaning, which is doubtless of a prophetic order. His books are warnings, especially on the loss of modern man's liberty, of many kinds: political, economic and humanistic. The extremely dramatic character he confers on belief in Christ will alienate the non-believer, as it has done for the work of Léon Bloy.

Bernanos is perhaps, today, the supreme example of a literary presence in French literature. He recalls and even reincarnates one aspect of French civilization, the baptistry of Rheims and the adventure of the crusaders. Nothing in his work can really be understood, unless it is seen from a Christian perspective, as engaging a real man behind a fictional character and, behind him, a nation, and behind it, the entire world.

Although Antoine de Saint-Exupéry is not a Catholic writer in the sense that Bernanos is, he is being read fervently by the younger public and seems to be considered a spiritual leader for the new generation. His posthumous work, *Citadelle,* was published in 1948, from a manuscript of almost one thousand pages. He is looked upon, more and more, as a spiritual writer who has described in his work the essential stages which unite the individual with God: the family, the house, the trade, the community. One of his most often-quoted sentences is: *"L'homme vent donner un sens à son coup de pioche."* (Man wishes to give meaning to his toil [to the blow of his pick ax].)

The man himself remains mysterious and enigmatic, despite the fact that his friends have begun to write about him. His legend of heroism and mystery is still pretty much intact. He is the poet of aviation, an archangel suspended between heaven and earth. The text of *Citadelle* is not much more than a series of notes and improvisations. The publication has been premature, and, probably because no one yet knows how to read the work, it has disappointed and puzzled. Many of Saint-Exupéry's essential themes are in it, however: his belief in the virtue of the heart, in intuition, in sentiment, in greatness, which one day will cause him to be compared to Corneille. Things and beings in themselves are nothing, according to his belief. What does count is the bond that unites them.

Among the living writers of this generation of Bernanos and Saint-Exupéry, the one who for twenty years has been representing the Catholic tradition, has of recent years lost his high position of influence. I doubt very much if the younger generation in France reads François Mauriac. The fame he knew in the thirties, in France, exists, however, today in England, where his entire works are being translated. Mauriac has given to French literature the most complete and stark picture of provincial Pharisaism that exists. He wrote, as early as 1926, *"la province est pharisienne,"* and continued to study this theme in each of his successive books.

In 1939, Jean Paul Sartre published, in the *Nouvelle Revue Française* of February, an analysis of Mauriac which, more than anything else, I would guess, has diminished Mauriac's position in French letters and discouraged the younger readers from continuing with him. It is this essay, included in *Situations, I,* where Sartre tries to prove that Mauriac leaves no liberty to his characters. The end of the article has been quoted so often that it has become a cliché: *"Dieu n'est pas un artiste; M. Mauriac non plus."* [1] (God is not an artist; nor is Mauriac.) Mauriac is a far more personal writer and more limited than the two who have replaced him today, Sartre and Camus. Mauriac has written only about his own personal torment, and that is precisely what Sartre has never revealed.

Midway in his career, Mauriac was strongly accused by his Catholic readers of being an immoral novelist. They claimed that not only did he make perceptible and tangible the universe of evil, but that he often made it appear seductive. The charge was not so much against the subject matter of his writings as it was against the tone with which he treated the subject matter. They felt his books revealed a secret sympathy, a connivance with sin. When his novel, *Destins,* appeared in 1928, Gide wrote him a letter of congratulation saying, "the objective of your novel is not so much to bring sinners to Chris-

[1] Jean Paul Sartre, *Situations, I,* Gallimard, Paris, 1948.

tianity as to remind Christians that there is something on earth beside heaven. Doubtless if I were more of a Christian, I should be less your disciple." At the same time, Jacques Maritain gave solemn warning to Mauriac. The novelist made a serious examination of conscience, and replied to both Gide and Maritain in his book, *Dieu et Mammon.* Maritain's principal point had been that it is important to know at "what altitude the novelist is when he makes his portrayal of evil, and whether his art and his soul are pure enough to make it without conniving with it." Maritain summarizes his point by adding that "to write the work of a Proust as it should be written would require the inner light of a St. Augustine." [2]

No younger novelist today in France has replaced Mauriac or Bernanos. In the purely Catholic tradition, there is a surprising lack of leaders and writers. In their absence, other writers are being read and interpreted as if they belonged more literally than they do to the spirit of Catholicism. This phenomenon is part of the paradox of Catholicism in France where literature often demonstrates deep religious fervor, as well as a strong tendency to anti-clericalism. I am thinking particularly in this respect of André Malraux, whose career has undergone a more curious and a more complicated development than Mauriac's.

Before the war, Malraux's position was solidly established as one of the leading novelists, whose large social frescoes of *La Condition Humaine* and *L'Espoir* had revealed a world torn by the worst catastrophes. During the war, and immediately afterward, his prestige declined, more in France perhaps than in America. His political alliance with De Gaulle might explain this to some degree. But then, in 1948, appeared his two-volume work, *La Psychologie de l'Art,* which is far more than art history or art criticism. Malraux is the most recent man of letters in France who undertakes to write on art. The lineage is a noble one: Diderot, Baudelaire, Taine, Alain, Valéry. The book has recaptured for Malraux a place of high esteem in the younger generation.

Malraux believes that a struggle or battle is at the origin of artistic

[2] Jacques Maritain, *Art et Scolastique,* 3rd edition, revised, Louis Rouart, Paris, 1935, p. 298.

creation. A young artist will first imitate a master and then react against him and create an individual style. This theory of the struggle for beauty, whereby a revolt lies at the beginning of each new art, is a familiar theory, but Malraux turns the history of art into a dramatic story that has something of the character of *The Iliad* or a *Chanson de Geste*. He is particularly fond of the revolutionaries: Goya, Manet, the Christian sculptors. He has a tendency to feel and, therefore, to stress the pathetic and the catastrophic in art. Malraux exalts those painters who depicted the lowest examples of humanity, Franz Hals, for example. He exalts those painters who efface their subject. Malraux dilates on the theme that the princes and the bourgeois who are painted disappear from the face of the earth and only the painter remains. He is in total agreement with Valéry when he writes: "A painter is not a man who first loves figures and landscapes, he is first a man who loves paintings." [3]

The long work on the psychology of art, written in an opulent, almost Bossuet-like style, is exacting and stimulating. To participate in a work of art is comparable to plunging into a conflagration. There is something almost Satanic in Malraux's belief that art reveals to us a secret way of possessing the world. He sees the artist as one who creates another universe, who corrects or reorganizes the work of *Genesis*. The book is really on the subject of human genius. Because of its tone and fervor, Malraux is already being considered a kind of spiritual guide in France.

Catholicism in France has always defined itself in the work of those who oppose it, and who, by opposing it, according to those within the Church, are testifying to a nostalgia for the Christian life. In the study of each of the major writers, whatever his religious affiliation or lack of it, French criticism emphasizes first the religious problem. Critics are still exploring and studying the religious attitude and conviction of Rabelais and Montaigne, of Pascal and Descartes, of Voltaire and Rousseau, of Chateaubriand and Renan. Important books will be written when there is more time for perspective on the religious ideas of Péguy and Gide.

[3] André Malraux, *The Psychology of Art,* translated by Stuart Gilbert, Pantheon Books, New York, 1949.

A study could be written on the subtle influence of Catholicism on Gide, or on the invigorating way he has redefined Christian doctrine by refusing to accept it according to its orthodox form. Gide represents to an exceptional degree the conflict between a heart formed by the Bible and an intellect stimulated by Nietzsche and Goethe. His soul is imbued with the Christian spirit, but his senses are pagan. For an entire generation Gide has been the prodigal son, inciting it to some kind of escape and self-revelation. He has been called the demon corrupter of youth. But already such accusations are being softened, and even by Catholic critics his message is seen to be, not one of flagrant immorality, but one of detachment and of spiritual courage.

During the years of the First World War, Gide's thought was constantly being nourished on the Gospels. His little tract, *Numquid et tu,* based on the St. John Gospel, "Are you a Galilean, too?", written at a time when he was very close to Catholicism, has a mystical fervor in its search for the word of life. His novel, *Les Faux-Monnayeurs,* written soon after this, is about those men who, in society and in their religious life, falsify the word of life and pervert it for selfish reasons. They are the counterfeiters. Whatever form Gide's writing took, tale, novel, story, parable, journal, sociological reporting, it was always concerned with man in his complex relationships with the Eternal and the transitory, with God and time. Much remains to be said about the self-discipline and the esthetic discipline Gide imposed upon himself and his writings. Distrustful of philosophies and doctrines, Gide has never succinctly defined his own, but it will probably turn out to be a lesson on intellectual and spiritual liberty, on tolerance and man's need to reconcile the extremes in himself and in other men.

II

For the past hundred years, the religious problem in French literature has been more profoundly reflected in poetry, although it has often been poetry not rigorously, not doctrinally Catholic. For this period of a century, when the Catholic spirit has not been universally persuasive in France, when it has been put to many tests and undergone many attacks, its particular expression in poetry (and especially in the three poets who seem to testify to three cardinal aspects of its problem) is the most valid, because it is at once bound up with the eternal spirit of Catholicism and with the specific drama and dilemma of modern man.

Charles Baudelaire is the source of modern poetry, and the poet in whom the spiritual problem appears both in its most agonized and most transcendent form. The creation of beauty for Baudelaire contains the promise of a spiritual deliverance. He was haunted all his life by a sense of tragic dualism and a need to discover a way to effect a unity and harmony between these two opposing forces of good and evil. The foundation of Baudelaire's esthetics, as well as the foundation of his personal moral problem, is stated in his *Journaux Intimes,* when he says that as a child he felt two contradictory sentiments, the horror and the ecstasy of life. The opening sentence of *Mon coeur mis à nu* states the same idea: "Everything is in the vaporization and the centralization of the self." Honest with himself, Baudelaire never claimed to have known the mystical form of ecstasy, the result of assiduous prayer and religious ardor. His ecstasy was more sensational, more voluptuary, and at the end of it he sought not love, nor truth, but some revelation of beauty, beauty the source of the unknown. His way is mystical in only the very broadest sense. It is really a poetical mysticism. He calls the principle of poetry, human aspiration toward a superior beauty. Its manifestation is in an enthusiasm, a rapture of the soul.

This instinct or aspiration toward beauty makes us, according to Baudelaire, consider the world a "correspondence" of heaven. Our yearning for another life is the proof of our immortality. By means of poetry, we half see the beauty of the purely spiritual world. Swedenborg had helped Baudelaire formulate this theory. The notion of analogy leads one to the doctrine of "correspondences," which, in its turn, leads to the theory of symbolism. Nature is a temple, each part of which has a symbolic meaning. The poet is the one who finds in nature a "dark profound unity." Baudelaire's book, *Les Fleurs du Mal,* reveals a constant search, impeded by velleity or impotency, to get out from himself and master his fate. He certainly believed in artistic creation containing the possibility of his salvation. When he speaks of religion in his *Journaux,* it seems to be a last recourse of a desperate man, not an experience which engages his entire being. He was always skilful at forming resolutions and incapable of following them out. His destiny was that of a seeker, a voyager, moving toward the unknown, the different. He made no arrival. He was unable to change his original condition. His was the ambition of the poet-priest, capable of changing the world, of recreating the world by the word. His system was one of analogies and correspondences, where the poet appears as decipherer of hieroglyphics, as reader of the book of creation. All the elements of Baudelaire's great ambition, which have guided subsequent poets, were felt and practiced by him as a means of uniting his life with that of the world, of discovering behind the individual and the ephemeral, the universal and the eternal. Baudelaire's is the myth of a lost paradise, of an Orpheus no longer able to enchant the animals and bewitch all nature.

The second case history in modern French poetry and infinitely more mysterious than that of Baudelaire, is Rimbaud's. His life as poet was a dazzling brief period of four or five years. Ever since it terminated, it has been examined by countless critics and historians, each anxious to arrive at a solution, an explanation of the adolescent destiny. There seem to be as many solutions as there are critics, but all agree on the essential mystery of this life, a mystery of a spiritual order, and one that may well contain the clue to modern man's spirituality or search for a spiritual absolute.

Rimbaud has been defined by all the opposites: Catholic and pagan, visionary and rascal, surrealist and Marxist, the devil and God. He has been compared to Julien Sorel, to Villon, Faust, Prometheus, Icarus, Peer Gynt, Adam, the Good Samaritan, John the Baptist, Job, Joan of Arc, the two St. Theresas, the four Evangelists, Ezekiel, Isaiah, Orestes, the Messiah. Rather than using any one of these names, or discovering a further prototype, let us consider him the modern poet, the almost purely intuitive poet who repudiated the logic of philosophers and doctrinaires. He was the visual poet, the voyant, aggressive and revolutionary by temperament, who had alienated the conventional approaches to God and to love. He willed to make himself into a magus, a magician, a voyant. But the magic he learned to control was poetry. Although he scorned the trivial exercise of writing poetry in the usual way.

For Rimbaud the true poet has not yet arisen. We do not yet know what a poet is. But he tells us that the first study of a man is to know himself, the true self, to cultivate himself. In this process of self-knowing, poetry will be acquired, through an act of the will. The creation of poetry depends on the discovering of the hidden self, of the other personality that we are. *"Je est un autre,"* (I am another) wrote Rimbaud, and I suppose that no sentence of modern times has elicited so much commentary. In this work of a poet man finally reaches the unknown, according to Rimbaud's formula, which is reminiscent of Baudelaire. The world we live in is conventional and fabricated. We have to reach another realer world. One would not have to go farther than this to sense the deep spirituality of all of Rimbaud's formulas. His poetic experience was always close to the mystical, although I do not believe it ever became that, literally. The poet he defined as the re-creator of the world. Before engaging upon such a destiny, his life was characterized by a denial of everything, by insults, insolences, vagabond voyages, seductions. From today's perspective, it is possible to see this violent period as a *chasse spirituelle,* a name given to a manuscript which has been lost. If Rimbaud was not the illuminated mystic, he was the hallucinated poet, who created a whole new world in his *Illuminations,* only to find that it was really a subjective world and the confession of the deepest part of himself. What he thought was self-exploration and self-knowledge was, in part at least, nostalgia for some lost purity, for some original innocency.

The importance of Rimbaud, and especially the spiritual significance of his work, was first revealed by a poet who is still living, Paul Claudel. The precise way in which Rimbaud helped Claudel, in revealing to him his mission as a religious poet, will always remain a mystery. Deep within a poetic work which seems largely to be composed of revolt and blasphemy, Claudel discovered traces of a religious drama which spoke directly to him and to which he owed his return to Catholicism. In his preface to the work of Rimbaud, he tries to analyze systematically the phases of Rimbaud's drama which had taken on such limitless importance for him. Rimbaud's violent period, Claudel interprets as the necessary mutation of genius, the sentimental reaction to his world. The visionary phase, the *voyance* of Rimbaud, Claudel calls the way of the spirit. The magnificent images of the literal *Illuminations* were preparation to seeing truth. The final phase Claudel calls that of belief where, as in the last pages of *Une Saison en Enfer,* Rimbaud greets beauty and its radiating simplicity. Claudel believes that Rimbaud accomplished a mission in the world, that of a violent reaction against positivism. His theory of Rimbaud being a Catholic poet has been developed by other subsequent critics. The value of this interpretation, which I do not myself share, has been to invest Rimbaud's poetic imagination with a profundity that it deserves.

The most ardent admirers of Claudel have not hesitated to compare him with Dante. The reading of Rimbaud and the religious experience he underwent at the age of eighteen, changed the world for Claudel. These were revelations whereby he saw the world as the work of God and worthy of the song and praise of the poet. This was the genesis of his great theme of joy, the one reality for Claudel, the one requirement for the making of an artistic work. Without it, he believes that man has nothing to say. But a conversion—Claudel's occurred in Notre Dame on Christmas, 1886—is only a beginning. A new Catholic has to learn two things, a way of renouncing the world, of giving up all passions except the Divine Passion, and the way of acquiring spiritual powers—*membres spirituels,* as Claudel calls them —with which to reconstruct all of one's former knowledge. There are many ways to do this, ways dependent on the individual's temperament and aptitude, but they have to include the two pivotal forces of love and knowledge.

Claudel has not been reluctant in describing the stages of his spiritual development which in many instances resemble those of an authentic mystical experience. In China, his *Vers d'Exil* described his boredom and disgust with his early suffering, the solitude he needed, and the Presence he finally came to. There, he studied attentively the two *Summas* of St. Thomas, which encouraged his love for syntheses and unifications. Mallarmé had taught him something of the symbolic structure of the universe and Rimbaud something of the creative power of language. These two lessons were gradually illuminated by medieval philosophy. He discovered that religious symbolism and poetic symbolism are the same, and that in addition to the logic of a syllogism, there exists the logic of analogy and metaphor. Aquinas had called the universe "a general sacrament which speaks to us of God, of all good and all beauty, principle of the ideal which the artist tries to reproduce, supreme end of all that was, is and will be, sovereign rule of all that we should do."

Such a text was for Claudel both a discovery and a confirmation of what he had learned through the poets. St. Thomas completed the work of Mallarmé, in providing Claudel with a theocentric esthetics according to which the universe is the mirror of God. The world for Claudel with his faith of a medieval artisan, is a textbook which can be read and must be read. It speaks to us of two things. First, of its own limitation, of its own "absence," as Mallarmé would say. And secondly, of the presence of its Creator. Claudel contrasts the sorcerer's book, *le grimoire* of the symbolist poets, with the Word, the *Logos* in which everything has been uttered. He was not, in any profound sense, the disciple of the symbolists, and yet his work represents the accomplishment and the culmination of many themes of symbolism, especially those whose purpose was the understanding and the demonstration of the poetic act.

By temperament Claudel belongs to the race of revolutionaries and conquerors, poets such as D'Aubigné and Rimbaud, but also close to Mallarmé, in his will to define poetry in its essence. From Mallarmé Claudel learned especially his lesson on the metaphor, the essential element of his poetics. He learned that a metaphor is a relationship between two objects. It may even be a relationship between God and the world. The poet's role is to apprehend, to seize the metaphors which exist in the world. This means naming each object and restoring it to its rightful place in a new ordering of the universe, in a new lexicon of the world. Each time that Claudel states that with each new breath of a man, the world should appear new to him, as fresh and virginal as it appeared to the first man, with his first breath, he is reiterating Mallarmé's belief about the metaphor, about the endless metaphorical richness of the world. By naming an object, the poet gives it its meaning, as God had originally done when He created the world by naming it. The total word, or the total poem, is, therefore, the universe. Each poet bears in himself a picture of the universe, a subjective maze of images which have relationships with one another. Mallarmé follows an instinctive quest in naming various objects and seeking to understand their metaphorical meaning. Claudel goes farther in willing this quest as if it were a religious obligation. Symbolism, under the initial guidance of Mallarmé, was a spiritual way of understanding and celebrating the universe. It became later in the art of Paul Claudel a more frankly religious way of discovering in the midst of endless variety a secret unity. In his *Art Poétique* of 1903, Claudel states that the metaphor is the logic of the new poetry, comparable to the syllogism of the older logic. Things in the world are not only objects to be known, they are means by which man is being constantly reborn. He had not altered his basic belief when, in 1925, he commented on Mallarmé's *Igitur* and (as indicated above) called the world not a sorcerer's handbook, *grimoire,* but the Word engendering all things.

III

The literary expression in novels and poetry given to Catholicism today can hardly be studied without some knowledge of what it means to be a Christian in the contemporary world. The Christian is both very old and very young, by his dual participation in time and eternity. By comparison with the Sartrian man, about ten years old, and the Marxian and the Nietzschean man, both about a hundred years old, the Christian is 2,000 years old. If Christ really lives in him, the Christian is the type of perfect man, the center of history, the reason why the world was created. The Christian does not expect any other Messiah. What he has to do, through the centuries which began with the Incarnation and will end with the end of the world, is to use the virtues and powers which are divinely his. Péguy warned Christians against speaking in just this way, with such pomposity and assurance. If the message of Christianity is not heeded universally today, the

Christians themselves are to blame. They have not been very skilful in solving the problem of the relationships between man and the world of history and the world of science.

What is the Christian meaning of history? Marxists particularly have accused Christians of turning their backs on life, of repudiating what is now called collectivism. This complaint can be justified. The Christian is torn between his nostalgia for the kingdom of God and his conscience urging him to participate in the temporal political unfolding of history. But this conflict does not date from our period. Roman magistrates accused the earliest Christians of undermining the Empire, of stressing the individual conscience to the detriment of the state worship. The same remarks have been used by Marx, Lenin, Mussolini, Hitler. The Christian will always, to some extent, be unassimilated, falsely nationalist, falsely revolutionary. He will always be a public danger, in the sense that his mind is more fixed on eternity than on the imperious and pressing needs of any society or race or class or clan. He will always be tempted by the desert. God's love has made him a captive, and the very weight of that love draws him out of the world, toward invisible things. He belongs to that other society of the saints, and he is always repeating as did the earliest Christians, "May this world pass and may grace come!"

Even if he does not fully realize it, the Christian is always secretly an anchorite fleeing the world. Certain phrases from the Gospels have branded themselves in his soul and he can do nothing about them, sentences about the insignificance of gaining the world if he lose his soul, about the kingdom of Christ not being of this world, about the need to lose one's life in order to save it. St. Paul taught that the façade of the world is crumbling, and St. John wrote that "the world rests in evil." The lives and writings of saints and ascetics for centuries have underscored this Christian impulse toward retirement and pessimism. But that is only one aspect of the Christian revelation. The other, equally important and forming the great paradox, is the central mystery of the Christian faith, that of the Incarnation, by which God became man and dwelt among men in this world of iniquity. If the Christian excluded himself from the world and history, he would betray Christ as the incarnate word. The Christian's position is not easy to hold, because he belongs both to heaven and earth. He must first fill himself with the spirit of God and then cause it to live in the midst of sin and matter. Supernaturalism and naturalism are his two worlds, in neither one of which he is allowed to live exclusively. Supernaturalism alone would separate him from the world, and naturalism alone would separate him from God.

The great lesson of the Incarnation has become the pivotal theme of contemporary Catholic literature. It teaches that the supernatural destiny of the Christian is, to a large degree, ordered and governed by the particular condition of human life he knows. Time itself is a kind of determinant for eternity. Péguy has written in one of his most moving passages that we lead a life temporally eternal: *"Nous menons une vie temporellement éternelle."* The tree of grace is deeply rooted. *"L'arbre de la grâce est raciné profond."* This is why the Catholic believes he has chosen everything by joining the two kingdoms of God and the world. To a Catholic the Marxian solution which states that materialism will lead to a society without class distinctions and where the exploitation of man by man will be abolished, seems oversimplified, unwarrantedly optimistic. History is made by men, and like them, is a complex of good and evil. In it there are forces of disintegration and selfishness which lead to its ruin, and also forces of generosity and love which transform the world and are constantly saving it. The same kind of struggle is going on in the heart of each man. The Christian believes that the powers of truth and justice are always deeply working in the world, even if at times they are not visible and not felt. History is as ambivalent as man. The artist, who works more in darkness than in light, will be more apt to depict the man unaware of the forces of good working in him. This is true of many contemporary French Catholic artists.

In the Incarnation is the central doctrine of the Christian faith, two other doctrines are placed as extreme poles of the faith, protecting and defining it. First, the Creation, which plunges us back in history long before the flood, affirming the dependence of the world on God Who made all things. And the other, the resurrection of the body, which forces us to look way ahead into the future toward a cosmic optimism that exceeds all our powers of imagination and which leads us to believe that, thanks to our body, the material universe may be saved. St. Paul, on this doctrine, said, "Nature will be delivered from the bondage of corruption." This text contradicts the over familiar opposition of body and soul, flesh and spirit. Existentialism has called attention to the Christian belief in the abjection of man. Pascal, long before Sartrian Existentialism, wrote of the old opposition of Nature and Grace. This Catholic tradition in which the body is considered evil has been exaggerated by Catholic literature. For some time, Catholic literature has been one of original sin and concupiscence. One wonders if Claudel, of all the authors mentioned in this essay, is the only one close to the Dominican interpretation: Grace does not destroy nature, but perfects and raises it. Despair is not the ultimate secret. Claudel believes in a theocentric humanism. Nothing is more exultant than this conception of the universe. When the Word became Flesh, it assumed the universe.

XVII

PROTESTANT ORIENTATION IN CONTEMPORARY POETRY

BY

AMOS NIVEN WILDER

What affirmations are made, what affirmations are possible, in this age of crisis, this age of anxiety in which we live? This would appear to be our fundamental concern in this part of the present series of discussions. It is not, first of all, a question of doctrinal beliefs. It is the question: What do men live by today? And we rightly turn to literature and the arts in seeking an answer. The present discussion will restrict itself in two respects. We shall give our attention in the central part of the paper to characteristic poems of two of our contemporary poets. We believe that we can generalize significantly from this selection. In the second place we shall focus on writers who would not be identified with an orthodox or dogmatic position.

I

The conditions of our time make for a wide gamut of patterns of belief. Many groups have found themselves alienated from the great religious and cultural traditions. They have thus been led, negatively, to disbelief, but also, positively, to shape their own alternate faiths. It is important for us to understand the difficulties men have today with traditional patterns of belief, indeed, their difficulties in making any affirmations at all. It is also of interest to see that the exiles from tradition, the heretics if such they are, the explorers—writers who represent so many men of our modern world—are often not so far from the great faiths of the past as may at first sight appear.

We must preface our discussion with certain observations and cautions. In the first place, we should not underestimate the value of affirmations that are not expressly dogmatic or confessional. In faiths which some might be disposed to call merely esthetic or at least ambiguous, we, nevertheless, draw near to the hungers and aspirations of countless souls today. We live in a catastrophic period. The foundations have been shaken, and multitudes of men can find no home either for their minds or their hearts in the older religious institutions. It is a matter of poignant and grave interest to observe how they deal with the harshness of the age and the ambiguities of its loyalties.

We would also caution against the view that optimism is a fair test of art or poetry. It is true that in the greatest literature we look for great affirmation. But, if we exclude all art or poetry that lacks such explicit faith, we rule out a vast amount of profoundly significant work. Especially in a time like ours, it is inevitable that the experience of evil will occupy a large place in the contribution of the imaginative artist. No doubt ultimately "poetry is praise" and poetry is joy, but real poetry must take up into its praise and joy the negative aspects of our experience as men.

Moreover, the affirmation in art is properly implicit, rather than explicit. The poet is an imagemaker rather than a preacher, a celebrant rather than a teacher. It is true that poetry and religion are consubstantial in their origins. The poet, at the risk of being a magician in the bad sense, cannot finally be distinguished from the seer and prophet. Yet the poet ministers to true belief and right conduct not by indoctrination or didactic, but by enabling us to *see*—in the sense that Goethe ascribed to it: *schauen*.

Affirmation in modern works is then often only implicit. It is also, granted, often swamped in negation or even despair. This only underlines the fact that faith here is hard won. The implicit courage or affirmation is all the more significant. Men too often want easy solutions, even in our noblest religions. But Judaism and Christianity should be able to recognize the rights of pain and dismay.

That the Victorians were protected or exempt from some of the shocks that we have had to meet, explains why much of their literature has qualified appeal to us. They had their troubles like all the sons of Adam, but different kinds of troubles. Perhaps the Victorians who had the distresses most like our own did not write or publish. The Christian affirmation of the great Victorians, as of more recent writers such as Francis Thompson, Vachel Lindsay and John Masefield, appears to us now to have suffered from a limited context and experience. We have only to name contemporaries of some of them: Dostoievski, Baudelaire, Melville, men who broke out of the framework of their age, to recognize these limitations.

Thus modern affirmation is hard won. It speaks out of intimate initiation into our cultural and spiritual crisis. This means, of course, the social crisis of world wars and economic costs. But, more deeply, it means the psychological strains that have accompanied the crisis: the dehumanization and lostness of the modern soul. There is something peculiarly poignant and magnificent in the spectacle of men wringing art and celebration out of these nightmares, and saying "Nevertheless," in the midst of the distempers that afflict the spirit today, and which afflict particularly the most gifted and sensitive.

II

Let us begin our documentation by looking at a study of our topic by a contemporary American poet. I refer to Karl Shapiro's poem, "Essay on Rime," whose third section is entitled, "The Confusion of Belief."

Shapiro begins this section with a passage on Hart Crane, the strange and gifted ecstatic whose poem, *The Bridge,* is recognized as one of the few near great achievements of our century in poetry. Crane sought in this work to project an American myth; having in mind, indeed, Walt Whitman, but using other methods, and giving a larger place to the reality of evil. Crane makes no special use of the Christian tradition, but seeks to build his encompassing vision out of the local myth and legend of the American scene, and the promise of technological achievement. Here is a faith, indeed, but interpreters of the work have connected its miscarriage with its utopianism. As one critic has suggested, Crane was strong when he leaned on Melville, weak when he leaned on Whitman. Moreover, he sought not only to build a myth but to make a religion of his art. Here he is typical of many modern poets. Unable to believe in any of our inherited faiths, and driven into a corner by the immense sway of science and rationalism, they have perforce been led to explore and exploit their subjective and irrational experience as a religious substitute.

Shapiro then turns to D. H. Lawrence. With a geniune religious vision this writer raged against the devitalized secularism and moralism of his day. He espoused an affirmative paganism more substantial than that of Crane, which may have something to do with the fact that he could survive, while Crane's effort ended in suicide.

Shapiro then lists what he calls "new and substitute beliefs," beginning with the faith in inevitable progress and its Marxian version, and following on with the Freudian phase of naturalism. In the twenties a transition to "poetry of disbelief" is registered, including the early work of T. S. Eliot. But this led to a period of "personal systems" in which each poet wrote out his own synthetic myth, but one in which he could not genuinely believe. Shapiro then concludes with an indictment of the esoteric and impoverished character of the work of a host of moderns of the second rank.

III

What are the causes for the difficulty of affirmation in our time? The prevailing explanation is that the older faiths are no longer meaningful. To put it in current terms: the myths are dead. By myths here are meant the older pictures of the world and of life, so long a part of our cultural and religious heritage in the West, pictures which offered an explanation of things and in which generations have found security and meaning. This means, above all, the Bible's story of the world, the drama basic to Milton's *Paradise Lost,* but also the interpretations of human existence offered in classical literature. These roots of our culture, these structural elements of life-affirming faith—it is said—have lost their claim upon us. The causes lie, above all, in the diffusion of the rationalistic, positivistic outlook since the seventeenth century. Science and its outcomes have destroyed the myths and the faiths connected with them. But a second factor bears especially on the

Christian world-view. The modern man and the modern artist have found the Christian outlook ascetic and world denying, despite its message of eternal salvation. Let us now examine certain writings of two contemporary poets in their bearing on these matters.

We turn first to Allen Tate's "Sonnets at Christmas." Here we have the cogitation of a modern upon the ambiguity of the Christian faith today. The two sonnets express the difficulty of believing the Christian story and yet the need to believe it. We are reminded of Hardy's well known poem, "The Oxen." There, it will be recalled, the poet, on Christmas Eve, is reminded of the pretty superstition that at midnight the cattle kneel, and he writes,

> I should go with him in the gloom,
> Hoping it might be so.[1]

But instead of being merely wistful as Hardy is, Tate is dead serious, though after an ironical fashion. It is not possible for him, despite a sense of "crime and punishment" to be shriven.

> Therefore with idle hands and head I sit
> In late December before the fire's daze
> Punished by crimes of which I would be quit.[2]

The trouble, he implies, is connected with our modern overemphasis on knowledge:

> Man, dull critter of enormous head,
> What would he look at in the coiling sky? [3]

That is, our kind of sophistication can see no heavenly host nor can it hear the angels' song. For us Christ is not alive but dead, and the bells of Christmas are only the tinsel bells hung in the living room, and they ring out only silence.

> But I must kneel again unto the Dead
> While Christmas bells of paper white and red,

[1] Thomas Hardy, "The Oxen," *Collected Poems,* copyright, 1925, by The Macmillan Company, New York, p. 439, and used with their permission.

[2] Allen Tate, "Sonnets at Christmas," *Selected Poems,* Charles Scribner's Sons, New York, 1937, pp. 47 f.

[3] *Ibid.*

> Figured with boys and girls spilt from a sled
> Ring out the silence I am nourished by.[4]

Notice the symbolism: the "boys and girls spilt from a sled"—pictured on the gay decorations, represent the lives of men and women spilt by death. And the poet, ironically and tragically, is nourished by silence, that is, he is not nourished at all.

As Delmore Schwartz reads the poem: "the ego of the poem is incapable of enjoying this Christmas as a day of feast partly because he is a dull critter of enormous head, an intellectual animal: partly because of the great difficulty of belief. He cannot believe, nor can he disbelieve. His difficult case is that he must kneel—to one whom he must call the Dead, with but an hour of life—he must look at the sky and he must argue his difficulty. . . . It is easier to believe or to disbelieve than it is to maintain this poise between belief and disbelief which the sonnet presents. The honesty in question at the outset is fully exemplified in this difficult case." [5]

In a series called "More Sonnets at Christmas: Ten Years Later," [6] Tate records the same dilemma. In one impulse he would free himself from being haunted and inquisitioned by a Christ who never rose:

> Ten years is enough time to be dismayed
> By mummy Christ, head crammed between his knees.[7]

But then he considers the other options open to him. Why should he not give himself entirely to an uninhibited pagan freedom, say, some reckless arrogant life of action, perhaps of a bombardier, whose fear, if any,

[4] *Ibid.*

[5] Delmore Schwartz, "Poetry of Allen Tate," *Southern Review*, V, 3, Winter, 1940, p. 426.

[6] Allen Tate, "More Sonnets at Christmas: Ten Years Later," *Poems, 1922–1947*, copyright 1932, 1937, by Charles Scribner's Sons, New York, 1948, pp. 52–55, and used with their permission.

[7] *Ibid.*, p. 33. In one of his more recent poems the "I" of the poem makes his appeal to "Venus"—as "the vital principle of love"—to return to the world, since Christianity is no longer potent:

> the drying God above
> Hanged in his windy steeple
> No longer bears for us
> The living wound of love.

Is of an enemy in remote oceans
Unstalked by Christ: these are the better notions.[8]

But these sonnets end in an admission that it is too late. We have been
captives too long—condemned to a starved and meager fare. Even if
we emancipate ourselves at this late date, we shall find that we are still
helpless in the chains of habit.

Your ghosts are Plato's Christians in the cave.
Unfix your necks, turn to the door: the nave
Gives back the cheated and light dividend
So long sequestered; now, new-rich, you'll
                spend
Flesh for reality inside a stone
Whose light obstruction, like a gossamer bone,
Dead or still living, will not break or bend.[9]

That is, we have lived too long facing away from reality like those
in Plato's allegory of the cave. If now we turn toward the light rather
than the shadows—the light so long "sequestered," that is, held off—
and if we seek to live the full free life that should be ours, we shall
find that we are still prisoners of the cave. All sorts of intangible,
gossamerlike fears and scruples and habits will still rule us.

You will be Plato's kept philosopher,
Albino man bleached from the mortal clay.[10]

The secular man of today, says Tate, the man who seeks to cast off
his Christian past cannot be a good pagan made of rich red earth, but
only an albino whose mortal clay is bleached!

We have here an ever recurring protest of the modern artist, not
against Christianity as such necessarily, but against the impoverished
forms of it that have held such wide sway in the modern world, both
Protestant and Catholic. Thus we get the scorn of the Jewess Rosetta
in Auden's "Age of Anxiety," spoken to the Christian, condemned

To a locker-room life at low tension. . . .
(Dowdy they'll die who have so dimly lived.) [11]

[8] *Ibid.*
[9] *Ibid.*
[10] *Ibid.*
[11] W. H. Auden, *Age of Anxiety*, Random House, New York, 1947, p. 44.

The second illustration of the difficulties of Christian faith in our time is found in Wallace Stevens's "Sunday Morning," one of the most quoted of his poems. It offers us the soliloquy of a woman having her late coffee and oranges on a sunny porch on Sunday morning. Her enjoyment of the calm scene is invaded by thoughts of "the ancient sacrifice" of Christ, and her revery deals with what we would call "the offense of the cross," the contradiction between the natural joys of men and the harshness of the Christian story and claim.

> She dreams a little, and she feels the dark
> Encroachment of that old catastrophe,
> As a calm darkens among water-lights.[12]

And her dreaming passes

> Over the seas, to silent Palestine,
> Dominion of the blood and sepulchre.
>
> Why should she give her bounty to the dead?
> What is divinity if it can come
> Only in silent shadows and in dreams?
> Shall she not find in comforts of the sun
> In pungent fruit and bright, green wings, or else
> In any balm or beauty of the earth,
> Things to be cherished like the thought of heaven? [13]

The speaker in the poem speculates as to whether we should set our hope on Paradise after the present life. But no, she is content with earthly beauties. After all, no old legends of Paradise or the Hesperides have "endured/As April's green endures." And yet

> She says, "But in contentment I still feel
> The need of some imperishable bliss."
> Death is the mother of beauty; hence from her,
> Alone, shall come fulfilment to our dreams
> And our desires.[14]

[12] Wallace Stevens, "Sunday Morning." Reprinted from *Harmonium*, copyright 1923, 1931, by Alfred A. Knopf, Inc., New York, pp. 89–94, and used with their permission.
[13] *Ibid.*
[14] *Ibid.*

Paradise itself would become insipid without death. Thus, she decides, our best hope is here on earth, and our best ritual is a chant to the sun. And the poem draws to its conclusion as follows:

> "The tomb in Palestine
> Is not the porch of spirits lingering.
> It is the grave of Jesus, where he lay."
> We live in an old chaos of the sun,
> Or old dependency of day and night,
> Or island solitude, unsponsored, free
> Of that wide water, inescapable.
> Deer walk upon our mountains, and the quail
> Whistle about us their spontaneous cries;
> Sweet berries ripen in the wilderness;
> And, in the isolation of the sky,
> At evening, casual flocks of pigeons make
> Ambiguous undulations as they sink
> Downward to darkness, on extended wings.[15]

The waiving of the Christian faith here would seem to be connected with its alleged anti-naturalism, asceticism, refusal of the beauty and goodness of our creaturely life. As we have said elsewhere in connection with Yeats: "For the poets the scandal of Christ is his asceticism. The very medium of their art as poets; indeed, the very element of their experience as men, is the gamut of human living, emotions, drama. 'Man's resinous heart' and the loves, loyalties, the pride, the grief it feeds—these are the stuff of poetry and the sense of life. And the Cross lays its shadow on this; it draws away all the blood from the glowing body of existence and leaves it mutilated and charred in the hope of some thin ethereal felicity. The wine of life is changed to water. The spectrum, incredibly enough, is surrendered for an undifferentiated and commonplace white light. The 'dramatic caves' of the human heart and imagination are renounced for some wan empyrean of spiritual revery." [16] Illustration of this view is found in Yeats's colloquy with the great Catholic, Baron Von Huegel. In one of

---

[15] *Ibid.*

[16] Amos N. Wilder, *Spiritual Aspects of the New Poetry*, Harper & Brothers, New York, 1940, p. 196.

his poems Yeats takes his leave of the latter and his faith, with the explanation that his role of poet predestines him to his unbelief—only out of the lion can come forth sweetness:

> I—though heart might find relief
> Did I become a Christian man and choose for my belief
> What seems most welcome in the tomb—play a predestined part.
> Homer is my example and his unchristened heart.
> The lion and the honeycomb, what has Scripture said?
> So get you gone, Von Huegel, though with blessings on your head.[17]

"The implication is that a Christian so sterilizes his heart that there is no concern left for art and the rich play, the riot and fecundity of life. It is as though the only treasury of poetry was 'the lust of the flesh, and the lust of the eyes, and the pride of life.' " [18]

IV

Thus in the matter of Christian belief there are today major obstacles for the poet and artist, as there are for the modern man generally. We have illustrated two such obstacles. In the case of Tate, attention is given to modern man's rationalism, with its counterpart of the "uneducated heart." Man is a "dull critter with enormous head"; his intellect, his sophistication, has taken on a disproportionate role. He has become critic, observer, analyst, scientist, to such an extent that a seal has been placed upon the springs of impulse, upon the mythmaking and mythbelieving faculties, upon the vital prodigality of the unconscious, upon the eternal child that man should always remain, upon the organic, intuitive, spontaneous sense of life which man should always have as a creature in the great web of being.

In the case of Stevens, as in that of Yeats, we see a second great obstacle to Christian affirmation: the supposed world denial or false asceticism of Christianity. Our faith appears to say "no" to life, to be a blasphemy against the beauty and goodness of the natural order. Here, indeed, a basic issue is raised, even when we recognize that

---

[17] W. B. Yeats, "Vacillation, VIII," *Winding Stair,* copyright, 1933, by The Macmillan Company, New York, p. 290, and used with their permission.

[18] Wilder, *op. cit.,* pp. 197 f.

many such charges are superficial. The Christian cannot but admit that the poet is partly right. The Christian religion as men meet it too often justifies the criticism. What we have said about Stevens and Yeats could be said of D. H. Lawrence and others. Indeed, the rebellions against formal Christianity of older poets and prophets of the nineteenth century here falls into line.

The best literary expressions of our secular culture can be understood on one side as the protest of the modern soul against the starved and meager aspects of the Christian heritage in this period. These writers, whether romantic or transcendentalist, symbolist or surrealist, from Blake and Shelley down to Yeats and Joyce, can be understood as Christian voices, heretical, indeed, protesting against the narrowing and stifling of the Christian faith. They demand, if often on the basis of misunderstandings, and often in ways that are erroneous and even perilous, that the yea-saying impulse of the biblical faith and its moment of creative play be given their due place, and that this "yea" should be spoken not only to the spirit but also to the flesh, not only to grace but to nature. This is a necessary protest even if a dangerous one. It has a strong element of antinomianism in it. But there is a genuine kind of antinomianism in the gospel itself and in St. Paul in particular. Despite the tension occasioned by the sense of cosmic drama and catastrophic outcomes, the first Christians exhibit a simplicity and liberality of spirit (*haplotēs*) and an uninhibited confidence (*parrēsia*) which were incompatible with moralism or insensitivity. Christianity represented, indeed, a prodigious release of faith, and its crowning theme was the glory of God. The great rebirths of Christianity in the midst of the years, whether in St. Francis or the Reformation, have in their various ways recognized that the chief end of man is to glorify God and enjoy Him forever. This means that the end of life is lifted above all self-centeredness and moralism into a sharing in the works of the Creator.

Much of the best witness of the modern poets, novelists, and artists whom I have mentioned, including many lesser figures, represents a groping for this richer content of the Christian tradition, indeed of the Christian faith itself, and stands as a warning to the theologian and churchman. It has been said by way of paradox and scandal that "the blood of the *heretics* is the seed of the church." We should not overlook the element of truth in this dictum. It is true, moreover, that these heretics have been martyrs, secular martyrs. The struggle, persecution, loneliness, of figures like Shelley, Nietzsche, D. H. Lawrence, James Joyce, or of some of the modern painters like Van Gogh, represents an anguish of the modern cultural crisis, and these men have known what it costs to say "yes" to life when even the church, not to mention our Philistine dehumanized age, has said "no."

In saying these things, we must, of course, be very clear that the characteristic work of these modern voices is compounded with genuine heresy, is in various ways, neo-pagan, antinomian in a bad sense, sometimes blasphemous. Thus Shelley, like Santayana, platonizes radically in his conception of redemption. Nietzsche, like Jeffers, confuses the poor in spirit and the meek with the slave or the craven. D. H. Lawrence is not content to recognize the sacredness of the flesh and the wisdom of the dark powers of the blood, but exalts these at the expense of the full personal life. Yeats would seem to fail of the Christian perspective as appears in his cyclical conception of history and his dualism of world and spirit. But the definition of heresy is not always easy with changes in the dominant philosophies and categories. Milton was heretical in important particulars. Pascal's thought roamed across the recognized limits of his day. Especially in a time like ours when the landmarks are in disarray, our task is, indeed, always to "test the spirits," but our test will be by the Holy Spirit, rather than by the formulations of particular periods in the past.

V

We have spoken of reasons why modern writers find it difficult to make specific Christian affirmations. There are of course those who do but we are not here dealing with them. But even the others do have their affirmation. Tate and Stevens, for example,[19] both praise and celebrate man's life. Tate is concerned with that full richness of our

---

[19] Mr. Tate has more recently identified himself with an explicit Christian position. The work cited may still, however, be taken as significant for the modern crisis of faith.

human experience which science cannot lay hold of, and with the repossession of the religious and cultural values of his Southern tradition as a way of meeting both the enigmas of life itself and the bleakness of our present culture. Like T. S. Eliot in this respect he affirms tradition in reactionary wise. Spokesman of a "fierce latinity," he is a debtor to Christian Mediterranean culture, and though seemingly thwarted on the threshold of explicit confession, he values the Christian rites and symbols as expressions of that essential significance which a modern has such a hard time possessing. In his Christmas poems and in his extraordinary poem, "The Cross," he shows both how worldshaking was the coming of Christ, and what profound intimations of existence it opens up to the imagination.

Stevens's affirmation of the world has been at least suggested by the citations from his "Sunday Morning." He wonderfully conveys the glorious play of the imagination in its marriage with reality. Thus in his "The Auroras of Autumn" he meditates on the aurora borealis. A man, he says,

> opens the door of his house
> On flames. The scholar of one candle sees
> An Arctic effulgence flaring on the frame
> Of everything he is. And he feels afraid.[20]

"Is there," he asks, "an imagination that sits enthroned" behind all that is—"as crown and diamond cabala?" [21] The reality behind the Northern Lights, the original Beauty, the pure principle of Innocence, is not an illusion. For

> it exists,
> It exists, it is visible, it is, it is.

> So, then, these lights are not a spell of light,
> A saying out of a cloud, but innocence.
> An innocence of the earth and no false sign

> Or symbol of malice. That we partake thereof,

[20] Wallace Stevens, "The Auroras of Autumn," *Kenyon Review,* X, 1, Winter, 1948, pp. 1-10.
[21] *Ibid.*

Lie down like children in this holiness,
As if, awake, we lay in the quiet of sleep,

As if the innocent mother sang in the dark
Of the room and on an accordion, half heard,
Created the time and the place in which we breathed.[22]

It is true, Stevens acknowledges, that "this imagination that sits enthroned" [23] brings us all and the planets and suns to death. Yet

these heavens adorn
And proclaim it . . .
by way of majesty
In the sky, as crown and diamond cabala.[24]

The movement of W. H. Auden's work toward an explicit Christian statement may be taken as significant for the direction if not the goal of much of the wrestling with the modern situation. This would agree with Silone's remark that "the rediscovery of a Christian heritage in the revolution of our time remains the most important gain that has been made in these last years for the conscience of our generation." [25] As few others Auden has been in position to register the intellectual, as well as the spiritual predicaments of the time, both because of the alertness of his intelligence and of the social conscience which characterized his circle. His writing for a considerable period echoed both the dehumanization and anguish of modern men, as well as the confusion of belief.

In his "Christmas Oratorio" we can observe not only these moods but their transmutation into faith, and so have a revealing presentation of both sides of the same coin. It is one theme of this work that the initiation into estrangement and the exploration of the mistaken alternative must proceed to their limit before the way out presents itself.

---

[22] *Ibid.*
[23] *Ibid.*
[24] *Ibid.*
[25] Ignazio Silone, *And He Hid Himself: A Play in Four Acts,* Harper & Brothers, New York, 1946, p. v.

> For the garden is the only place there is, but you will not find it
> Until you have looked for it everywhere and found nowhere that is
>   not a desert.[26]

What comes with the necessary "miracle" is not a different world, but the same world in a different light.

What is here of particular interest is the way Auden deals with the two issues our discussion has raised: the tyranny of intellect and the dilemma between affirmation and negation of the natural order. The "Christmas Oratorio" follows the episodes of the nativity narratives in the Gospels, and orchestrates their implications by means of discourses placed in the mouths of the participants in the familiar scenes and of narrators, choruses and other additions to the cast.

On the eve of the annunciation, a moment at which the secular world always stands, the Four Faculties of man, Intuition, Feeling, Sensation, and Thought—corresponding to the four elements in Blake's "Gates of Paradise": earth, water, air, and fire—are represented as sundered from each other since the fall of man, and, therefore, in their separate anarchic self-assertion, as false guides. The condition of Thought is presented as follows, and here we are to bear in mind the inhibition of imagination and faith by intellect in Tate's "Sonnets at Christmas." It is the emptiness of intellect, and, therefore, the vacuity of the life of the autonomous mind that Auden emphasizes. "Thought" speaks:

> . . . where I was,
> The haunting ghosts were figures with no ground,
> Areas of wide omission and vast regions
> Of passive colour; higher than any squeak,
> One note went on forever; an embarrassed sum
> Stuck on the stutter of a decimal,
> And points almost coincident already
> Approached so slowly they could never meet.
> There nothing could be stated or constructed:
> To Be was an archaic nuisance.[27]

[26] W. H. Auden, "Christmas Oratorio," *The Collected Poetry of W. H. Auden,* Random House, New York, 1945, pp. 407 ff.

[27] *Ibid.*

What the incarnation must mean to sophistication is stated by the Star
of the Nativity:

> I am that star most dreaded by the wise,
> For they are drawn against their will to me,
> Yet read in my procession through the skies
> The doom of orthodox sophrosyne. . . .
>
> All those who follow me are led
> Onto that Glassy Mountain where are no
> Footholds for logic, to that Bridge of Dread
> Where knowledge but increases vertigo. . . .[28]

But the "Oratorio" also deals with the issues of sense and imagination, the renewal of innocence in man's enjoyment of the natural
order, thus excluding all false asceticism. The "romantics," caught
in an unredeemed "Time and Space" which, therefore, change Love
into voluptuousness, intercede for each other:

> Joseph, Mary, pray for those
> Misled by moonlight and the rose,
> For all in our perplexity. . . .
> Pray for us, enchanted with
> The green Bohemia of that myth
> Where knowledge of the flesh can take
> The guilt of being born away,
> Simultaneous passions make
> One eternal chastity:
> Pray for us romantics, pray.[29]

The answer is found in the acclamation of the Wise Men at the
manger:

> O Living Love replacing phantasy,
> O Joy of life revealed in Love's creation;
> Our mood of longing turns to indication:
> Space is the Whom our loves are needed by,
> Time is our choice of How to love and Why.[30]

[28] *Ibid.*
[29] *Ibid.*
[30] *Ibid.*

In the word of Simeon the two deliverances are summed up:

Because in Him the Word is united to the Flesh without loss of perfection, Reason is redeemed from incestuous fixation on her own Logic, for the One and the Many are simultaneously revealed as real. . . .

Because in Him the Flesh is united to the Word without magical transformation, Imagination is redeemed from promiscuous fornication with her own images. . . .[31]

Thus the warring faculties of man are restored to a harmonious unity by the incarnation.

We may draw three brief conclusions from the evidence adduced. First, it is true that the larger part of the most significant poetry of today is ambiguous or heretical, if tested by our Christian tradition. But, secondly, such productions are offering a necessary criticism, correction, and protest. Thirdly, such productions when scrutinized more deeply surprise us, for we discover how far they are, after all, rooted in our religious tradition, witness to it, and in some cases move toward its fuller recovery.

[31] *Ibid.*

XVIII

THE LITERARY MIND AND RELIGIOUS RESPONSIBILITY

BY

ÉMILE CAILLIET

If I sense aright the mood of the busy men who took time out to think about art and literature, they are not essentially motivated by feelings of empathy or urges for temporary orgies of wish fulfilment. They are not mere *dilettanti* lending themselves to all sorts of mental attitudes without surrendering to any cause whatsoever. The fact is they are at opposite poles from that Aristotelian gourmand of the *Nicomachean Ethics* who prayed that his throat might become longer than a crane's, implying that it was the *contact* he took pleasure in.

Those who stimulated and organized the lectures which led to this volume were essentially concerned with the problem of the literary mind and religious responsibility—the responsibility of the men of letters under consideration, to be sure; yet, ultimately their own responsibility within sight of the ever widening and deepening gap now yawning between the realm of culture and the realm of religion.

I

The basic issue involved in our problem was brought to a head in France by Bourget's novel, *The Disciple*. The work presented, under the guise of fiction, one of the two intellectual leaders of the nineties —and I mean Taine, the other being Renan—in the person of an intellectually honest philosopher of science, strictly deterministic in his views. An unknown disciple was supposed to have taken eagerly to the new teaching. Thereupon the youth had become convinced of these two essential truths: first, that science requires experimentation, even and especially in the study of man; second, that our traditional notions of good and evil are obsolete, inasmuch as virtue and vice prove to be mere byproducts, just like sugar and vitriol. And so the disciple proceeded to experiment on a candid young lady, with the result that she committed suicide.

The book created an uproar. Was the old philosopher responsible for the girl's death? Brunetière, the mouthpiece for the traditionalists, exalted Bourget's novel for having exposed at long last the danger of reckless publications, even if such recklessness were candidly meant to further the cause of science. To which Anatole France retorted in the name of liberalism that this was pure nonsense: a writer could not be held responsible for the overt acts of psychopathic self-styled disciples. The resulting exchange of letters between Bourget and Taine on the subject was also most interesting. Although detached in tone, Taine's letters revealed a man touched to the quick. His defense consisted in questioning the validity of his own replica in the old philosopher of the novel. Think of it! A man of abstractions, never having done as much in science as a single monograph. It must have been for such lack of actual practice that the character had lost contact with any sense of reality. Passing next to the offensive, Taine added for good measure that only the extension of the scientific notion of determinism to the study of ethics could safeguard the cause of morality by undergirding a genuine sense of responsibility. The debate lasted for generations, as anyone who knows the delight of the French for a good argument will readily understand. Yet even the most hopeless sophists could not help being haunted by the final scene of the novel, where the old philosopher caught himself muttering the Lord's Prayer as he watched with the mother over the body of his dead disciple.

I have not been in France recently. Yet I suppose that comments on Bourget's *Disciple* still proceed in about the same way in academic circles, even after the terrible tragedy of the past war—or should I say, on account of it? The old country finds it hard to break away from tradition, from that wisdom unaware of itself in which centuries of experience transmit their ultimate witness. Paul Souriau, at one time my professor of philosophy at the university, who was an agnostic of Protestant heritage, spoke on this matter of responsibility very much like his Roman Catholic colleague in a near by seminary: a man who *publishes,* he used to say, underlining the last word with an unforgettable tone of gravity—a man who *publishes, ipso facto* contracts a direct responsibility to the public. And he went on drawing a sharp contrast between what he called "small art" and "great art." To him, "small art" was any form of artistic expression catering to the lower instincts or passions of the public; whereas "great art" would ultimately prove to be noble in thought and intention. Emphatically the unethical could never attain to true greatness. We sometimes objected with reference to a certain type of literature meant for edification, which did not even deserve the name of literature. To this Souriau agreed. He had never said that edifying literature was great literature, or even literature at all. He merely maintained that baseness had no place in truly great forms of art. I leave it to the reader to disagree or to acquiesce. I, for one, have always felt, even in the darkest days of France, that you cannot quite despair of a country where critics and university professors will unite deep within on such views as are backed by our entire Western tradition at its best.

Since coming to this country, I have delighted in finding an echo of beloved voices in the motto of one of New York's morning newspapers: "All the News That's Fit to Print." As I wake up to read this motto every morning that God makes, I know that I am still a citizen of this Western world.

II

I take it that on this general principle of the responsibility of the writer we are all agreed. But we are agreed, some will say, because the principle is so broad in scope that it hardly affects any specific aspect of our contemporary scene. One is reminded of the poet's imagined long tirade to the one who set fire to the great library at Alexandria. When the discourse on the unique value of the great books destroyed by the blaze was over, the individual to whom it was addressed answered simply: "I can't read."

And so, many a man of letters familiar with the situation in America today may politely stifle a yawn at this point of our discussion, and say in effect: "Well and good; but the books we write remain for the most part unread, and when they are read, those who read them have sense enough to see through them. Our first and foremost responsibility is to our own selves and families; in other words, to our publishers. We must write what will stand a fair chance to sell. To be useful, therefore, any discussion of our so-called responsibility should begin at this level—admittedly a low level but this situation is hardly one of our own making."

There is a strong feeling abroad among our contemporaries that literature is impractical and unimportant. It is regarded at best as a pastime which would compare more favorably with bridge, the radio, the movies, or television, were it not for the fact that it makes severe demands on the reader. Thus an insistence on every side on fragmentation, dilution, and popularization. Let us look closer into such subnormal or even abnormal aspects of our subject, and thereby secure more relevant insights into what may be called the contemporary climate of the literary mind.

There is the first fact that America spends far more on magazines than it does on books. Besides, except for the *Saturday Review of Literature* and a few others with a genuine literary concern, most of such periodicals are devoted to some kind of trade, recreation, hobby, or sport. Even in serious reviews interested in literature, essays are out of question. Emerson would hardly get a chance with magazine editors today. As for poets, everyone knows that they have generally been out of business for quite some time, the only outstanding exception being T. S. Eliot, and we may see in this a sign of the perennial character of religious literature. But more about this in a moment. The fact remains that the ten leading American reviews which are at all interested in literature put together, do not succeed in publishing an average of one short poem a day. Longer poems would of course draw only rejection slips. Fragmentation implies shrinkage. This is the age of the short poem, the short story, and the one act play. We have even by now a number of short Bibles. Ours is a hurried generation, and so time itself is cut to bits. We have so much to get in today.

Morris Bishop, to whom I owe some of my statistics, wittily points out that we may nowadays buy modernized Chaucers, dehydrated Shakespeares, Karl Marx for children, and that "the stories of Greek mythology have been retold in a comic strip, under the general title of Alley-Oop."

Dilution further entices the unwilling reader easily discouraged by the number of new words he encounters in so-called great literature. Why should not writers use the words of everybody? This suggestion was already made by Pascal; but his context was different. Said Pascal: "When we play tennis, we both play with the same ball, but one places it better. I had as soon it were said that I used words employed before." The accent is evidently placed by him on the use of the pertinent word. As every writer worth his salt very well knows, there is only one specific, irreplaceable term that fits into a certain situation. It is the knack of hitting upon such terms continually, often by dint of laborious effort, which distinguishes the great stylist and helps dress the truth in beautiful garb. And this is, properly, the function of the artist. But then, suppose that a work be reduced to the mere factual values of its raw material, the substance being forcibly isolated from the form. What will remain will be valuable still, no doubt, more especially in certain cases such as that of an author forcefully pleading a case. Steinbeck's *Grapes of Wrath* offers a good illustration of a work which could be thus processed. The number of "digest" magazines already in existence would tend to show that such a type of processing has already been promoted to the rank of a national industry. Yet high is the price our culture must pay in terms of literary values. Have you ever read the Sermon on the Mount in Basic English?

The criterion behind all such barbarism has by now come within view. Many of us know it to be well in force on the American campus in such matters as those of curriculum or evaluation of teaching personnel—namely the criterion of popularity. Our ultimate reference is of course to progressive education, with due regard for the undeniable merits of the same. To illustrate, there is the example of that young college instructor who achieved popularity by telling the story of literature in terms of the most catching samples he could find, every rough spot being eliminated—and this meant at times whole areas of writing. He was finally found out and became a successful columnist. There could obviously be no equivalent to collegiate authorities to watch over the growing demand for popular literature in our day.

A rather amusing outcome of some of the tendencies we have just seen at work is the reduction and ultimate elimination of reading material in magazines and books. The vogue of pictorial periodicals is typical of this same trend which kept for weeks *White Collar Zoo* at the top of all best seller lists. It was duly classified under "general reading" which is supposed to be of a more serious nature than "fiction." And to be sure there was no fiction there, and I myself enjoyed it. The tensions of modern life helping, we all gladly revert to that more tender age when we turned the pages to look at the pictures. The thing to do is to keep this inclination under control.

Those who feel the pressure most directly are the publishers. It is fair to say that, generally speaking, neither the public at large nor the authors themselves, especially in the academic world, realize the plight of publishing firms today. While it is true that 3,000,000 out of 150,000,000 people in America buy one of the six or seven leading magazines every week or every month, those who buy books may be counted only by the thousands, rarely in terms of hundreds of thousands. The plain fact is that any large department store in New York does three times as much business as the total book trade in the United States.

Curiously enough, and this is of special interest to our subject, the all time best sellers in English are to be found in the religious field, the Bible and Bunyan's *Pilgrim's Progress* heading the list. Such books as Sheldon's *In His Steps* have sold by millions of copies. And it is still true in our day, especially since the war. *Peace of Mind* is nearing the million mark. Others are well on their way: *The Big Fisherman, The Greatest Story Ever Told, The Seven Storey Mountain* and *The Screwtape Letters,* to name only a few. There is more at stake here than what a recent critic called "the scramble for serenity," more than "a fad" or an "ersatz faith" as he diagnosed it. Neither is it sufficient to speak of escapism. As Nash K. Burger, a member of the book review staff of the *New York Times,* brought out recently, the real question is to know from what people want to escape, and to what. Do we not all spend a large part of our time in "escaping"—from hunger, sickness, and ignorance? His diagnosis went far deeper—in fact, to the very roots of our own problem. To him, readers are turning once more to books that explain or portray the Judeo-Christian world-view because the current, purely humanistic views have been found inadequate.

We may rest assured that publishers will be only too glad to continue looking for more such books as beautifully express their author's views on God and human nature. We ourselves may well exult in the vindication of the fact that a sense of religious responsibility will ultimately prove rewarding to both authors and publishers. Nevertheless this is another way of stating that before we pass any harsh judgment on contemporary literature, we had better realize what are some of the characteristics of the climate in which it tries to subsist. The word, "exist," would obviously fail to do justice to what must be called in the main the present day plight of literature.

III

Could it be that the difficult situation confronting contemporary men of letters and their publishers is that they have lost the appreciative, highly qualified patronage enjoyed in another age, only to be reduced to a regime of near slavery to a somewhat unappreciative, unqualified multitude? But such a statement would obviously be unfair to the small elite of readers who appreciate both the profit and the pleasure derived from genuine literary values.

The question then is: do we, as intellectual and spiritual leaders, belong to this elite? Do we take full advantage of the possibilities available in the world of letters, or do we in effect, through some aloofness, actually join hands with those millions who make life difficult for literary minded men of goodwill? Upon the answers we are ready to make to such heart searching questions may depend the solution to the problem of the literary mind and religious responsibility. Denunciation will simply not do. We will get the literature we deserve. It now becomes clear that the responsibility involved at this point is first and foremost our own. Yet responsibility works both ways, and the possibilities at stake are apparently of considerable magnitude.

What is most to be deplored in the plight of men of letters in our day also becomes clear, and it is this: the majority of our contemporaries will not volunteer the time and initial effort required to make reading profitable as well as enjoyable. This is already true in school and college, although it would be unfair to blame this state of mind on the teaching profession. Granted that there are too many uninspired and uninspiring teachers, that the type of preparation for the Ph.D. degree granting access to the teaching of literature in colleges and universities is for the most part detrimental to the end in view, the roots of this situation go deeper yet. They must be traced to the various sets of circumstances which are rapidly transforming this land of pioneers into a land of boy-men. This appellation I borrow from the title of a poem by Karl Shapiro in a recent number of *The New Yorker*, "Boy-Man":

> He knows the application of the book
> But not who wrote it; shuts it like a shot.
> Rather than read, he thinks that he will look;
> Rather than look, he thinks that he will talk;
> Rather than talk, he thinks that he will not
> Bother at all; would rather ride than walk.[1]

Matthew Arnold reminded another generation that some men waste all of their spare time, that most waste much, but that all of us waste some. He pointed out that should any man be given all the time that he now wastes, he would have plenty left for culture, that is, according to our author, for the best that was thought and said in the world.

But, frankly, there is no problem of time involved here. Thanks to our labor saving devices we have more leisure than we ever had. The grievous thing is that boy-men will not volunteer time and initial effort, because they are by now persuaded that "the real thing" lies elsewhere. A study of the ways in which time and money are being

[1] Karl Shapiro, "Boy-Man," *The New Yorker*, New York, 22, January 11, 1947, p. 26. Excerpt, reprinted by permission. Copyright, 1947, The New Yorker Magazine, Inc.

spent in our contemporary world would go a long way to reveal our actual scale of values. But then few readers of this paper would begin to compare with such boxers, blues singers, or even horses which I could name. "Where your treasure is, there will your heart be also."

A great shift of interest has been taking place in our civilization, causing it to drift away from literature, to seek its gratification in a new industrial and political order; in sex, in sports, in streamlined automobiles, and non-contributory pension plans, along with ballots, lobbies, blueprints, and balance sheets. This involves, as so many counterparts, aversion for dependence upon God, for such notions as those of family, purity, self-denial, the traditional idea of the gentleman. With the frontiers vanished the pioneering conditions of American life. The expression of virility is lost in literature, because virility itself has been lost. So also the intellectual and spiritual assurances which carried a man through a well ordered life become intimidated by the loud publicity of counseling services, guidance clinics, mental hygiene and adjustment programs. And, lo and behold, this last sentence reads like a literary manifesto.

It would seem that the transition is all the more painful to those with a moral and religious concern, that it began at a time when determinism and mechanism still held the scientific field. No intellectual leader as yet could foresee the aftermath of Maxwell's electromagnetic theory of light. To all practical purpose the universe was still conceived of by the intelligentsia on the model of a Newtonian big clock whose regularity was now seen to be reflected in the human soul as a principle of order. These were the days when such scholars as Fechner and Foucauld proceeded with the elaboration of a science known as psychophysics based on Weber's law, the experimental basis of the measurement of sensations. Henceforth tests and measurements were on our horizon. Contemporary man was well on his way to becoming a walking set of equations. In such circumstances any reference to the freedom of his will became merely a convenient way of speech, just as one spoke of "sunrise" and of "sunset." So was any reference to the spirituality of the soul in the human animal. For contemporary man was by now known to be also a walking museum of antiquities, with no less than 180 vestigial structures, including the vermiform appendix and the abbreviated tail with its set of caudal muscles. Harry A. Overstreet's best seller, *The Mature Mind,* gives one to understand that in such a context the "goodness-badness" theory now belongs to what he calls "the pre-psychological ages." In other words, the very notions of good and evil are ultimately found to be also museum pieces. The author adds for good measure the "knowledge-ignorance" theory.

Contemporary man, then, is thought of increasingly as an animal unfolding in a social environment in which such obsolete scales of measurement as good and evil, knowledge and ignorance, should make room for the "maturity-immaturity" view. Such notions are being generalized to such a degree that they are made to extend even to theology. Once Henry N. Wieman, for example, defined God as that character of events to which man must adjust himself in order to attain the greatest goods and avoid the greatest ills.

These rapid indications are not to be construed as suggesting that the sense of responsibility is disintegrating in our society. Such men as we have mentioned write under the compulsion of a high sense of duty. It just means that for better or for worse the *climate* of responsibility has changed. This fact should be brought out even in so brief an analysis as this. It is evident that no evaluation of the contemporary scene should in all honesty be made according to a frame of reference which our contemporaries feel inclined to ignore as obsolete. The issue as to whether or not it *is* obsolete, remains of course entirely in a world of thought where the dangers of expediency are also being increasingly appreciated.

"Responsibility" calls for a complement, *i.e.,* for what? or to whom? The new contemporary notion of responsibility is modern to the core. As such, it implies a redefinition in terms of empirically verifiable processes of what proves to be a basic, practical, concern. Concern, first and foremost for what such men as Professor Burtt call *Right Thinking* in the light of the best which a candid approach to the whole process of scientific methodology can teach. Or one may think of the type of thinking suggested by President James B. Conant of Harvard University, under the title "Certain principles of the tactics and strategy of science," in the fourth chapter of his book *On Under-*

standing Science. In spite of the hopeful signs already pointed out with relation to the present popularity of religious books, it appears that the whole intellectual drift of our age is still very much under the sway of science. The obvious reason for this is that science knows how to do things so as to get results.

Responsibility, then, is seen to be first and foremost to that kind of truth which everyone concerned has been given a chance to discuss and criticize, until nobody can any longer find fault with the outcome, at least for the time being. Fresh information being brought forward, a reconsideration will have to take place, the whole issue being re-opened. Responsibility, as our contemporaries see it, is to the best that can be known and thought empirically by the intellectually honest. In this context, moreover, the best imperative is seen to be a clear indicative.

Once set in this new light, the responsibility of the literary mind to many a man of letters remains directly involved in a clear guidance through the intricacies of the human heart, and in the corresponding duty to vivify life and illuminate its meaning.

IV

And so we are led to think afresh in terms of contemporary categories, which is the perennial task of literature. In other words, our men of letters may be said to fulfil their mission to the best of their ability with the light they have. In so doing they are anxious to keep in close touch with the world of men and affairs on which they depend in every way, more especially for their work and for their own sustenance. Although they try to vivify and illuminate its life, this world is not of their own making. They use all forms of available popularized scientific disciplines to understand it and to guide it, in the constant awareness that literature deals with the whole of man, and, therefore, need not be restrained by the specifications of scientific disciplines. Above all, they neglect no point of contact which a candid observation may suggest.

Those religious circles which certain extreme theological views imported from Switzerland are isolating more and more from the world of men and affairs, and more especially from the elite, would do well to ponder over the example thus given to us by men of letters in our own day. It is a significant fact that the books on theological subjects which really succeed in establishing contact with the reading public are those of literary men. The well known work of popularization achieved by C. S. Lewis constitutes a fine example of this. More recently it took a Harvard man of letters to write at long last the book which would do justice to the much caricatured Jonathan Edwards.

Nobody would deny that our literary world is greatly confused and lacks leadership. So also its sense of responsibility seems too sensitive to changes of weather in public opinion. For such weaknesses, however, theologians and churchmen have chiefly themselves to blame. Let them resume proper contacts with the world of culture in general, and with the literary world in particular, and they will soon come to the realization that a sense of religious responsibility was mostly wanting on their own part, with the result that religion and culture became more and more estranged.

It is evident in all this that as I have reached the point of passing, or rather, suggesting, what seems to me pertinent judgments, I limit myself to what concerns the Reformed faith to which I belong. In so doing I can hardly refrain an expression of admiration, if not of envy, for what has already been done by our Jewish and Roman Catholic brethren. This is said also in the awareness of the great heritage which continues to bind us together at a time when the high values we cherish are being threatened by a common enemy already infiltrating within our gates.

A few years ago, some of the leading Protestant theologians of this country were called together in one of our great American centers of learning, to be constituted as the editorial board of a new review. The editor-in-chief, who was also the founder, made it clear that his aim was to restore theology to its former rank and dignity as the "Queen of the Sciences." The boldness of this statement overwhelmed the group. There was a hush, then a murmur in which timid wonder became articulate: "How can this be brought about—nay, how can this even be uttered in our day?" Many a listener evidently would have been satisfied with less, with at least some kind of recognition for theology as a science in our day. All he would concede was that if true theology is queenly in rank and dignity, its superiority must become manifest not by many arrogant claims to veneration, but by the validation of its worth in humble, effective service.

The discussion had by now become lively. Some kind of opposition was crystallizing, the gist of the objection being that an immediate claim to her lost throne by theology may be somewhat unwise, at least for the present. For on the true status of theology in rank and dignity everyone seemed to agree. The area of disagreement was merely around the messianic secret: was it or was it not advisable to reveal it at the outset and proceed without any more ado to call theology the "Queen of the Sciences"?

The nays seemed to have it although there was not as yet any motion on the floor. A theologian need not have any motion on the floor before he starts arguing.

Then something happened. A quiet, retiring man who had been increasingly drawing the attention of everyone because he had thus far kept his peace, gently cleared his throat as if to speak. There was a silence. For everyone had by now recognized Walter Lowrie, the Kierkegaardian scholar. Yet Walter Lowrie was evidently not in a hurry to have his mind known. He took time for a deep puff from his pipe, and then, with an infinitely conciliatory tone, while a spark of light brightened the twinkle of his left eye, he suggested meekly:

"Gentlemen, could not you at least call *her* the First-Lady-in-Waiting?"

I, for one, never forgot Walter Lowrie's remark. Theology has now been the First-Lady-in-Waiting for a long time. Science managed to break away from its Aristotelian stagnation ever since the days of Galileo, and has progressed by leaps and bounds down to our day. Meanwhile literature has managed with various fortunes and emphases, to remain in touch with man and his world, providing inspiration and at least some kind of leadership. Where both scientists and men of letters have missed a higher mark with reference to their respective duties to individuals and to groups, the reason has been the absence of that genuine leadership which only theologians and churchmen could give. Let me repeat that at this point I merely speak as a Protestant of my Protestant brethren, and this, allow me to insist, in a spirit of constructive criticism.

The conclusion as to where responsibility is found to be wanting may now be safely drawn. I, for one, have no stone to cast at our contemporary men of letters. Neither do I condemn them in any way. And it would take One, the latchet of Whose shoes I am not worthy to unloose, to say to them, "Go, and sin no more."

V

Only the laborious formulation of a long range program will remedy the situation in which our culture finds itself as a result of such shortcomings. The time is hardly ripe, moreover, for the constitution of theology as a science. The human sciences (*Geisteswissenschaften*) from which such a full fledged science will have to draw a varied and extensive amount of information, have themselves hardly reached a scientific status as yet. A frank acknowledgment of the resulting situation will go a long way toward a realistic evaluation of the difficulties which confront us. This much is clear: the fulness of time is not yet. One of the worst mistakes that could be made would be to believe that we have solved the problems, while the truth is that these same problems have hardly been formulated. *It is not that theology is obsolete, then, but that it still is, and for an unpredictable length of time, in the embryonic stage.* In similar circumstances great philosophers of the past—Descartes being probably the most outstanding illustration of this—have found it advisable to provide themselves with a temporary house where they could live during the time of building and rebuilding. But there is more here than the advisability of adopting provisional views and safe maxims which would allow us to be resolute in our actions while we have to remain uncertain in many of our judgments.

Our Hebrew-Christian tradition does not primarily proceed upon theological speculation, but upon the reality of God—more specifically upon the four opening words of the Bible which *ipso facto* become the motto of all straight and relevant thinking, "In the beginning God." This is the norm. Neither need we apologize or feel that we must come forth with proofs before anything else is done. The burden of proof truly rests upon these creatures who feel bold enough to question the reality of the Creator. The true way originates in Him Who is the Principle and End of all things, the only One, therefore, Who can give meaning to the world of nature and of man. Only He can help map out the path, because He is the Lord of the Hill and the Originator of the Map.

The resulting corollary was formulated by Matthew Arnold in this pungent, three word axiom: "Religion is given." If the author of *Literature and Dogma* were asked, "What is the object of basic religion thus understood," he would reply, "Conduct." And when asked further, "What is conduct in this connection," he would answer, "Righteousness," which is the master word of the Old Testament and the object of Bible religion. Before attempts are made to define God in the debatable terms of metaphysics, therefore, this much may be said of Him, *i.e.,* that He is "the Eternal not ourselves Who makes for righteousness." In the words of Micah which unite us all in a common call, "He hath showed thee, O man, what is good: and what doth the Lord require of thee, but to do justly, and to love mercy, and to walk humbly with thy God?" It is noteworthy that for the past one hundred years some of the most highly cultured men concerned with religion in colleges and universities, in this country and abroad, who have submitted religion to the harshest criticism, have struck the rock roughly at this point. In other words, agnosticism having been given full sway, we are allowed to uncover, as it were, the rockbed on which a sane Hebrew-Christian tradition might be rebuilt, and there precisely because it had been built on it originally according to the Providence of the Living God. Hence the consciousness of continuity preserved down to our day in our cultural heritage, as, for instance, in the language of prayers drawn from all parts of the Bible, the singing of Hebrew psalms in Christian churches, and the liturgy. C. H. Dodd thus calls attention to those churches following the traditional Western rite where they sing on Easter Eve the hymn called *Exultet,* which commemorates God's dealings with His people in history. "This is the night in which Thou didst first lead our fathers, the children of Israel, out of Egypt, and didst make them pass dryshod through the Red Sea." And so "the Eternal not ourselves Who makes for righteousness" is also the Covenanter God, "the great Doer of redeeming things." Such is the spiritual context of the cultural tradition we call our Western culture. As such, it needs to be restated and reaffirmed afresh today in the face of Communist aggression.

VI

The main implication for the individual of what has just been brought out, is that our thinking at its best is existential thinking. Let us not be afraid of that word, "existential." Kierkegaard—and he was supposed to know—traced his own use of the notion back to Socrates, as well as to the Hebrew prophets. Should the men of Athens offer Socrates his life on condition that he betray his call? His answer would be, "I shall obey God rather than you." And we know that these were not empty words for him. This pagan who knew God only through general revelation was actually obedient to the divine voice unto death. This was his way to fulfil what he called "the philosopher's mission of searching into myself and other men." Truly the quest of a committed soul. And this is existential thinking at its highest. To be sure, there is ample room for delusion in the notion, as evidenced all through the trend down to our day. We are emphatically not saying that Existentialism is Hebrew-Christian, or even Socratic, but we would insist that our Hebrew-Christian tradition, with the Socratic heritage it assimilated on its way, is genuinely existential. As such it is a committed way of thought and life which makes no room for the *dilettante,* that is, the man who lends himself to all sorts of theoretical attitudes without ever surrendering to any cause.

We may follow this high road of our cultural heritage through such men as Augustine and Pascal. By their works we shall know them. Augustine's treatises remain closed books until they are read in the context of his *Confessions.* They all express in one way or another the basic attitude expressed in the famous dictum, "Our hearts are uneasy until they find their rest in Thee." Henceforth the first and foremost duty of each one of us is the duty of inquiry, with the whole of our destiny at stake. Pascal developed this thought to the point of classifying men on the basis of the attitude each one takes with regard to this primary concern. There are, as he came to see it, three kinds of persons: those who serve God, having found Him; those who are busy seeking Him, without having found Him; and finally those who live without seeking Him, and without having found Him. He felt overcome with consternation at the sight of those insensate persons who, not having found God, yet live without seeking Him. He spoke of them as being, in all respects, like men in chains, all of them condemned to death; every day some are killed in the sight of others; those who remain see their fate in that of their fellows, and yet all they do is to await their turn, looking at one another sorrowfully and without hope. To read pages such as these—but more, to see how they became flesh and blood in the heroic life from which they proceeded, is truly to come under the Shadow of the Almighty, invisible but constantly present on the human scene.

About two centuries later, Kierkegaard, the Danish Pascal, rediscovered this same passionate outlook. His thought also is inseparable from a poignant concern with all that is at stake in a committed life of righteousness under the Living God of Scripture. That is what we mean when we call it genuinely existential. It was the thought of a man who, at the age of twenty-two, wanted clarity with respect to what he ought to do; who, ten years later, had come to the realization that "existence constitutes the highest interest of the existing individual," so that "his interest in his existence constitutes his reality." Such genuine existential thinking, then, proceeds from a basic either/or, with all that is involved in such a life/death issue —the same age old issue of Joshua, "choose you this day whom ye will serve"; the same issue dramatically put by Pascal in the terms of an ultimate Wager with everything at stake. And these men, all of them, very well knew the high cost of such genuine thinking. Pascal believed only those witnesses who stand ready to have their throats cut open for the sake of their testimony. So also along the path of Kierkegaard's philosophical itinerary, the stations were called *Fear and Trembling, The Concept of Dread,* and *The Sickness unto Death*. This much is as sure as it is profoundly moving: such a life-view makes sense only in the context of the Book which opens with the four words now seen to be the charter of all relevant thinking, "In the beginning God."

Could it be, then, that our contemporaries are adrift because this genuine religious context of our culture has been lost as a whole? Philosophers and literary men, try as they may, merely succeed in restoring, or rather, distorting, shreds and partial perspectives here and there. Thus, Karl Marx, having forgotten the tongue he originally learned from Augustine, blurted out in a vernacular of his own. Some debris of our religious tradition were revived in monstrous ideological organisms in Berlin, Rome, and Moscow. Man will always pay in terms of such ideologies for the loss of his faith in God. And here is the resulting paradox: we now live in a world where it takes less "nerve" to be a Communist than a Jew or a Christian. While the portraits of Lenin and Stalin are being proudly paraded in Europe and in Asia, almost any sophomore in our own colleges would blush to be seen with a Bible under his arm.

No wonder virility has been lost. It is still less surprising that responsibility has been allowed to degenerate into a problem. The whole problem of the literary mind and religious responsibility may now be viewed as a mere symptom pointing to the deeper nature of the malady: we no longer see our cultural heritage as a whole in its divine context. To say that as a result the leaders of public opinion do not live up to their responsibilities, would amount to making a glaring understatement. The truth is that we have become basically unrighteous in the biblical sense of the word. This Western world which we like to call our own, reminds one of a city called Babel which remained unfinished. And so once more the sons of Noah are being scattered abroad upon the face of the earth.

Let a man of letters of our age speak the closing word on this, in the awareness that such a word can only be the outcry of a burdened soul:

> If drunk with sight of power, we loose
>   Wild tongues that have not Thee in awe,
> Such boastings as the Gentiles use,
>   Or lesser breeds without the Law—

Lord God of Hosts, be with us yet,
Lest we forget, lest we forget.[2]

[2] Rudyard Kipling, "Recessional," *The Five Nations*. Copyright, 1903, by Rudyard Kipling. Reprinted by permission of Mrs. George Bambridge and Doubleday & Company, Inc.

BIOGRAPHICAL SKETCHES

James Johnson Sweeney. Born Brooklyn, New York, 1900; studied at Georgetown University, Jesus College (Cambridge, England), Sorbonne, University of Siena (Italy); married and has three sons and two daughters; Contributor to *The New York Times,* 1929–1933, New York correspondent of the Chicago Evening Post Art World, 1931–1932; Director of Exhibition, Twentieth Century Painting and Sculpture, The University of Chicago, 1933–1934; Lecturer on Fine Arts, Institute of Fine Arts, New York University, 1935–1940; Director of Painting and Sculpture, Museum of Modern Art, New York, 1945–1946; Director of the Solomon R. Guggenheim Museum, since 1952; Director of Picasso Exhibition, Art Gallery of Toronto, 1949; Director exhibition, *American Painting 1950,* Virginia Museum of Fine Art, Richmond, 1950; Director of Exhibition *Masterpieces of the XXth Century,* Musée d'Art Moderne, Paris and the Tate Gallery, London, 1950; Installation of the U.S. Pavilion, Venice Biennale, 1952; vice-president, International Association of Art Critics since 1948; associate editor, *Transition,* 1935–1938; advisory editor *Partisan Review* since 1948; Director of *The Burlington Magazine,* London, since 1951; author of *Plastic Redirections in Twentieth Century Painting, African Negro Art, Alexander Calder, Marc Chagall, Burri, Antoni Gaudi* (With José Luis Sert), etc.; contributor of articles to American and European periodicals.

Albert Salomon. Born Berlin, Germany, 1891; studied at the University of Berlin, Freiburg, Heidelberg; married and has a son and a daughter; Professor of Sociology, Graduate Faculty, The New School for Social Research; Lecturer in Philosophy, Columbia University, 1950–1951; Lecturer, Brandeis University, 1951–1952; author of *The Tyranny of Progress* and articles in *Social Research, Journal of Social*

Philosophy, Philosophy and Phenomenological Research, Political Science Quarterly; editor of *Die Gesellschaft,* 1928–1931.

IRWIN EDMAN. Born New York City, 1896, died 1954; studied at Columbia University; unmarried; Lecturer on Philosophy, Columbia University, 1918–1919, Professor, 1935–1954; Executive Officer Department of Philosophy, Columbia University, 1945, Lecturer at Amherst College, University of California, Harvard University, Wesleyan University; Visiting Professor at Hamilton College, 1942, National University of Brazil, 1945; awarded gold medal by New York University Society of Libraries, 1949; LL.D. Goucher College, 1949; Johnsonian Professor of Philosophy, Columbia University, 1950; appointed a Fulbright Lecturer (France), 1951; author of *Arts and the Man, Fountainheads of Freedom, Philosopher's Quest,* etc.: editor of *The Philosophy of Santayana,* etc., contributor to *The Nation, New Republic, New York Times, New York Herald Tribune, Harper's Magazine, The Saturday Review of Literature, Atlantic Monthly,* and *The New Yorker*; member, editorial board, *The American Scholar.*

HORACE (VICTOR) GREGORY. Born Milwaukee, Wisconsin, 1898; studied at Milwaukee School of Fine Arts, University of Wisconsin; married and has a son and daughter; free lance writer from 1923 to 1934, contributing to *New Republic, The Nation, Atlantic Monthly, Hound and Horn, Poetry* (Chicago), *New Verse* (London), etc. Lecturer on Poetry and Critical Theory at Sarah Lawrence College since 1934; awarded Lyric Prize by *Poetry* Magazine, 1928, Helen Haire Levinson Prize by same, 1934, and the Russell Loines award for poetry from the American Institute of Arts and Letters, 1942; author of five books of poems, including *Selected Poems* (1951), translator *The Poems of Catullus* (new edition with new introduction, 1956), author in collaboration with Marya Zaturenska *A History of American Poetry 1900–1940, D. H. Lawrence: Pilgrim of the Apocalypse* (new edition with new introduction, 1957), editor *The Portable Sherwood Anderson,* (with Marya Zaturenska) *The Mentor Book of Religious Verse.*

THEODORE SPENCER. Born Villa Nova, Pennsylvania, 1902; died, 1949; studied at Princeton University, Cambridge University, Harvard University; married, one son; was Instructor and Tutor in English at Harvard University, 1927–1933; Assistant Professor, 1933–1939; was appointed Lecturer in English Literature at Cambridge in 1939, but because of the war remained at Harvard as Visiting Lecturer from Cambridge, 1939–1940; resigned Cambridge lectureship, becoming Associate Professor of English at Harvard, 1940–1946; from 1946 until his death was Boylston Professor of Rhetoric and Oratory at Harvard. He was Lowell Lecturer at Harvard in 1942; Phi Beta Kappa poet, College of William and Mary, 1942; Tufts College, 1943, and Harvard, 1943; trustee, Boston Athenaeum, New England Conservatory of Music, Wellesley College; Fellow in American Letters, Library of Congress; author of *Death and Elizabethan Tragedy, Shakespeare and the Nature of Man, The Paradox in the Circle* (verse), etc.; editor; contributor of articles and verse to *Atlantic Monthly, New Republic, The New Yorker,* and other magazines.

DELMORE SCHWARTZ. Born Brooklyn, New York, 1913; studied at University of Wisconsin, New York University, Harvard University; formerly associate editor, *Partisan Review*; author, *In Dreams Begin Responsibilities, Shenandoah* (verse play), *Genesis, The World is a Wedding,* and *Vaudeville for a Princess.*

DAVID DAICHES. Born Sunderland, England, 1912; studied at University of Edinburgh, Balliol College, Oxford University; married and has a son and two daughters; taught English at the University of Edinburgh, Andrew Bradley Fellow at Balliol College, Oxford University, Assistant Professor of English at The University of Chicago, Second Secretary, British Embassy, Washington, D.C., 1944–1946, Professor of English at Cornell University, 1946–1951, University Lecturer in English at Cambridge, England, 1951– , Visiting Professor of Criticism, Indiana University, 1956–1957. Contributor of poetry, articles, and essays to various periodicals; author of *The Novel and the Modern World, Robert Burns, Two Worlds,* etc.

KENNETH BURKE. Born Pittsburgh, Pennsylvania, 1897; studied at Ohio State University and Columbia University; married and has three daughters and two sons; did research work with the Laura Spelman Rockefeller Memorial, 1926–1927, was music critic of *The Dial,* 1927–1929, did editorial work, Bureau of Social Hygiene, 1928–1929, was music critic of *The Nation,* 1934–1936, in 1937 lectured on practice and theory of literary criticism, New School for Social Research; lectured on psychology of literary form and on Samuel Taylor Coleridge at the University of Chicago in 1938, Visiting Professor of English, 1949–1950; lecturer on theory and practice of literary criticism at Bennington College since 1943; taught at Kenyon School of English, summer, 1950; at School of English, Indiana University, summer, 1952; winner of Dial Award for distinguished service to American letters, 1928, recipient of Guggenheim Memorial Fellowship in 1935; recipient of a grant from the American Academy of Arts and Letters and National Institute of Arts and Letters in 1946; member, National Institute of Arts and Letters; author of *A Grammar of Motives, A Rhetoric of Motives, Counter-Statement, Permanence and Change, Attitudes toward History, Philosophy of Literary Form, The White Oxen and Other Stories, Towards a Better Life, Book of Moments, Poems 1915-54*; critical articles, book reviews; contributor to leading magazines.

STANLEY ROMAINE HOPPER. Born Fresno, California, 1907; studied at the University of Southern California, Boston University School of Theology, Harvard University, The University of Zurich, Switzerland, Mansfield College (Oxford), Drew Theological Seminary; married and has four sons; Lecturer in English Bible, Brothers College, Drew University, 1932-1935; Instructor, Assistant Professor and Associate Professor of Homiletics and the Christian Criticism of Life, 1935-1945, in Drew Theological Seminary; Assistant to the Dean, 1935-1945; Professor of Christian Ethics to 1952; Professor of Christian Philosophy and Letters since 1952; Dean of the Graduate School, Drew University, since July 1954. Ordained Methodist minister 1931. Pastor of First Congregational Church, Farmington, New Hampshire, 1928-1931; Tranquility-San Joaquin, California, Methodist Churches, 1927, Dinuba, California, 1928, Clifford, Pennsylvania, 1932-1933; Park Church, New Haven, Connecticut, 1933-1935. Editor, *The Drew Gateway*, since 1938. American delegate to the International Conference on Christianity and Art, at the Ecumenical Institute, Chateau de Bossey, Celigny, Switzerland, 1950. Chairman of the Commission on Literature of the Department of Worship and the Arts of the National Council of Churches. Author of *The Crisis of Faith*, Introduction to *The Riverside Poetry*, 1953, chapter on "The Future of Religious Symbolism—A Protestant View" in Religious Symbolism, edited by F. Ernest Johnson, 1954, chapter on "Augustine's Anti-Manichean Writings" in *Augustine Studies*, edited by Roy Battenhouse, 1955, exposition for Book of Jeremiah for *Interpreter's Bible*, 1956, chapter on "The Naming of the Gods in Hölderlin and Rilke," in *Christian-*

ity and the Existentialists, edited by Carl Michalson; 1956, introduction to *Riverside Poetry 2,* 1956, articles, poems, reviews, etc.

HARRY SLOCHOWER. Born in Austria, 1900; studied at the Universities of Berlin, Heidelberg, College of the City of New York, Columbia University; formerly with the William Alanson White Institute for Psychiatry; former Assistant Professor, Brooklyn College; Lecturer, The New School for Social Research; author of *No Voice is Wholly Lost, Three Ways of Modern Man, Thomas Mann's Joseph Story: An Interpretation*; contributing editor of *Philosophic Abstracts*; contributor to *Encyclopedia of the Social Sciences,* editor of *The Guide to Psychiatric and Psychological Literature,* and other American and European journals. Currently engaged in the practice of psychoanalysis.

CLEANTH BROOKS. Born Murray, Kentucky, 1906; studied at Vanderbilt University, Tulane University, Oxford University (Rhodes Scholar); married, no children; Lecturer and Professor of English at The Louisiana State University, 1932–1947; Lecturer and Visiting Professor at University of Texas, University of Michigan, and The University of Chicago; Professor of English at Yale University since 1947; managing editor and later editor (with Robert Penn Warren) of *The Southern Review,* 1935–1942; fellow of the Kenyon School of English, 1948–1952; author of *The Well Wrought Urn, Modern Poetry and the Tradition, Literary Criticism: a Short History* (with W. K. Wimsatt, Jr.), and others; editor and co-editor of many volumes on literary topics; contributor to *The Sewanee Review, The Kenyon Review, Partisan Review,* etc.

WILLIAM BARRETT. Born New York City, 1913; studied at the College of the City of New York and Columbia University; married, one child; taught at the University of Illinois, Brown University, served in the Diplomatic Service of the State Department during World War II, now Associate Professor Philosophy at New York University; a former Editor of *Partisan Review*; author of *What is Existentialism? Aristotle's Theory of Nature,* and numerous articles on philosophy and literature; contributor to *Commentary, Kenyon Review, Atlantic Monthly,* etc.

DENIS DE ROUGEMONT. Born Neuchâtel, Switzerland, 1906; studied at Neuchâtel, Vienna, Geneva; married and has one son and one daughter; Lecturer at the University of Frankfort, 1935–1936; publisher in Paris; writer OWI, New York, 1942–1943; Director, "Centre

Européen de la Culture," Geneva, 1950; Chairman Executive Committee, Congress for Cultural Freedom; author of *La Part du Diable,* (*The Devil's Share*), *Penser avec les mains, Politique de la Personne, L'Amour en l'Occident* (*Love in The Western World*), *Vivre en Amérique, Journal des Deux Mondes, Doctrine fabuleuse, Suites Neuchâteloises, L'Europe en Jeu, Lettres aux Députés Européens, Man's Western Quest,* and others; contributor to leading periodicals in Europe, the United States, and Latin America.

GEORGE R. KERNODLE. Born Camp Hill, Alabama, 1907; studied at Carnegie Institute of Technology, The University of Chicago, and Yale University; married, no children; taught at Western Reserve University, University of California at Los Angeles, State University of Iowa, University of Tulsa, University of Colorado, since 1952, in the Speech and Dramatic Arts Department at the University of Arkansas; author of *From Art to Theatre*; contributor to *Yale Review, Theatre Arts, Quarterly Journal of Speech,* and others.

JUDAH GOLDIN. Born New York City, 1914; studied at College of the City of New York, Seminary College of Jewish Studies, The Jewish Theological Seminary of America, Columbia University; married and has a daughter and son; Lecturer and Visiting·Associate Professor of Jewish Literature and History at Duke University, 1943–1945; Associate Professor of Religion, School of Religion, The State University of Iowa, 1946–1952; Dean of the Teachers Institute and Seminary College, The Jewish Theological Seminary of America, since 1952; author of *The Fathers According to Rabbi Nathan* (1955), *The Wisdom of the Fathers*; contributor of monographs and articles to *The Hebrew Union College Annual, The Journal of Religion, The Menorah Journal, Jewish Frontier,* and others; contributor to symposium, *The Jews: Their History, Culture and Religion.*

WALLACE FOWLIE. Born Brookline, Massachusetts, 1908; studied at Harvard University; Assistant Professor of French at Yale University, Associate Professor of French at The University of Chicago, now Chairman of French Department at Bennington College; author of *Rimbaud, The Clown's Grail, Clowns and Angels, Rimbaud's Illuminations, Mallarmé, Pantomime,* and others; editor of *Sixty Poems of Scève, Mid-Century French Poems, Journals of Jean Cocteau*; contributor to *The Sewanee Review, Accent, Partisan Review, The·Commonweal, Poetry,* and others.

AMOS NIVEN WILDER. Born, Madison, Wisconsin, 1895; studied at Oberlin College, Yale University, Mansfield College (Oxford), Harvard University, married and has a son and daughter; served with the American Ambulance Field Service, 1916–1917, with Seventeenth Field Artillery, Second Division in France, 1917–1919; recipient of Croix de Guerre; fellow, Belgian-American Foundation, University of Brussels, 1920–1921; ordained Congregational minister, 1926, serving as pastor of the First Church of Christ, North Conway, New Hampshire, until 1928; Associate Professor of Ethics and Christian Evidences at Hamilton College, 1930–1933; Professor of New Testament Interpretation at Andover-Newton Theological School, 1933–1943; Professor of New Testament Interpretation at the Chicago Theological Seminary and Federated Theological Faculty, The University of Chicago, 1943–1954; Visiting Professor, University of Frankfort, 1951 (spring) and 1952 (fall); Professor of New Testament Interpretation, Harvard Divinity School, 1954– ; Hollis Professor of Divinity in the Harvard Divinity School, 1956– ; also chairman, department of New Testament and early Christian literature; fellow, National Council on Religion in Higher Education; author, *The Healing of the Waters: Poems, Spiritual Aspects of the New Poetry, Eschatology and Ethics in the Teaching of Jesus, Modern Poetry and the Christian Tradition, Otherworldliness and the New Testament, New Testament Faith for Today,* Introduction and Exegesis of the Johannine Epistles (*Interpreter's Bible*).

ÉMILE CAILLIET. Born Dampierre, France, 1894; studied at College of Châlons, University of Nancy, University of Montpellier, University of Strasbourg (France); married and has three daughters and a son; served in 44th Infantry Regiment, French Army, in World War I, wounded in action was rescued by an American field ambulance, came to United States, 1927, citizen, 1937; taught French literature and philosophy at the University of Pennsylvania, Scripps College, Wesleyan University; lectured at Davidson College, McGill University; Stuart Professor of Christian Philosophy, Princeton Theological Seminary, since 1947; National Fellow French Academy of Colonial Sciences, 1932; Officier d'académie (France) for service in the field of letters, 1934; author of several works published in France dealing with primitive thinking and symbolistic expression, especially *Symbolisme et âmes primitives,* Paris, 1936; contributor of book reviews and articles. Author of *The Life of the Mind; Pascal: Genius in the Light of Scripture; Great Shorter Works of Pascal, The Literary Tradition of Ideology,* and other works.

Grateful acknowledgment is made for use of the quotations on the half-title pages, with the generous permission of the publishers as follows:

Longmans Green & Company for the quotation by Charles Péguy from their book, *Péguy and Les Cahiers de la Quinzaine*; Random House for the quotation by W. H. Auden from their book, *The Collected Poetry of W. H. Auden,* and for the quotation by Stephen Spender from their book, *The Edge of Being.*

INDEX

"Abyss, The," Tiutchev, 155
Adding Machine, The, Elmer Rice, 51-52
Affinity, channels of, 112
Affirmation, in modern poetry, 243-245
After Strange Gods, T. S. Eliot, 167
Age of Anxiety, W. H. Auden, 249-250
Alexander, Samuel, 194
Anderson, Maxwell, 198; on essence of tragedy, 49-50; *Key Largo,* 196-197; *Winterset,* 56, 196
Antic Hay, A. Huxley, 88-89
"Aphorisms," Franz Kafka, 158-159
Aquinas, St. Thomas, 34
Aristophanes, comedy of, 22
Aristotle, 60; function of tragedy, 79; *Rhetoric,* 118
Arnold, Matthew, 132, 137; "Dover Beach," 80-81, 82; on religion, 275; on science and religion, 128-131; on waste of time, 268
Arrival and Departure, Arthur Koestler, 203
Art: beauty and, 177; concepts of, 173-174; psychology of, 230-231; religion and, 128; science and, 129; sincerity and, 180; spiritual value of, 4-5; surface aspects of, 3, 8; vulgarization of, 176; work of, defined, 176, 177
Artist, 175; creativity of, 183-184; false, 177; incarnation of realities by, 183, 184; inspiration of, 183, 184-185; mission of, when fulfilled, 179-182; and other "makers," 175
Ash Wednesday, T. S. Eliot, 84, 103-104, 154, 163, 164, 167
As I Lay Dying, William Faulkner, 43
Auden, W. H., 26, 134, 156, 161, 162, 163; *Age of Anxiety,* 249-250; "Christmas Oratorio," 256-259; *Double Man,*

Auden, W. H. (*cont.*)
The, 154; quoted, 162, 169
Augustine, Saint, *Confessions,* 276
"Auroras of Autumn, The," Wallace Stevens, 255-256
Auschwitz, 123
Ayalti, J., "The Eternal Values," 220

Balzac, Honoré de, 18, 23-24
Barrett, William, 139-152, 285
Barretts of Wimpole Street, The, 189
Barry, Philip, 198-199
Basic English, Sermon on the Mount in, 265
Baudelaire, Charles, 180, 233-234; *Flowers of Evil,* 154
"Bazaar of the Senses," Isaac Rosenfeld, 218
Beautiful People, The, William Saroyan, 200
Beauty: and art, 6, 177; in Bible, 177-178; Greek concept of, 178; true, 110
Behaviorism, and personality, 91
Bell for Adano, A, John Hersey, 198
Berdyaev, Nicholas, 169, 170
Bergelson, David, "The Revolution and the Zussmans," 211-212
Bergson, Henri, 26, 27, 145, 148, 194; *Matter and Memory,* 32; *Time and Free Will,* 32
Bernanos, Georges, 227-228, 230
Best sellers, 266
Bible, 278; beauty in, 177-178; short, 264
Big Fisherman, The, 266
Blackmur, R. P., 134, 135
Blake, William, 117, 147, 148, 253
Bloy, Léon, 228
Bourget, *The Disciple,* 261, 262
"Boy-Man," Karl Shapiro, 268
Bread and Wine, Ignazio Silone, 207-209